WOMEN'S HIGHER EDUCATION IN THE 19TH CENTURY

About the Author

Dr. Gouri Srivastava is a Reader in Education in the Department of Women's Studies, National Council of Educational Research and Training, New Delhi, since completing her M.A. and M.Phil. with high grade points at Jawaharlal Nehru University and Ph.D. at Delhi University. She has published widely in academic journals and is the author of Women Who Created History. She is also a recipient of scholarship from Indian Council of Historical Research (ICHR) and from Indian Council of Social Science Research (ICSSR) for completing her doctoral work. Currently she is working on the Role of Begums of Bhopal in promoting Education of Muslim Girl's in the 19th and 20th century.

WOMEN'S HIGHER EDUCATION IN THE 19TH CENTURY

GOURI SRIVASTAVA
Reader in Education, Department of Women's Studies,
NCERT, New Delhi

CONCEPT PUBLISHING COMPANY, NEW DELHI-110059

ISBN : 81-7022-823-9

First Published 2000

Published and Printed by
Ashok Kumar Mittal
Concept Publishing Company
A/15-16, Commercial Block, Mohan Garden,
NEW DELHI-110059

Phones : 5648039, 5649024
Fax : 091-11-5648053
E-mail : publishing@conceptpub.com

DEDICATED
TO
MY PARENTS

PREFACE

The book is a revision of my thesis, "The Socio-Economic Political Aspects of the Growth of Higher Education of Women in Bombay Presidency 1857-1921", which was submitted to the Delhi University in partial fulfilment of the requirement of the Doctor of Philosophy.

The present book gives a graphic account of contunity and change regarding women's education in Western India in the 19th century with a backdrop of what existed in the ancient past i.e. the Rigvedic period. The book examines how women's education declined in later Vedic and Medieval period and once again became prominent during the 19th century as a result of conscious efforts made by the christian missionaries, male intelligentsia and the British Government. This work is not restricted to Western India alone, which along with Bengal became a meteor of women's education but a comparative picture of the status of women's education is drawn at the all India level.

The present work is restricted to 19th and 20th century because certain significant changes were witnessed during this period which had a significant bearing on the evolution of women's education. It was a period which saw the establishment of the three important universities at Calcutta, Bombay and Madras and the beginning of Dyarchical form of government in which education became a provincial and transferred subject incharge of Indians. In the political sphere it saw the beginning of the non-cooperation movement under Gandhiji in 1921.

The book attempts to show how a few women in the late 19th century and early 20th century succeeded in breaking the barriers to education, what were the agencies that helped them and what change education brought in their lives, attitude and consciousness and finally their successful participation in the struggle for *Swaraj* under Gandhiji.

I am deeply indebted to my Supervisor, Professor Aparna Basu, my parents who have inspired me to write this book. I owe a debt of gratitude to my husband Dr. Ved Prakash Srivastava who has taken great pains in going through each and every aspect of my draft and in helping me with useful suggestions and criticism. I am grateful to Dr. Vijaya Joshi who has helped me in translating most of my Marathi sources and my sister Mrs. Meenakshi Dhote for the help she has rendered in preparing relevant graphs.

I would like to express my heart felt gratitude to my father-in-law late Shree J. N. Srivastava who could not live to see this work of mine and my mother-in-law whose blessings have helped me to complete my work. My son Gaurav Prakash has been responsible in keeping me cheerful throughout my research work.

I express my sincere thanks to the members and staff of the National Archives, Nehru Memorial Museum and Library, Central Secretariat Library, N.C.E.R.T. Library, Library at the All India Women's Conference and Jawaharlal Nehru University Library. I would also like to express my thanks to the staff of S.N.D.T. University Library, Bombay University Library, Bombay Archives and Elphinstone College Library.

GOURI SRIVASTAVA

CONTENTS

LIST OF ABBREVIATIONS

B.C.	Bombay Chronicle
I.S.R.	The Indian Social Reformer
N.A.I.	National Archives of India
N.M.M.L.	Nehru Memorial Museum and Library
S.N.D.T.	Shreemati Nathibai Damodher Thackersey

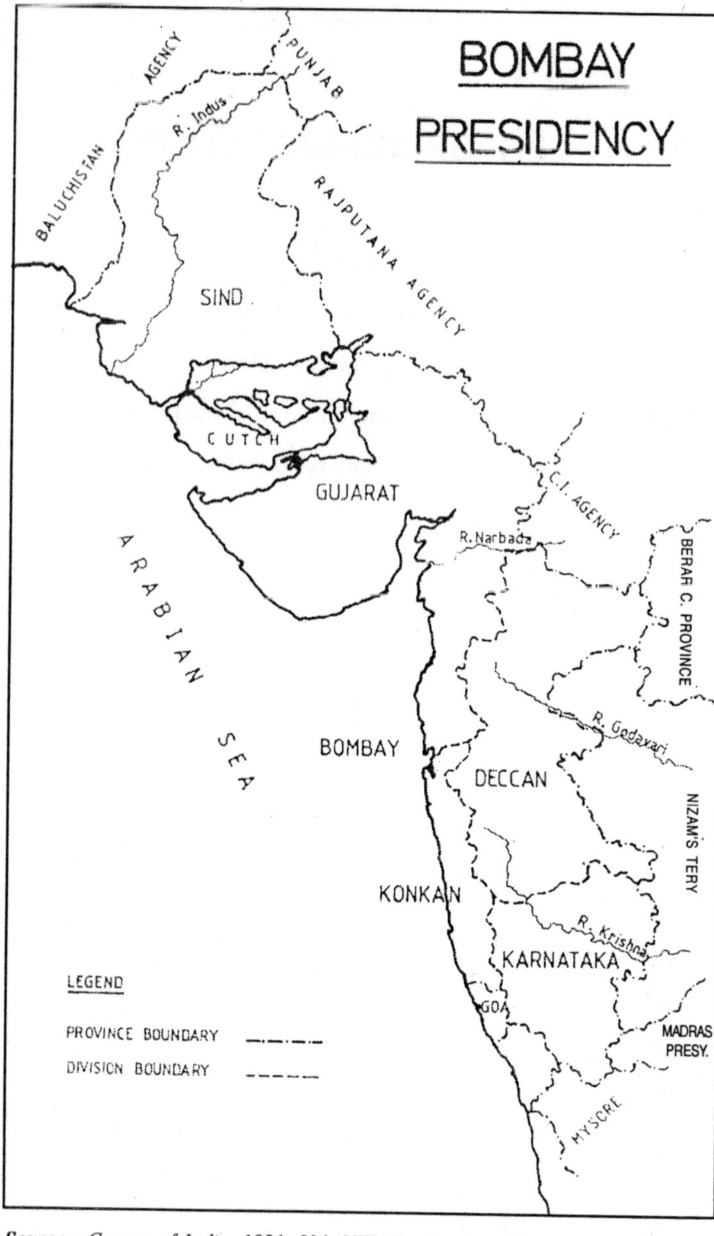

Source : *Census of India*, 1921, Vol. VIII, Bombay Presidency (Part II).

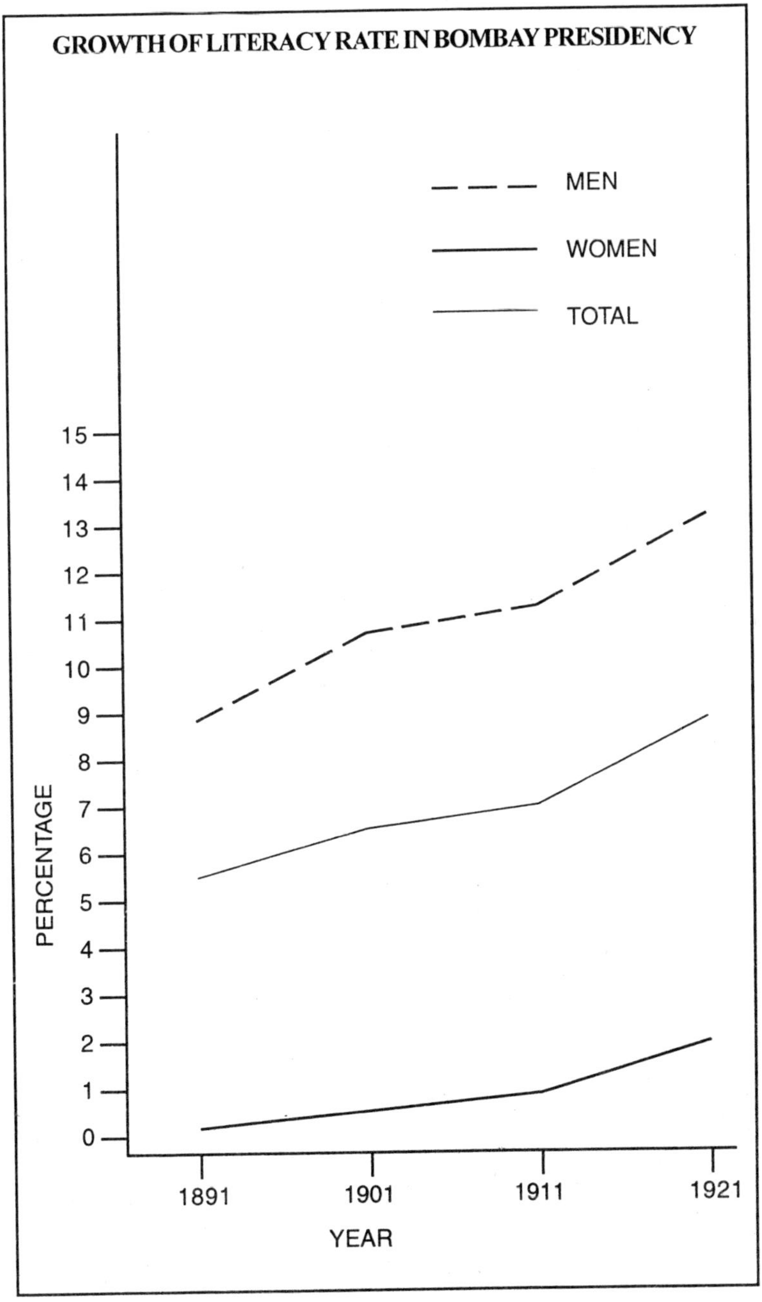
GROWTH OF LITERACY RATE IN BOMBAY PRESIDENCY
MEN
WOMEN
TOTAL
15
14
13
12
11
10
9
8
7
6
5
4
3
2
1
0
PERCENTAGE
1891
1901
1911
1921
YEAR

1

INTRODUCTION

The present book emphasises on the status of women's education in the 19th and 20th century in western India. The 19th century particularly can be called an age of women, for all over the world their rights and wrongs, their nature capacities and potential were the subjects of heated discussions. In Europe feminist consciousness began spreading during and after French Revolution, and by the end of the century feminist ideas were being expressed by radicals in England, France and Germany. By mid-nineteenth century the 'woman question' had become a central issue for Russian reformers and anarchists; while in India the wrongs of women began to be deplored by social reformers mainly in Bengal and Maharashtra.

For a student of history of education it is important to know that before 19th and 20th century when very conscious efforts were made by the christian missionaries, male intelligentsia (those who were educated in the western system of education) and the British Government for promoting women education among different sections of society, India had already a very rich tradition of women's education.

It was in the Rig Vedic period that complete educational facilities were available to women and some of them attained very high educational levels and distinguished themselves Lopamudra Apala, Vishivavara, Sikata, Nivavari and Ghosha are few names that was constantly referred to in the Vedas. It is interesting to note that girls like boys underwent the Upanayana ceremony (Sacred initiation at an early age perhaps about the age of eight) and began the vedic studies. As recorded in *Sarvamukramika*, there were 20 women 'seers' or authors of Rigveda. There were women sages who had gone through the discipline of *Brahmacharya*. Further, there were two classes of women students, Brahmavadinis who were life long students of theology and sadyodvahas, who studied up to the age of 16 or 18 years and learnt Vedic hymns by heart. Specialist in theological work were considered Kasakritsni.

Education was mainly centred in the family and girls studied along with family males. Women were initiated into 3 Rs when writing came into vogue. Women participated in democratic assemblies. The marriage hymn expressed the hope that the bride would be able to speak with composure and success in public assemblies during old age. This importance of women's education and confidence about their ability is evidenced in early Upanishads recommending a certain ritual to the householder for ensuring the birth of a scholarly daughter. Further we are told in the *Atharva Samhita* that "by Vedic studentship a girl wins a young husband". This shows that higher education was regarded as a necessary accomplishment for being well placed in life. It is interesting to note that the list of great Vedic teachers to whom tribute of respect had to be paid at the time of Brahmayajna includes the name of some ladies viz. Gargi Vachaknavi, Vadava Pratitheyi, Sulabha Maitreyi.

The above evidence, shows that the highest education, including vedic studies was open equally to men and women and many ladies distinguished themselves not only as vedic scholars but also as great philosophers, debaters and teachers.

It may, therefore, be stated that educational status along with their overall status of women in the vedic ages was much higher than in any other ancient society that we know, those of Greece and Rome.

This high point of women's education witnessed a gradual decline during the Brahmanical period. The all pervasive Brahmanic codes took a constrictive view of the position and rights of women, prescribed various forms of restriction generally limiting their roles to *grihasti* (domestic realm) as nurturers and bearers of progeny. Women were forbidden to join public assemblies. Certain derogatory customs like child marriage enforced widowhood were prescribed (interestingly this was absent in the Rig-Vedic period) and all forms of women's education particularly formal education continued to be the preserve of men. It is significant to note that kshatriyas did resist this trend as close to one millennium B.C. and women from amongst this particularly princely family receieved military and administrative training some of them even receieved higher education.

The emergence of Buddhism and Jainism tried to reverse the prevalent inferior status of women. Both of them promised salvation to men and women and opened their monastic order to them. In fact, women during this period enjoyed greater freedom. Education of women was well looked after. The religious discussions of Khema and Dhamnadiny reveal high intellectual capacities women could attain when given freedom and opportunity. Further, the presence of a widow was not considered inauspicious.

Once again during the Puranic age the status of women got relegated to the background. Puranic writers contended that the husband is god for women and devotion to him is equivalent to mans devotion to god. Women and Sudras could no longer listen to Vedas. From 200 A.D. onwards pre-puberty marriages became quite popular. Widow remarriage was prohibited and women had hardly any access to education. The *pathsalas* and Tols were devoid of female scholars.

During the medieval period this trend regarding women's education continued. Interestingly though Islam had nothing to say about women's education the *maktabs* and *madrasas* (primary and higher centres of learning) had no women scholars.

There were various reasons that was responsible for the above mentioned phenomena. The prevalence of polygamy and *purdah* (symbol of segregation) particularly among the muslim women prevailed to such an extent that, in the ultimate analysis, the social status of muslim women was not better than that among the Hindus. Also, certain superstitious beliefs like education leading to early widowhood was common among the Hindus and Muslims and went a long way in discouraging women's education.

Also, the patriarchal nature of Indian, society barring some areas such as Kerala restricted women's entry into educational institutions. In such a society men controlled decision-making not only within the family but in society in general. Since they were the bread earners, the educational system, particularly formal education catered to their requirements. The curriculum was framed in such a manner that after acquiring the necessary knowledge, a person could earn his livelihood. Apart from formal education which catered to the requirements of the higher castes, vocational education also served the some purpose. In such an educational system, there was little room for women's formal education, it was felt, formal education was not essential for a woman because she was not seeking employment. The home or the domestic sphere was regarded as her domain and hence the only education considered necessary for her was cooking child care, home management etc. This could be taught by mothers or some other older women and could be learnt at home.

It is significant to note that when the survey of indigenous education was undertaken in Madras, Bombay and Calcutta by the British officials in the early 19th century they found complete absence of female students in the formal institutions of learning M.S. Elphistone, the Governor of Bombay in his long minute of eight paragraphs (1819-27), made no reference to women's education. Also, when the Bombay government undertook an inquiry into the state of indigenous education in the 1820's and when the first reports were receieved in 1824 from the districts, there was no mention of a single female scholar attending any of the common schools of the province. These schools were exclusively meant for boys. In the 9 taluks of the South Konkan districts, thc absence of female education was once again depicted. However, it was only in Madras that Sir Thomas Munro in his report mentioned a few female scholars attending day schools.

Despite, the complete apathy and neglect of female education in the 18th and early 19th century we find that a few women did acquire education. These women mainly belonged to the upper caste. In western India few names that became very prominent during our period was Pandita Ramabai Saraswati, Ramabai Ranade, Anandibai Joshi, Vidyagauri Nilkanth, her sister Sharda Mehta and Cornelia Sorabji. While the first three belonged to the Chitpavan Brahmin community, the last three were Vadnagra and Parsi; respectively. The Parsis, because of their commercial and social contacts with the English and influence of western ideas were the first to take to women's education. An example set by Framji Cowasji Banajee who gave his daughter instruction in English, Maneekjee Cursetjee followed by educating his daughter Sirinbai Cursetjee.

The earliest to promote women's education as mentioned earlier during the period where the Christian missionaries followed by social reformers and later by the British Government. Missionaries belonging to the American missionary society, Church missionary society and Scottish missionaries established schools for girls. Apart from schools, they also established orphanages and boarding establishments were formal as well as some kind of vocational education was imparted. Domestic or zenana system of education was also encouraged by the missionaries. It was largely informal and was meant for women belonging to the higher caste families who did not go to schools. The missionaries took up this sensitive issue on humanitarian grounds and also because of their desire to proselytize. There was a realization on their part that education was an important channel through which they could influence pupils, particularly women, and thereby convert them to Christianity. Infact, they hoped that by converting women, the entire family would be converted to Christianity. Missionaries played a pioneering role both in Bengal and Bombay Presidencies.

The work begun by the Christian missionaries was picked up by the Indian social reformer who in their individual capacities encouraged women's education. Most of them acquired western education and were deeply influenced by the new values and beliefs it emphasised and upheld, viz. liberalism, rationalism, democracy, equality and so on. These ideas made them critically examine their society as well as the educational system. There was a realization on their part that not only was Indian society steeped in tradition but also the indigenous system of education had become outdated. Thus refomers like Rammohan Roy advocated modern education based on liberal and rational values. In Bengal, Ishwarchandra Vidyasagar was one of the earliest reformers to take up the cause of women's education by establishing thirty-six school for girls. It was largely because of the favourable public opinion created by Rammohan Roy that Lord William Bentinck could pass an Act abolishing *Sati* in 1829 and Ishwarchandra Vidyasagar's effort led to the passing of the Widow Remarriage Act in 1856. A similar movement in Maharashtra was spearheaded by Vishnu Shastri Pandit who was called the Vidyasagar of Maharashtra, Jotiba Phule, Gopal Hari Deshmukh, Behramji Malabari, Justice Mahadev Govind Ranade, G. K. Deodher, Badruddin Tyabji and Maharishi Karve. Most of them took up social as well as educational issues. With the help of journals, newspapers and speeches they brought into sharp focus the various evil customs and taboos of the society. While on the one hand, they were critical of Indian society as it existed in the 19th century at the sametime, they wanted to prove that such customs did not exist in the past and they wanted to restore the high position enjoyed by women in society.

Most of the intelligentsia in western India particularly in Bombay Presidency were Brahmins, the Parsis and the Muslims also did not lag behind. There were exceptions such as Jotiba Phule who belonged to the mali caste which was almost an untouchable caste. The need to promote womens education was keenly felt by all of them. Educated men found that their illiterate wives could share none of their interests. One reason for encouraging women's education was that they would have wives as intelligent companions.

Many of the reformers felt that without social change, political freedom would have no meaning. Women's education, according to them, was the crucial channel through which social evils would be gradually eradicated and women would be able to acquire a better status in society like the missionaries they also opened educational institutions for women. However, it was D.K. Karve who succeded in laying the foundation of a separate University for women known as the S.N.D.T. University.

Apart from individual efforts, various organizations and associations were begun during our period which not only worked for social welfare of women but also promoted women's education. In other words, the groundwork for higher education of women was laid by them. One of the earliest such association was the Students Literary and Scientific Society of Bombay, founded in 1848 by the students of Elphinstone college, which in turn opened several girl's school, members of the society taught in these schools.

Similarly, the Servants of Indian Society, Poona; the Deccan Educational Society, *Arya Samaj, Seva-Sadan,* in Bombay and the National Social Conference were organizations which focussed on women's education. Education was regarded as a vital means of raising women's status and in kindling in them the desire to improve their position. These organizations motivated many women to go in for higher education.

Unlike the Christian missionaries and the intelligentsia the British Government took the responsibility of educating women as late as 1854. Infact, the Educational Despatch of 1854 not only mentioned governments support to female education but also stated that grant-in-aid would be given to female schools. A similar sentiment was echoed in the Hunter Commissions Report (1882). Among other things, it clearly mentioned that women's education should be encouraged in all aspects, viz. syllabus, teaching staff, women inspectors and others. In other words, its recommendations included an improvement in all aspects regarding women's education. Lord Curzon also supported this view and the Simla Conference of 1901 and the Educational Policy of 1913 carried a similar message.

Thus, the efforts of Chrisian missionaries, male and female intelligentsia and the British Government, led to an overall expansion of primary, secondary and collegiate education of women. Also a very significant development that took place during our period was the beginning of professional education for women with the establishment of two training colleges for women in Poona (1870) and Ahmedabad (1871). Midwifery classes were started in the Grant Medical College (1875-76) and women students began to be admitted to degree courses in medicine. In short, women began to be trained as doctors, nurses and midwives. Similarly, the Art courses in the J. J. School of Art, Bombay, attracted several women students. It is true that the number of girls attending professional colleges was very small and that a very large percentage of them belonged to the European, Anglo-Indian, Indian-Christian and the Parsi communities.

As a result of the formal as well as informal education received by women, they succeeded in laying the foundation of organizations which promoted social welfare and educational work. Some significant organizations established by women intelligentsia whose work came into prominence were Pandita Ramabai's *Sharda-Sadan* (Home of learning) – Ramabai Ranade's *Seva-Sadan* (Home of service) this Sadan was opened with the cooperation of Byramji Malabari and Dayaram Gidumal. The other significant association established by Ramabai Ranade was the Hindu Ladies Social and Literary Club. This was cosmopolitian in nature an promoted reading habits amongst women by establishing various libraries. Essay and debates were also conducted and the themes generally chosen was closely related to women's issues. A significant development during the period was establishment of an all India organization for women known as the Women's Indian Association. It was founded on 8th of May 1917 at Adyar in Madras. Its members consisted of women belonging to different castes and communities. Most of the issues pertaining to women were decided through consensus. Its activity succeeded in promoting communal solidarity and national consciousness among women.

It is interesting to note that though the women intelligentsia constantly strove to improve the position of women, they did not desire to bring about a social revolution or question the very basic relationship in the family. A few women took up professions outside the four walls of their home. Professions like teaching, nursing, midwifery which were common among women were considered to be suitable for women's nurturing and caring nature. Technical professions continued to be dominated by men.

The female intelligentsia rejected western notion of feminism that women were an oppressed class and that there existed any kind of contradiction between male and female.

> "Indian women very definitely distrust the use of such phrases as "Women's Emancipation" or "Women's Movement". They have the feeling unconsciously or consciously that such terms imply something of feminine inferiority; whereas in India there is little of the sex antagonism that one often detects in accounts of women's activities in European and American periodicals."[1]

They further stated that —

> "The women's movement in India has thus differed very much

> from its sister movement in Europe. Man has not questioned women's right to enter any field of activity or any profession although he has held complete sway everywhere for many years now, keeping the women out and restricting their influence and scope of work by rigid rules and customs. But when the day came for her to emerge from seclusion imposed on her, and take her rightful place along with him, it did not strike him as being new or strange. Thus, this movement cannot in any sense be said to be a rebellion or a revolt against man; it is rather an attempt to regain lost ground. It is not actuated by any spirit of competition marked with violence; it is a movement of calm assertion."[2]

The movement among Indian women was one which sought to ensure a better position for women in the patriarchal family, to take them enlightened and responsible wives and mothers.

> ".... by the discharge of their responsibilities alone would they maintain their great and ancient ideals of womanhood; prove themselves worthy daughters of the Motherland. ...."[3]

It was not one directed towards asserting the individual status of one woman against one man which could take place only in an industrialized society where the notion of individualism were developed. Thus, the Indian women intelligentsia did not assert the independent individuality of women; it rejected the contradictions between male and female and it argued from a perception of their powerfulness not oppression.

Educated women became politically conscious and actively participated in the struggle for *Swaraj*. Their participation became significant in the *Swadeshi* movement, struggle for suffrage, home rule movement and finally under Gandhiji women in urban and rural areas joined hands and supported his *Satyagraha* and non-violent technique in winning *Swaraj*.

The main objective of this book is to examine in detail the role of the Christian missionaries, male intelligentsia, and the British government in promoting the growth of women's education in western India. The book also focuses attention on a comparative analysis of the growth of colleges, professional and training institutions not only in Western India but in the whole of India. The important themes that have been examined are:

(a) Social norms and customs that inhibited women's education.

(b) The contribution of various agencies like the missionaries, male intelligentsia and the British government in ameliorating social evils and promoting women education, their motives, and the degree of success they attained;
(c) Gradual evolution of collegiate and professional education in Western India and the whole of India;
(d) The beneficiaries of the new education is analysed in terms of caste, class, etc. Overall expenditure of the government on women's education; and
(e) The impact of education on the status of women and their participation in political life.

A detailed examination of these themes have enabled us to know not only the forces which led to the emergence of higher education of women but also whether there existed any kind of relationship between higher education of women and their status in society. The book also provides insight into some of the problems that plague the present society e.g. lesser participation of women in higher education. Further, the book also portrays how customs and traditions that got institutionalized after Vedic period continued to retard the participation of women at all the levels of education. It is interesting to note that till recently several E.F.A. (Education For All) initiatives have shown that one of the reasons for the discontinuance of girls in education is the existence of the above mentioned customs and traditions.

The important contemporary sources on the growth of higher education of women are the Gazetteers, Educational Records, the Report of the Director of Public Instruction, Quinquennial review, Census Reports, contemporary speeches and biographical accounts of some of the pioneers regarding the growth of women's education. Some of the biographical accounts are in vernacular, i.e. Marathi and Gujarati, though few have been translated into English, Newspapers like the Indian Social Reformer, the Bombay Chronicle, the Kesari and the Hindu magazine also provide accounts relating to women's education. A sharper focus was given to various social reform activities undertaken by the intelligentsia as well as the Governor-Generals and wide publicity and coverage were published and circulated in all the British Presidencies.

A combined study of these primary sources, along with the useful secondary works have enable us to construct the history of the growth of higher education of women during our period.

The subject matter of book has been divided into total of five

Chapters, according to the specific nature of the area covered by each. Chapter one is the Introduction.

The second chapter highlights social aspects. In this chapter detailed discussions is undertken regarding social norms and customs closely related to a woman's life from her very birth till her old age, i.e. infanticide, child marriage, *sati* and enforced widowhood. Its impact on education of women is examined. Also, pioneering contribution of Christian Missionary, male intelligentsia and Britsh Government's policies in promoting female education is dealt with.

The third chapter is devoted to the growth and development of higher education of women. An in-depth account of the development of collegiate and professional education are taken into account in Bombay Presidency and the other presidencies as well. Also extent of co-education, expenditure incurred by the government on higher institutions of learning, cost of education and the effectiveness of the system of educaiton are examined. Statistical and graphical methods are used to portray facts.

The fourth chapter gives a vivid account of the efforts of the women intelligentsia in forming organizations which undertook social and education works. It also encouraged professional education among women and increasingly made them aware of the unjust social customs. Organizations begun by women acquired an all India character and cut across caste, religious and linguistic barriers. It encouraged women to decide matters based on consensus and kindled political consciousness amongst them. Further, women's participation in the freedom struggle, the suffrage movement and their role under the leadership of Gandhiji are mentioned.

Finally, the last chapter or the conclusion summarises the findings of the investigation made on the evolution of higher education of women in Bombay Presidency during our period. By a careful and discretionary use of the materials available on the subject this work is able to throw new light on some of the aspects of the evolution of higher education of women already mentioned above.

REFERENCES

1. Gail, Olivia Pearson, *Women in Public Life in Bombay City with Special Reference to the Civil Disobedience Movement,* p. 34.
2. *Ibid.,* p. 35.
3. *Ramabai Kamdar at The Bombay Special Congress, B.C., September 29, 1930,* p. 9. in Gail Olivia Pearson, *Op.cit.,* p. 215.

2

SOCIAL ASPECTS

SIGNIFICANT CUSTOMS AND TRADITIONS AND THEIR IMPACT ON THE GROWTH OF WOMEN'S EDUCATION

In the 19th century prevalent customs and traditions associated with the different stages of women's life significantly influenced the education and status acquired by her in society. These stages were broadly classified as childhood, youth or married life and lastly widowhood or old age by the ancient law giver Manu. There was a thin line separating each stage from the other finally culminating in the last, i.e. widowhood. It is , therefore, important to know –

(a) Customs and traditions associated with each stage,
(b) Kind of impact it had on women belonging to different communities, and
(c) Its effect on the growth of education.

The first or the initial stage in the life of a woman was childhood. It stretched, from infancy, i.e. birth till the time of marriage. In a typically dominated patriarchal family, the birth of a girl child was not a very happy event. While sweets were distributed and songs were sung on the birth of a male child, it was totally absent in the case of a female child. Parents craved for having a son mainly because –

> "Through a son he conquers the world, through a son's son he obtains immortality but through his son's grandson he gains the world of the sun."[1]

It was commonly believed that there was no place for a man in heaven if he was destitute of male offspring. Therefore, in western and southern India whenever a girl or a woman saluted the elders and priests, they blessed her with these words - "Mayst thou have eight sons, and may thy husband survive thee."

Preference for a son also existed in the *Rig Vedic* hymns. A good number of sons along with cattle and land were constantly prayed for. In the concluding portion of the *Rig Vedic* hymn X.85 *Indra* is invoked to grant ten sons to the bride. In the age of the later *Samhitas* and the *Brahmanas* male progeny continued to be distinctly preferred to female ones. The *Aitareya Brahmaṇa* declares that a daughter is a source of misery while a son is the saviour of the family.[2]

It is interesting to note that favourable treatment meted by a husband towards his wife was also closely associated with the birth of a son. Often expectant mothers became superstitious and procured Rosaries from mothers of sons to pray; herbs and roots were regularly swallowed; trees and son giving gods were devoutly worshipped. Ceremonies honoured with the name of "sacrament", was administered to the mother between the third and the fourth month of her pregnancy for the purpose of converting the embryo into a boy.[3]

The birth of a son was preferred to a daughter because he always remained with his parents; continued the family line as lineage; for in a patriarchal family lineage was traced through a male descendant. Sons often offered oblations to their ancestors for spiritual benefits and added glory to the good name of the family by their noble and brilliant achievements. A girl on the other hand had to migrate to another family after marriage and was of no help for the spiritual benefit of her parents.

Thus, from the very beginning of her mortal existence the girl - child was not favourably looked at by her parents and society at large. In Gujarat the birth of a girl child was considered a curse. A girl was looked upon as a burden and a danger, like *sap no bharo* and many such epithets were given to her[4]. From their very birth parents were worried about getting their daughter married. Heavy expenditure involved in marriages and getting the daughter married into a particular family only, led to the inhuman practice of female infanticide, popularly known as *dudha piti.*[5] This custom was widely prevalent among the *Jadeja Rajputs* and the *Kulin-Kanabis* of Gujarat[6].

Few who escaped this inhuman custom were brought up with no special care in their parental household only to be married as soon as a suitor was found. Early or child marriage saw the beginning of second stage in the life of a women. Infact, a thine line separated the second stage from the previous one.

Marriage was regarded as the most important stage in the life of a women. For her life had no other interest or duties besides marriage. Such attitude also led to the custom of child marriages which was widely prevalent in our presidency. The widespread prevalence of this custom was mainly because performance of marriage in India was regarded as a sacrament. The giving of a daughter in marriage i.e. *Kanyadan* was regarded as the highest religious duty and most of the parents were anxious to marry their daughters early[7].

Also, the significance of marriage was enhanced because its underlying aim was namely *dharma* (religious duty), *praja* (progeny) and *rati* (sex). To save a man from going to hell after death, a son was required to offer certain oblations. Also, there were certain religious duties to be performed as a house holder and for this purpose also marriage was considered as inevitable[8].

It is interesting to note that the Hindu notion of marriage was summed up by the Bombay chronicle in an editorial that stated ---

> "While the Hindu pays homage to the sacramental conception of marriage, he tolerates the right of polygamy for husbands with indissoluble union and compulsory widowhood for women, caste prohibition, barter of girls, monstrous dowry system and child marriage. All such inequitable and anti-social customs and laws rest on the fact that proprietary right rather than personal self respect and love were deemed the basis of conjugal obligation in the earliest times and the Hindu have not still discarded that inheritance."[9]

Such was the little value of an individual identity for girls, that during the marriage ceremony of Maharashtrians the young bride's name was changed from that given in her natal home to one more suitable to her new family, e.g. Anandibai Joshi was earlier called Yamuna and Anandibai Karve was known as Godhubai.

Girls were usually married between the age of three and eleven. Thirteen was the limit beyond which no girl was unmarried. Prepuberty marriages were institutionalized in our presidency as early as 17th century. In Maharashtra, particularly the Peshwa Balaji Bajirao issued an order in 1735, by which he fixed the marriage age of *Brahmin* girls between seven and ten years[10]. During our period this practice not only continued but many of the prominent women intelligentsia in the Bombay Presidency were married at a very early age. Ramabai Ranade was married at the age of eleven; Tarabai Modak's mother Durga was married at the age of ten[11]. Anandibai Karve first got married at the age of seven and her sister Parvatibai Athavale on the other hand was married at the age of eleven[12]. Their younger sister, Baya was married when she was nine. Anandibai Joshi was also married at the age of nine. Similarly, Vidyagauri Nilkanth and her sister Sharda Mehta were married at the age of twelve and thirteen respectively. Being married at such a young age the child bride hardly knew what marriage really meant. Many of the girls when playfully asked whether they would like soon to be married innocently answered in the affirmative. They often saw their sisters, cousins or playmates married, the occasion was one to remember with pleasure. There are gorgeous dresses, bright coloured clothes, beautiful decorations, music, songs and so on. What can be more tempting to a child's mind than these[13] ? The responsibilities brought along with marriage was hardly realized by her.

It is ironical to note that while performing marriage rites the consent of the bride (i.e. girl child) was hardly taken. Since parents were very anxious to get their daughters married at an early age, physical fitness and occupation of the groom was hardly taken into account. However, caste was the only guiding factor in selecting bridegrooms. It did not matter even if the groom possessed few wives. This naturally resulted in ill-assorted marriages. A girl might be eight while her husband might be even eighty. M. Malabari in his work states that ". . . . The wife may outgrow the husband, or the husband may become fit for the grave when the wife becomes fit for his home. . . ."[14]. He further states that ". . . it was generally found that girls of eight or nine were given to men of sixty or seventy, sometimes to men totally unworthy of them. . ."[15]. Also at times parents were compelled to marry their daughters to physically handicapped men. Infact, Parvatibai Athavale was married to a lame man[16]. The unhappy lot of the child wife was very movingly portrayed in a poem by the 18th century poet Vallabha Bhatt. In his open addressed to mother-goddess (*gorma*) he states that ". . . . Mother, mine are just sixteen year and he has seen his eighty. Mother, my hair is black and his head is all white or grey, my youth is at its blooming and already my life is wrecked. Goddess mother why was not I strangled at birth, why was not I poisoned?. . . . "

. . . .Yet if my husband dies it is my part to be true to death. My goddess mother, with joined hands I pray at thy feet when I am born again, give me a husband that is young and strong[17].

Sometimes the girl's were senior in age to the boy. This kind of mismatched marriages were often recorded in Gujarati folk songs. One of them maintains that ". . . . I have passed twelve springs, and he is only a child of fifteen months. How shall I pull on." Another folk song conveys the hearts yearning in rather enigmatic way: the girl requests passers by to give one swing to a cradle in which a child is sleeping; some think it is her son, others think it is her infant brother; the bitter truth is that it is her husband[18].

It is ironical to note that although the ancient law givers thought it desirable to marry girls when quite young, and consequently ignored their right to choose their own husbands, yet they were not altogether void of human feelings. They have positively forbidden parents and guardians to give away girls in marriage unless good suitors were offered to them –

> "To a distinguished, handsome suitor of equal caste should a father give his daughter in accordance with the prescribed rule, though she may not have attained the proper age . . . ."
> "But the maiden though marriageable, should rather stop in the father's house until death, than he should ever give her to a man destitute of good qualities . . . ."[19]

These laws however defied by prevalent customs that governed society in the 19th century.

It is interesting to note that the institution of child marriage and ill assorted marriages were absent in the *Rig-Vedic* period. Girls normally married after puberty, as can be judged from the frequent mention of unmarried ones such as Ghosha who grew up in the house of their parents. In some cases a woman could freely mix with young men and carry on love affairs[20].

The widespread prevalence of child marriages in the 19th century had a very harmful impact on the girl-child. They became wives and mothers without realizing the seriousness of their position. Early consummation of marriage often led to the death of the girl, e.g. in 1890 in Bengal Phoolmani Dasi, a girl, of eleven, was forced by her husband to consummate their marriage. This resulted in her death and created widespread indignation.[22] It led to a whole lot of complications at child birth. As B.N.Malabari in his work states that ". . . . A too early consummation of the nupital troth, the breaking down of constitution and the ushering in of disease. The giving up of studies on the part of the boy, husband, the birth of sickly children the necessity of feeding too many mouths, poverty dependence, a disorganized household leading perhaps to sin. In short, it comes to wreck of two lives, grown old almost in youth, which might in favourable circumstances, have attained to happy and respectable age. . . .".[23] Parvatibai Athavale also gives a vivid account of the harmful effects of child marriage. In her autobiographical work she states that she had a child at a very early age, i.e. fifteen and he could not survive. A physician had to be called because of complication that arose at the child birth.

Thus, early marriage had a telling impact on the physique of the child wife. Very often it led to infant mortality and defects during child-birth.

Also, mentally the child wife was not placed in a better disposition. Soon after marriage the child wife had to reside at the back of the house, where darkness perpetually existed. There the child bride was brought to be forever confined. She occupied the humblest position in the family and was not allowed to talk or laugh loudly. She could not speak before her father and elder brother-in-law or for that matter any other distant male relative of her husband. The mother-in-law employed their daughter-in-law in all kinds of household work, in order to give them a thorough knowledge of domestic duties. The child bride of nine or ten years of age found it irksome to work hard all day long without the hope of hearing a word of praise from the mother-in-law[24]. As a rule, the bride was often scolded for every mistake committed, and often abusive speech were used by the mother-in-law. Thus, mortified and distressed, they seemed to console themselves by shedding bitter tears in silence[25].

Thus, child marriage led to mental, moral and physical degradation of the young bride. Perhaps the worst impact of such kind of marriage was widowhood. Married in infancy; the girl child had a perpetual widowhood before them. The joys of youth were unknown to her staying as a recluse in the patriarchal dominated family where women in any case were given a secondary place; the place of a widow, on the other hand, was next to that of a menial. Life to her was a bundle of miseries which had to be lived for the sake of living. A child-widow and a sonless widow were the worst effected. "A childless widow is a miserable, helpless creature, entirely at the mercy of her relations or priests or scheming and designing men. If she be so fortunate as to possess some riches inherited, she is soon and easily made to part with it and swindled by them, and if she be poor she has to beg from house to house in quest of food... In meek and humble submission, complete resignation under all adverse and critical circumstances, in the virtue of modesty, chastity, kindness, devotion and faithfulness they may stand as explars to future generations'[26].

It is of significance to note that in 1881, of every 10,000 women 1791 were widows and in 1901 the number rose to 1, 847. Thus, widowhood led to the final or the last stage in the life of women.

The final stage was the most pathetic in the life of a woman. She had either to physically annihilate herself or adopt a life of complete humiliation or enforced widowhood. It is ironical to note that just as the girl child had no hand in making matrimonial choices, similarly in the event of her becoming a widow her fate was to be decided by her husband's family.

In Bengal Presidency and to some extent in our Presidency *Sati*, or physical annihilation was practiced. A detailed description of the prevalence of this custom in Maharashtra is found in the marathi work of Dr. M.G. Mardi. In his work, he states that despite passing of the Widow Marriage Act, the *Brahmin* community in Maharashtra forced women to perform *Sati*. They were physically forced to commit this Act. He states that[27] —

> "....It was decided by the community that for a woman who is willing to commit *sati* a shed with a grass roof and dungcake along with sandlewood should be provided. Then the woman should be made to mount the pyre, she should be told about the legislation of the British and even after knowing about the legislation if the woman is ready to commit *sati* then only the pyre should be lit. Even after the pyre is well lit and is steadily burning if the woman jumps down from the fire she is not allowed to remain in her community; not only this her maternal relations are boycotted — this decision was finally taken up by the community".

However, it was enforced widowhood that was widely prevalent in Bombay Presidency. It led to physical deformation and mental torture of the widows. Customs and traditions associated with it have found poignant references in the works of few women intelligentsia, who themselves had undergone sufferings and pain of this stage of existence. Anandibai Karve in her autobiographical work gives a detailed account of the sufferings of a child widow. According to her a child widow was a laughing stock. She was made the embodiment of all kind of hatred. At every step it was impressed on her mind that *Brahmin* child widow could not cook for the family unless all her hair was removed from her head. If the hair was not removed, it was considered a great sin committed, since it was enjoined by the *shastras* that with each drop of water falling form the wet hair of a widow, her husband would take the life of an insect (a very lowly thing!) He would remain in hell for many birth cycles.[28]

About her own disfigurement, Anandibai writes :

> "…. My hair was not cut immediately after I became a widow, may be because I used to do menial labour on our farm and once the hair removing ceremony was performed I could not do so least the family will loose a free labour! I became a widow at the age of eight. My husband was twenty years old at the time of our marriage. He died when we were married only for three months. I was told not to put *kunkun* (*sindhoor*) red vermilion on my head any more; I could not understand why? The hair removing ceremony was performed when I was twenty-one. I knew by experience that a women who resisted this thing or custom was physically tortured beyond imagination. So I underwent that ghastly thing without any protest. I did not feel sorry when I actually became a widow in true sense but when I had to perform the above mentioned custom I felt that I had lost my identity and had become meek and submissive person without realizing what was correct for me till death approached"[29].

She further states that "…. After the hair removing ceremony my whole scalp burned with cuts and bruises; the thought of applying coconut oil or any other ointments did not occur to me. I would readily have accepted death to this pain and humiliation"[30].

Ramabai Saraswati also states that amongst the *Brahmin* widows of Deccan the heads of all widows were shaved regularly every fortnight. Similarly, widows were compelled to wear a single coarse garment, white red or brown. They were to eat one meal a day during twenty-four hours and never took part in family feasts and jubilee. Widows were generally considered as bad omen and on all auspicious occasions people shunned them and refused to look at them. Some people had become so superstitious that they would postpone their journey if a widow crossed their path[31].

The code of Manu gives in detail the duties of a widow[32] —

> "Until death let her be patient of hardships, self controlled and chaste and strive to fulfil that most excellent duty which is prescribed for wives who have one husband only"
>
> — Manu V., 157, 158

> "Nor is a second husband anywhere prescribed for virtuous women."
>
> — Manu V., 162

> "A virtuous wife who after the death of her husband constantly remains chaste, reaches heaven . . . . "
>
> —Manu V., 160

It is ironical to note that the code of Manu though assigned elaborate duties which a widow was required to perform; in case of a widower, on the other hand, it remains silent. According to the code, the widower was bereft of any kind of duties which a widow had to perform. Infact, the code gave full sanction to a widower to marry again . . . .

> "Having thus at the funeral, given the sacred fires to his wife who dies before him, he may marry again, and again kindle the (nuptial) fires."
>
> "...And having taken a wife, he must dwell in his own house during the second period of his life."[33]
>
> —Manu V., 167-169

Thus, a clear distinction was made in the code of Manu regarding the duties of a widow and a widower. While for the widow her life was full of miseries and agony, a widower's life, on the other hand was devoid of all such pain.

In the *Rigvedic* period widows were devoid of such kind of suffering. They were allowed to remarry (*niyoga*). However, in later years to come this privilege was lost and only the widower was allowed to marry. Thus, enforced widowhood had a telling impact on the women. Socially, as stated earlier they were treated as outcaste, shunned by all on important auspicious occasions, they were made to feel that they had committed grave sins in their previous life[34]. The harsh custom and tradition, that enveloped her life, was a constant reminder to her, that if she did not succumb to it, and perform her duties well, a similar kind of fate would be met by her in the next life.

Customs that were closely associated with the various stages in the life of a woman like infanticide, child-marriage leading to *sati* and enforced widowhood was by and large confined to the upper caste. Infanticide, as mentioned earlier, was confined amongst castes like the *Kulin Kanabis* and *Jadeja Rajputs* of Gujarat. Those who escaped this custom became victims of another, i.e. child marriage. This was widespread amongst the *Brahmins, Banias* and *Rajputs* in Gujarat.[35] In Maharashtra, on the other hand, it was prevalent among the *Brahmins, Shevni* and the *Prabhu* castes.[36]

The practice of *sati* and enforced widowhood which was the logical consequence of child marriage was practised amongst the above mentioned castes. In the Bengal Presidency also *sati* which was common was prevalent amongst the highest castes, i.e. *Kulin Brahmins*[37]. It is significant to note that in almost all the *Brahmin* families of our Presidency cases of *sati* or widows subjected enforced widowhood was found.[38]

Thus, customs and traditions assigned women a secondary place in society and denied her all kind of independence. The law-giver Manu states that — "Her father protects her in childhood, her husbands protects her in youth, and her sons protect her in old age; a woman is never fit for independence.".[39]

—Manu, IX.2, 3

Along with independence formal education was completely neglected for woman. Being married at a very early age girls were devoid of any kind of education. The role and function assigned to woman in a patriarchal household were such that it was generally believed that a women in different roles such as a child, bride and a widow needed no formal instruction. They could learn their varied roles through practice and inheritance. It was felt that household work needed no formal guidance. Therefore, women hardly went to schools. A similar view was depicted in Bombay chronicle in which Miss Eleanor McDougall Classical Lecturer at Westfield College, Hampstead states that ".... Very few girls however go to a high school and the merest handful to a University. Even the high school girls are sometime condemned on marriage to the traditional seclusion of the Hindu wife".[40]

Also, it was a commonly held view that the woman's role was to create a home where she could, with virtues of obedience and chastity, devote herself to her husband and family. For such duties, too, formal guidance was not essential. Tilak listed the virtues of the model Hindu woman in his *Maharatta*, as obedience to her husband and children; contentment with her lot in life, least important was her ability to read and write.[41] Even Gokhale in his introduction to the English translation of Ramabai Ranade's autobiography wirites :

> "A deep love between husband and wife is found in western society. That is a relationship of equality. But even when there is a similar deep love, that the wife should devote herself wholly to the service of the husband and consider this as the fulfilment of her life,

is a special characteristic of the women of the East and particularly of India. This characteristic is the fruit of the culture and tradition of thousand of years... This fundamental characteristic remains unaffected in women like Vahinibai, although the pattern of their life may be modified by new education, new ideas and new environment".[42] The Nawab of Bhopal outlines similar virtues —

"She should be the means of comfort to her husband; she should bring up and train the children; she sould make her home an abode of peace and rest for her husband and the male members of her family; she sould always be ready in time of need to undergo hardships and suffer privations . . . ."[43]

The poet, Narmada Shankar, a great champion of women's education regarded the first duty of a woman as obedience to her husband. "A wife should act according to the wishes of her husband. The parents should marry their daughters to a man only after full enquiries, but once married she should love her husband unquestioningly, she should forgive him for his trespasses and faults."[44]

Narmada admitted that the wife was not a slave of her hasband. Yet she should yield to his superior wisdom. "It is the wife's duty to get up before her husband to workship him, feed him and administer to all his needs and thus only can she attain heaven."[45]

Even the Parsis, regarded as a progressive community asserted that "a womens chief work is in her family and her chief virtue are modesty and devotion".[46]

Sir Charles Trevelyan made an interesting observation before the Parliamentary Committe in 1853, regarding the lack of female education. According to him the main reason for the lack of female education was that "in order to keep the women in subjection and seculusion, it was necessary to keep them ignorant".[47]

Also, there was a growing realization amongst the male members of the family that formal education of women should not be encouraged; for according to them it would lead to neglect of household duties and that it would be misused by women. Further it was felt that women on their part did not show any inclination towards it.[48]

Another added factor was a strong belief upheld by the people particularly those belonging to the Hindu and Muslim community that if a girl was taught to read and write they would soon become widow after marriage. Also, there was a common notion amongst the people that educated women would indulge in romantic intrigues and be unfaithful; that no man would marry a learned girl. It would spoil all feminine qualities and bring disgrace to the family. Educated girls were also less likely to submit to their parents choice of husband. It was held that women did not have enough intelligence to be able to receive education, ". . . . A women's intelligence does not rise higher than her foot, her rightful place was to serve her family, "tart with founding a high school for girls, said Tilak, it would soon lead to women running away from home".[49] In some cases poverty also become a contributing factor in hindering women's education in our Presidency.

Thus, prevelant customs and traditions along with the existing superstition went a long way in discouraging women's education.

Despite, this utterly gloomy picture, with regard to female education, there were rays of few examples which indicated that some kind of rudimentary knowledge, particularly regarding 3 R's were acquired by women. Most of them could handle house-old accounts properly. Few women were well versed with epic and mythological stories the knowledge of which was acquired by them from senior ladies of the house, i.e. grandmother, aunt, elder sister and so on.

". . . . There are not few Hindu ladies among the upper classes in this city Calcutta that can read and that do read. In such cases when they are children they attend the instruction of a *Guru mahasai*, either in their own house or at the house of some near neighbour . . . . By the time this is finished they are married. They are now removed from school and for want of paractice, soon forget to write. But they do not lose their knowledge of reading some of the matrons in the family — it may be an aunt — continue the study of Bengali with the little girl, and she soon learns fluently. The book with which the young women's mind are chiefly engaged are the following : *Ramayana, Mahabharata* . . . .

. . . . This was applicable to women belonging to Bombay Presidency also.[50] Even William Adam upholds the same argument that women in Bengal had acquired some kind of rudimentary knowledge at home. In his second Report on Vernacular education in Bengal, he writes : "...They (the *Zamindars*) in general instruct their daughters in the element of knowledge, although it is difficult to obtain from them an admission of this fact. They hope to marry their daughters into families of wealth of property and they perceive that without a knowledge of writing and accounts their daughters will, in the event of widowhood be incompetent to manage their deceased husbands estates and will unavoidably become a prey to the interested and unprincipled people. Instances sometime occur of young

Hindu female who have received no instruction under their parents roofs, taking lesson at the instigations of their parents, after they have become widows with a view to adequate protection of the families of which they have become members. . . ."[51]

This kind of knowledge was imparted to women in Bombay Presidency also. The Indian Social Reformer also states that ". . . . The Hindu girl is carefully instructed by words of mouth in the religious legends, especially those of the great epic poem, which place before her an ideal of duty and chiefly wifely duty. She is trained in those rites and ceremonies that women are permitted to take part in . . . . she learns to keep household accounts in some simple, but very practical fashion, occasionally she learns to read . . . . *Mohammadan* girl is taught needle work and to read *Koran* in Arabic . . . .[52]

Therefore, despite the existence of the institution of early marriage and existing superstitions against female education, women did acquire some kind of basic and practical knowledge. But the knowledge acquird was such that it could not promote rational and critical thinking amongst women.

This kind of knowledge acquired by women was in sharp contrast to that which had existed in the *Rig-Vedic* period. Many of the women during this period composed hymns. Lopamudra Apala, Vishivavara, Sikata, Nivavari and Ghosha are few names that were constantly referred to in the *Vedas*. It is interesting to note that girls, like boys underwent the *Upanayana* ceremony (sacred initiation at an early age perhaps about the age of eight) and began the *Vedic* studies. The *Atharva Samhita* states that "by *Vedic* studentship a girl wins a young husband". This shows that not only elementary education was regarded as important but higher education was regarded as a necessary accomplishment for being well placed in life. In later *Vedic* period we hear of two classes of women : (1) Sadyodivatas who prosecuted their studies till their marriage and (2) Brahmavadinis, who did not marry and pursued their studies throughout life.[53]

Perhaps formal education, particularly higher education, was possible in the *Rig-Vedic* period because the custom of child marriage and enforced widowhood did not exist then. However, with the development of these customs, as stated earlier, the formal education acquired by women in the *Rig-Vedic* period gradually began to decline.

However, it was the Christian missionaries, who instilled a ray of hope in the field of women's education.

Infact, they become the pioneer. An in-depth discussion of their activity and various institutions established to promote female education will be taken up in the next section.

PIONEERING CONTRIBUTIONS OF THE MISSIONARIES IN THE EVOLUTION OF WOMEN'S EDUCATION

The Christian missionaries played a poineering role in promoting female education in Western India[54]. Infact, they were the most important non-official agency who took up this issue. They became the initiators mainly because in the early 19th century the officials of the East India Company were reluctant to take up this issue for they feared that it would create unnecessary hostility amongst the people and would amount to interference in their social and religious activity. Therefore, they followed the policy of religious neutrality during the period. Though the Charter Act of 1813 compelled the East Indian Company to accept the responsibility for the education of the Indian people, the question of female education was completely ignored. The Indian intelligentsia who had received western education, on the other hand, had no clear perception of female education and it had not chalked out any programme of action.

The Christian missionaries not only entered the scene but took up this "dangerous" and senstitive issue. In order to further their objective, i.e. promotion of the female education they established formal institutions of learning and gradually paved the way for the growth of higher education of women in western India.

The main purpose which motivated the missionaries to undertake this risky venture despite strong opposition was a mixture of evangelical and humanitarian zeal. In the early stages of missionary activity, the former was given more importance. There was a general thinking amongst various missionary societies that education was a vital channel through which they could influence the people, particularly women and impress upon them the sayings and teaching of Christ and thereby convert them to their faith. There was a strong realization on their part that not only women alone but the entire family would eventually be converted to the folds of Christianity. Infact, education was considered as the cause and end of proselytization. Humanitarian considerations also encouraged them to undertake social and educational activities. Most of them upheld the view that education alone would help in developing the personality of women. Perhaps it would enlighten them and prevent them from submitting to irrational customs like *sati,* enforced widowhood and so on. Besides education could promote essential qualities in women such as natural tenderness, love, domestic and social virtues and above all ability to mould the character of their children. A popular poem entitled "Songs for the little ones at Home", reflects the above view —

> "See the heathen mother stand
> Where the sacred current flows
> with ther own materanl hands,
> Mid the wave her babe she throws.
> Send, Oh Send the Bible there, '
> Let its precepts reach the heart;
> She may then her children spare.
> Act the tender mothers part".[55]

A parallel was drawn between social regeneration, women's education with the general state of Indian society. In other words social progress was closely related to women's education. John Wilson who belonged to the Scottish missionary society clearly stated that "..... I am more and more convinced that in seeking for the moral renovation of India, we must make greater efforts than we have yet done to operate upon the female mind....In India it is the stronghold of superstition. Its enlightenment ought to be an object of first concern with us...."[56]

Similar views were upheld by the American Board of Commissioners for Foreign Missions and the Church missionary society..... In their opinion, Indian society was at its lowest ebb; so Christianity and Christianity alone, was the means of uplifting it morally. And one of the ways in which they tried to spread Christianity was by starting school for girls A. R. G. Wilder an American missionary wrote, "Vain will be the attempt to rescue men from the ruin and desolation which Hinduism creates, if women is still left to her cruel charities.... Only Christian eduation can take the Hindu female out of the lowest depth of degradation and sorrow which the human mind and human heart can know and elevate her to that dignified and blissful sphere for which God created her."[57]

The constant focus of missionaries on elevating the position of Indian women was an attempt to emphasize the superiority of British social systems over the prevailing Indian Social System. Missionaries were not only helmates of the Imperialist rulers but they were infact cultural imperialist, providing educational base entirely on English values. In the post Mutiny period, there was a deep concern of the rulers on "improving" the people by changing their habits thus making once for all, India safe for Europeans to rule.[58]

The important missionary societies whose work became prominent in the Bombay Presidency were the Roman Catholic Missionary, American Missionary Society, Anglican Church, the Church Missionary Society. Despite, the missionary organizations being varied their activity was more or less similar, i.e. spread of female education and proselytization.

There were three agencies through which the Christian missionaries worked for promoting female education, viz.

(i) Girls Day Schools
(ii) Orphanages and Boarding establishments.
(iii) Domestic teaching of women arranged in middle and higher class families popularly termed as "*zenana* teaching".

The period 1793 to 1813 was marked by great missionary activities. Evangelicals and Charles Grant, leader of the Clapham sect were against the neutral and anti-missionary policy followed by the Company. Charles Grant in his work "Observation on the State of Society among the Asiatic Subjects of Great Britain, particularly with respect to Morals; and on the Means of Improving it",[59] portrayed a very dismal picture of Indian society. According to him, the reedeming factor lay in spreading education and imparting the knowledge of Chistianity. Infact, the work of Grant became the basis of missionary agitation in England and in India. Thus, the Charter Act of 1813 opened India to missionary society for the first time.[60] During this period various missionary societies established formal institutions of learning, particularly schools meant for girls. A lead in this direction was taken in all the three Presidencies, i.e. Madras, Bengal and Bombay. In the Bengal Presidency, the Serampore Baptist missionaries took a lead in establishing schools for girls. They were responsible in setting up the Calcutta Female Juvenile Society in 1819 which later changed its name to Calcutta Baptist Female Society for the establishment and support of Native Female Schools. This society was reponsible in starting day schools for girls in Calcutta, Chitpore and Sibpore.[61]

In the Bombay Presidency, on the other hand, the American Missionary became the pioneers regarding female eduation. They established the first girls schools in 1824 and two years later they reported an increase of nine girls schools with an aggregate attendance of 340 pupils. In 1829 the number of pupils rose to four hundred of whom one hundred and twenty-two were able to read, write and cipher and also do plain needle work.[62] In 1831 a girl's school was opened at Ahmednagar. Similar kind of institution was established by the Church Missionary Society in 1826. In the course of next ten years it opened many schools, particularly elementay schools for boys and girls at Thana Bassein and Nasik.[63] The Scottish Missionary did not lag behind in this venture. Like the early missionay organizations, it established its first girls school in 1829. This school later came to be known as the St. Columba High School for girls. Infact, the school continues to retain the name even to this day. It was the sincere labour of Margaret Wilson, that gave a firm footing to the efforts of the Scottish missionaries. On her arrival in Bombay, she was determined to take up women's educations as a challenge. In her own words she stated ".... We have now come to Bombay the place destined to be the scene of our future labour and trails".[64] On her own initiative she established six day schools for girls and personally kept in touch with its growth and development.[65] In order to establish a closer rapport with her pupils she learned the local dialect, i.e. Marathi, and taught in this language. She also translated some books into Marathi, e.g. Rollin's "Ancient History" for the benefit of the students.[66]

By 1832 her school contained hundred and seventy-six girls. She gave her heart and soul to these schools because she felt that she was doing service to God and humanity by conveying the knowledge of the divine truth to the female of India. In her own words she stated that, ". . . . I take the entire superintendence of the school and consider that this affords me a most valuable opportunity of conveying a knowledge of divine truth to the female of India. I feel that every increase of occupation brings with it an increase of happiness and I see in this arrangement a wonderful illustration of the goodness of God. Had I contemplated at a distance the number and variety of duties which now devolve upon me, I should have been appalled at the prospect; but instead of lessening they greatly add to my enjoyment".[67]

The efforts of Mrs. Wilson were crowned with success and we find that the number of students in her school rose to two hundred by mid-19th century. After her death her work was taken up by her sisters Anna and Hay Bayne.[68] Perhaps the efforts of Margaret Wilson and her colleagues influenced Major St. Clair Jameson who appealed to the ladies of Scotland to help their Indian sisters. This gave rise to the "Ladies Society for Female Education in India" which supported girls schools in Bombay, Poona and other districts.[69]

Thus, we find that by 1833 the bulk of missionary enterprise succeeded in establishing elementary girls' school. However, this emphasis gradually under-went a change and we find that from 1833 onwards the missionaries concentrated on opening secondary schools and colleges[70]. In Bombay, Dr. John Wilson founded the magnificent college which afterwards bore his name. Infact, Wilson College was the first Arts College to admit lady students. In 1886, the first women student who entered Wilson College belonged to the Parsi community. They were Ratanbai Ardeshir Vakil and her sister Meherbai. Ratanbai specialized in French and was elected as a Fellow in 1890. From then till her early death in 1895, she taught French in the College. Meherbai took to medicine.[71] Gradually the college had a long roll of women graduates who had subsequently taken up medical sciences and law degrees.[72]

The Report of the Director of Public Instructions states that in the year 1897-98 there were fourteen lady students on the college rolls during the first term of 1898 of whom seven were studying for the previous examination, three for the intermediate and two for the B.A. examination. It is interesting to note that when Wood's Educational Despatch was received in 1854, mission institutions formed the bulk of educational enterprise in India. It is because of their efforts the Despatch specially mentioned liberal grants to mission schools.

The curriculum in mission schools mainly consisted of Reading, Writing, Arithmetic, Environmental education, General knowledge, Tailoring and even Knitting was taught. However, Bible formed the core subject. In some schools, music also formed an important part of the curriculum.[73] In colleges, on the other hand, professional education in medical sciences, law, different European languages and so on was emphasised.[74]

The day schools and institutions promoting higher education became popular among different sections of society. In the Bengal Presidency, they acquired a wider base among the lower castes. William Adam who conducted an in depth study into the state of Indigenous education in the Bengal Presidency clearly mentions that mission schools became popular among the *Bagdis, Muchis, Bauris, Domes, Haries, Vaishnavas, Tantis, Chandals, Kurmis* and so on.[75]

In the Bombay Presidency, on the other hand, pupils generally belonged to the Parsi, Muslim, Bene-Israel, Catholics and also from amongst Protestant converts. Gujarati and Marathi speaking Hindus also attended mission schools.[76] It is interesting to note that amongst the Hindus, the *Brahmins* who were the highest caste in social hierarchy attended mission schools. Mary Carpenter in her account states that in Poona twenty-five little *Brahmin* girls attended as day scholars in the Mission Boarding schools.[77]

Also, Margaret Wilson in her schools appointed *Brahmin* teachers not only to impart instructions to her pupils but also to help her in gathering more students from amongst this community.[78]

The second important agency through which the missionaries

carried their work of promoting female education were the orphanages and boarding establishments. This kind of institution was established by all the missionaries in Bombay Presidency. The Scottish missionaries, in particular the services of Margaret Wilson, deserves special mention in promoting these institutions. The earliest one was established by her in Bombay in 1832.

The main objectives of the institution were clearly specified by her, such as —

1. The object of the school shall be to afford support, and Christian instruction to destitute native girls, particularly widows and orphans.
2. The school shall be placed under the care of a committee, consisting of Mrs. William, Mrs. Money, Mrs. Webb and Mrs. Wilson, Mrs. Wilson was to act as general superintendent.
3. The children admitted shall be decently clothed and a small sum shall be allowed for their food.
4. When relatives are disposed to take proper charge of the girls, they shall be allowed to lodge with them; and when the case is otherwise and the girls are particularly destitute, some arrangements shall be made for their board.
5. When the girls have made a certain progress in reading, they shall be instructed in female work. Encouragement shall be given to such of them as may be disposed to become *Ayahs* (maid-servants); to acquire the requisite knowledge and practice.[79]

Thus, the boarding of schools and orphanages served twin purpose, i.e. promotion of education and carrying on humanitarian work amongst the destitute sections of society.

It is interesting to note that most of the pupils in the orphanages acquired vocational educational in lacemaking weaving, knitting, needle work, dress making and so on. The main idea behind such a training was to make the pupils self-reliant and self-sufficient. Some to the orphanages also trained pupils in agricultural and industrial work. The American Marathi Mission and the Anglican Church, particularly emphasised on such a kind of education.[80]

It is significant to note that some women missionaries in their own private capacities informally encouraged women to take to education. This can be clearly seen in the case of Vidyagauri Nilkant, the first Gujarati women graduate of the Bombay University who after finishing her primary education in Maganbhai *Kanyashala* (primary girls school) was helped by Mrs. Macaphee, the lady superintendent of the Mahalakshmi training college to continue with her education. Infact. Mr. Macaphee was the principal of the Christian mission school in Ahmedabad and informally taught Vidyagauri and her class mates Algebra and Geometry. Vidyagauri writes that but for the encouragement of Mrs. Macaphee, it would not have been possible for her to continue her education and appear for the matriculation examination. Perhaps such like encouragement was given to Cornelia Sorabji a Parsi Christian[81] and Anandi Gopal. The former became a legal advisor in the Bengal Government and the latter who was educated by Miss Maise graduated in 1886 from the Women's Medical College at Philadelphia.[82]

In order to widen their base amongst the people some of the women missionaries paid money to the students, particularly those tho were poor. In Gujarat, girls were given Rs. 45 worth of presents as dowry when they got married after leaving schools. In addition they got the *Bible* and two other Prayer books.[83] William Adam reported how in Bengal girls who joined Mrs. Paterson's school in Murshidabad were given one piece per week for attendance, every four months a piece of cloth and armlet every year[84]. At times force was employed to increase attendance. Peon known as *Hirkara* in Bengal Presidency were employed to search for those who were absent. Thus, at the close of 1850's, the various missionary effforts for female education in western as well as whole of India embraced three hundred and fifty-four day schools with eleven thousand five hundred and forty-nine girls; Boarding school with two thousand three hundred and forty-six girls; taught mostly in vernacular languages. The distribution of missionary schools in various provincess is given in Table 2.1

Table 2.1 : Missionary Schools in Provinces

	Day Schools	*Girls in Schools*	*Boarding Schools*	*Girls in Schools*
Bengal	26	690	28	836
N.W. Provinces	8	213	11	208
Madras Presidency	222	6,929	41	1,101
Bombay Presidency	28	1,087	6	129
Ceylon	70	2,630	5	72
	354	11,5491	91	2346

The Census of Mission institution 1851 also gives an in-depth account of mission activity in the whole of India at the time of the Despatch of 1854.[86] Table 2.2 gives the relevant statistics.

These statistics not only reveal the extent of mission activity but also support the view that by 1854 mission activity in education was almost equal to the official enterprise. Mission activity was particularly widespread in Madras, partly because it began very early (1706) and partly because the extremely hard plight of the *Harijans* in the south provided a more fruitful soil for conversion.[87]

Table 2.2 : Missionary Schools in Provinces

	Bombay	*Bengal*	*NWP*	*Madras*
1. No. of Station	23	61	19	111
2. Foreign ordained agents	38	95	45	147
3. Indian Ordained agents	4	21	1	12
4. Foreign & Europeanlay preachers	2	22	11	19
5. Indian lay preachers	15	132	37	306
6. Church or congregations	13	70	17	161
7. Indian Christians	638	14,177	1,732	—
8. Communicants	290	3,371	573	10,334
9. Anglo-Vernacular school & colleges for men	7	22	13	43
10. Pupils in Anglo Vern-acular school & college for men	907	6,054	1,029	4,096
11. Vernacular school for boys.....	85	126	47	824
12. Pupils in Vernacular schools for boys	4,679	6,319	2,640	24,178
13. Boarding school for boys	4	20	10	32
14. Pupils in Boarding school for boys	64	708	209	787
15. Day school for girls	31	26	8	217
16. Pupils in day school for girls	1,186	690	213	6,768
17. Boarding school for girls'	8	27	9	39
18. Pupils in Boarding school for girls	139	797	173	1,110
19. Grand Total of pupils - males and females (excluding sunday school)	6,975	14,568	4,264	36,939
20. Sunday schools	131	183	350	1,102
21. Pupils in Sunday school	13,711	6,938	16,671	61,688

However, the revolt of 1857 brought a sea change in the position acquired by the missionaries in 1854. The Queen's proclamation of 1858 emphasised on religious neutrality and gave assurance to the people that government had neither the right nor the desire to impose Christianity upon India.[88]

Thus between 1858 and 1882, the policy of the Department was marked by an unsympathetic attitude to mission schools and the officials of those days many of whom were agnostics or lacking in missionary zeal-made it difficult for the missionaries to work either within the system or without it. Some of the difficulties which missionaries experienced while working within the official system are as follows —

> "We cannot, however, pass over the fact that there were great disadvantages bound up with the new school system. Whereas in the first few years the Government preferred to appoint missionaries as inspectors of schools, yet later on, and especially after the great Mutiny of 1857, it turned its back almost entirely upon them, no doubt out of exaggerated religious neutrality, and chose with predilection Englishmen indifferent to religion or non-Christian *Brahmins*, for these positions. As the yearly grants-the hinge on which the new system turned-depended on the result of the annual visitations and examinations conducted by these gentlemen, it came about that mission schools, for instance, were often in a state of very undesirable dependence on the goodwill or the good temper of officials who were antagonistic to missions...."[89]

Similarly, the Education Department often followed a policy of direct competition which made it impossible for the missionaries to work independently of the official education system.

It was these difficulties that made the missionaries start an agitation, both in England and in India to the effect that the educational administration of India was not carried on in accordance with the Despatch of 1854 which had recommended the closure or transfer of government schools, that the officials were competing with mission enterprise to such an extent that the latter was threatened with extinction. It was this agitation that led to the appointment of the Indian Education Commission in 1882. The Commission after careful considerations came to the conclusion that missionary educational enterprise could occupy only a secondary place in Indian education and that the government should not withdraw in favour of missionary managements. Thus, the missionaries, particularly after 1882 adopted the policy of restricting their educational activities to the maintenance of a few educational institutions in high state of efficiency and abandoned their earlier dream of commanding the whole educational field in India.

Despite, adopting this policy, we find, that the missionary in larger provinces such as Bengal, Bombay, Madras numbered 10,461, namely, 42 colleges, 843 secondary schools 9,259 primary schools, 75 training institutions and 242 other schools. The Church of England mission educated some 113,000 pupils and contributed about 7.84 lakhs; Roman Catholic Mission approximately 108,000 pupils and 8.8 lakhs Baptist missions 54,000 pupils and 3 lakhs.[90] Scotish, American and other mission worked on a large scale. These figures indicate that missionaries continued to maintain primary and higher institutions of learning throughout India in a high state of efficiency.[91]

Apart from formal institutions of learning, the missionaries encouraged female education through the *zenana* system or domestic education which formed the third vital agency of promoting female education. This system catered for the education of women in middle and higher families who were denied access to formal institutions of learning owing to prevalent customs and traditions.[92] In certain cases it become a feasible alternative to a few years of formal schooling. Also, it was found that most of the Indian elites wanted their womenfolk educated in western manners and occupation of English Ladies. They were most anxious to have the missionaries visit and educated their wives and assist in introducing them to English clothing particularly shoes and stocking and also learn darning. The missionaries on their part contended themselves that by teaching such subjects to the "pure heathen" they were planting the seeds of Christianity.[93]

It is interesting to note that to most of the Europeans, the *zenana* was considered as bastions of ignorances, breeding places of disease, intrigues and prejudices. It was increasingly felt that only the Christian missionaries could cure this lacuna and shortcoming by educating and converting the women folk. While the missionaries succeeded in imparting education to women, they could not succeed in their second mission of converting women to Christianity.

The *zenana* system of education was widely prevalent in Bengal, although it was a common *modus operandi* with almost all the missionaries stationed in different parts of India. In Western India the earliest society to promote *zenana* education was the society for promotion of female education in the East. In 1842 it was the first to attempt *zenana* work. This society sent a lady to Bombay for the Parsis. Thus, it has been pioneers of all subsequent and kindred efforts. It had established a training school and home for the *zenana* workers in one of its stations in North West India and had selected agents to be sent out by other missionary society.[94]

The main advantage of this system of education was that even the grown up ladies could acquire the rudiments of learning without going to formal schools. They were instructed in their respective homes in reading, writing letter composition and ordinary accounts besides scriptural teaching. Regular examinations were held behind the screen or *purdah*. Suitable rewards were given to those who were successful in the examination.[95]

In the Bengal Presidency, the *zenana* system conducted by Rev. Fordyee and Mrs. Mullen's succeeded in getting access to some aristocratic families of Calcutta. The first successful teacher associated with *zenana* system in Bengal was Mrs. Toogood. In order to make her teaching effective she learned the local dialect, i.e. Bengali and taught pupil in it.[96]

For the *zenana* system of education to function properly a need of well trained teachers was strongly felt. Perhaps it was this realization along with a universal need for female teachers that compelled Mary Carpenter to suggest for the establishment of Female Normal Schools which would train female teachers. As a result of her endeavour training school for women were established in Bombay, Poona and Ahmedabad in 1862.[97]

In the initial stage very few young women applied for admission. Infact, there was no question of choosing students and everyone who applied was admitted. However, by 1882 these training schools succeeded in producing thirty-four trained teachers.[98]

Also, *zenana* teaching brought into sharp focus the need of women doctors and nurses who would look into the medical requirements of the womenfolk. It was found "…. During illhealth, unless women doctors are available, she cannot get any adequate advice. Messages are frequently sent describing her symptoms to male doctors through her husband or servants….. But it is in childbirth that the full horror of the *purdah* system is seen, when women are allowed to die undelivered sooner than show themselves to a man".[99]

Therefore, to meet the medical care for women poineering efforts in this direction was taken up by Miss Clara Swain who belonged to the Methodist Episcopal Church of America. She began her work initially at Bareilly in the United Province.[100] Her efforts bore fruits and we find that by 1887, 17 women were studying at the Grant Medical College of whom two were matriculates working for the LM&S degree, while the others were to be awarded diplomas and certificates.[101]

Hospitals exclusively meant for women were also established in the Bombay Presidency during our period. The earliest hospital was opened in Poona by the Church of Scotland. In 1892 St. Margaret hospital was opened which also dealt with medical problems faced by women; similar hospital was opened at Kolapur by the American Presbyterian Mission.

Thus, the *zenana* system of education led to the establishment of Normal schools for training teachers and it also motivated women to go in for medical profession and we find that during our period women were trained as doctors, nurses and mid-wives. Some of the significant women personalities who took to medical education were Anandibai Joshi, Annie Jagannadhan, Rukhmabai and others.

As mentioned earlier Anandi Gopal graduated in 1886 from the Women's Medical College at Philadelphia. She returned to India having been appointed to the charge of the Women's ward of the Albert Edward Hospital at Kolapur. She could not take up the new assigment because she suffered from tubercular disease, which took toll of her life in 1887.

Miss Annie Jagannadhan went to Edinburgh School of Medicine in 1888. She obtained the triple qualification of the Scottish College in 1892, and after successfully completing her course, she took up the post of house surgeon in the Cama Hospital. She too could not pursue her career for a longer time because she suffered from pulmonary tuberculosis and passed away in 1894.

Rukhmabai like the earlier ladies pursued her medical study at the London School of Medicine in 1889. She took her qualification from the Scottish College and returned to India in 1895. She took charge of the Women's hospital at Surat. In 1918 she was selected for the Womens Medical Service and at the same time she received the offer of appointment of Medical Officer in charge of the *zenana* state hospital, Rajkot which she decided to accept and began her work there.

The importance of the *zenana* or domestic education found reflection in Woods Despatch of 1854 and in the Hunter Commission Report of 1882. The former recommended that all the schools for girls including *zenana* teaching, be brought under a comprehensive educational system and assisted through grant-in-aid. The latter also echoed similar message. Infact, a separate section was devoted to *zenana* teaching. It stated that.......

"But in the existing circumstances of the women of India, the mere establishments of schools will be by no means sufficient to bring about the general spread of education among them. Public sentiment keeps them secluded in the *zenana;* many from their infancy and many more from the age of eleven or twelve. For this it follows that the education of girls of the better classes cannot be carried on in schools to anything like completion, and that in the case of many it cannot even be begun. Some plan is needed for conveying instruction to those who cannot leave their homes to seek for it and for prosecuting further the teaching which may have been begun in schools. Agencies for *zenana* teaching are conducting this work with considerable success. Actuated in many cases by religious motive, *zenana* teachers have brought some measures of secular instruction into the homes of those who would otherwise have been wholly debarred form it. We see no reason why this secular instruction, imparted under the supervision of ladies worthy of confidence, should not be recognized and assisted so far as it can be tested by a proper inspecting agency".[102]

Thus, the *zenana* system of education gave encouragement not only to female education but also to the growth of professional education, particularly teaching and medicine.

Therefore, the various missionary agencies in their respective capacity succeeded in laying the foundation of female education in western India. Infact, few women who received education formed a class known as the "Intelligentsia" who were educated in the Western sytem of education that emphasised on rational and scientific aspects. These women who were in receipt of such a kind of education were inspired to carry on similar kind of work undertaken by the missionaries, i.e. humanitarian work. Infact, they carried the thread of missionary activity to its logical consequence by founding organization which undertook social and educational work. In this connection the names of Ramabai Saraswati and Ramabai Ranade deserve special mention.[103] The former is credited to have established the *Sharda Sadan* (home of learning) especially meant for the widows in 1889.

Despite, the growing popularity of the *Sadan,* amongst the people, Ramabai Saraswati, had to face stiff opposition from the nationalist group headed by B.G. Tilak when it became public that a number of inmates had got attracted towards Christianity and been ultimately baptized.[104] She was often dubbed as a "demon" however widows and young girls continued to enroll themselves. In their own words they said "....... Let her be a demon! We don't mind! Atleast she looks after us well. That is enough for us......."[105]

Undaunted by social criticism Ramabai Saraswati carried her selfless and humanitarian work by laying the foundation of *Mukti Sadan* (Home of Salvation) and *Kripa Sadan* (Home of Mercy) which particularly emphasised on humanitarian work.

Ramabai Ranade closely followed Ramabai Saraswati in carrying out similar kind of work founding the *Seva-Sadan* (Home dedicated to self - less service for women).

It is interesting to note that not only the women but even male intelligentsia drew inspirations from the missionaries. Despite, social opposition, they continued to send their wards to mission schools. In this connection the name of Dadoba Paṇdurang became important. He was a superintendent of Government Vernacular School and the founder of *Paramhans Mandali* in 1840. He continued to send his daughter and those of his friends to Mrs. Wilson's schools, though he was often criticized for it.

It is ironical to note that though the missionaries succeeded in inspiring male and female intelligentsia to undertake social and educational work among the people they failed to convert them to christianity. Infact, the earlier assumption they held, i.e. education would be the cause and end of proselytization was belied in years to come. The institutions that were established by the male and later on by the female intelligentsia though carried on humanitarian and education activities of the missionary; they did not propagate Christianity or include *Bible* teaching in the Syllabus.

Therefore, though the missionaries failed on proselytization ground they did play a positive role in encouraging not only primary schools for girls and professional education, particularly training of teachers but here again the success of their efforts should not be over exaggerated as the custom of child marriage and deep rooted social prejudices and fear of conversion continued to hinder women from acquiring education in our Presidency. Despite, the limited nature of thier activity, they continued to be the pioneers in female education. Their activities motivated the male intelligentsia who formed the second non-official agency in promoting female education. An in-depth discussion of their activity will be taken up in the next section.

ROLE OF THE MALE INTELLIGENTSIA IN AMELIORATING SOCIAL EVILS AND PROMOTION OF HIGHER EDUCATION

In the Bombay Presidency during our period, the second important non-official agency next to the missionaries who undertook social and educational work among women were the male intelligentsia. They mainly consisted of individuals, who were the recipients of western system of education.[106] This system of education laid emphasis on democratic, liberal, rational and humanitarian principles[107] which found reflection in the works of James Mill, Comte, Herbert Spencer and so on.

Mills, "Subjection of Women" (1869) became popular amongst the educated circle. Infact, the argument in favour of female equality was often taken up by the intelligentsia. Similar views were found in the work of Comte who emphasised on the absolute necessity of women's equality. The ideas upheld by these authors had a far reaching impact on the intelligentsia. It helped them critically examine their society and find out the reasons which retarded its progress. A detailed examination of the social, educational and political institutions of the country was undertaken by them. In the social sphere, it was found that the practice of caste system, and the existing customs, and traditions followed, particularly, with regard to women, i.e. child marriage, leading to enforced widowhood, *purdah* went a long way in hindering social advancement. In the field of education there was a realization that knowledge imparted only emphasised on religious aspects and failed to promote any rational and logical thinking. Also, it was confined to the upper castes. Raja Ram Mohun Roy who is aptly described as the Father of "Modern India" not only upheld this view about traditional system of education but felt that if the Indian mind had to be regenerated, western literature and sciences should be propagated. Infact, he petitioned the government to abandon its project for oriental education and to undertake the teaching of western sciences and literature.[108]

Similarly, like the social and educational institutions, it was found that the political system reflected feudal tendencies for it supported those ideas and beliefs which did not encourage experimental methods or promote the spirit of inquiry.

Therefore, for any kind of advancement it was felt that institutional changes had to be first brought about. How were these changed to be brought about? In this connection various methods were suggested.

The first method was termed as the method of rebellion. The followers of this school of thought believed in outright and sudden change in the existing social institutions.[109] They were against any gradual methods of change. The creed of this school of thought was based upon the principle that conscience after all must be the supreme guide of human conduct and the followers of this school declined to allow any other consideration to affect or influence their proceedings.

The second method was the method of interpretaion, implying the interpretaion of sacred text. The upholders of this method strongly felt that the malice that had crept in social, educational and political institutions did not exist in the *Vedic* period, particularly in the *Rig-Vedic* period. They sought to bring about reformation by drawing parallels from earlier period and by interpreting sacred text, e.g. Raja Ram Mohun Roy[110] was against the practice of *sati* that was widely prevalent in the Bengal Presidency. He tried to do away with this custom by stating neither the *Vedas,* nor *Yajnavalkya* supported it. Infact, it was forbidden both by the *Bhagwad-Gita, Manu* and *Raghunanada;* even the author of *Mitakshara* considered it inferior to eternal beauty or virtuous life. He further argued that even *Harita* and other advocates of *sati* did not support it if it was not voluntarly.[111]

Ishwar Chand Vidyasagar, the pioneer of widow remarriage stated that widow remarriage was sanctioned by the *Shastras*. According to him, the *Parasara Samhita* sanctioned widow remarriage.[112] On the other hand, Ranade believed that –

> "a true reformer has not to write upon a clean slate.His work is more often to complete the half written sentence. We cannot break with the past altogether for it is a rich inheritance and we have no reason to be ashamed of it. But while respecting the past we must ever seek to correct the practical growth that have encrusted it".[113]

The third was the method of pledges. The followers of this method appealed to men's sense of honour, irrespective of the opinions of society, the command of religious or personal convenience and comfort. Maharshi Karve, the follower of this method pledged to marry a widow when his first wife expired. In his own words, he stated that "...... the question of second marriage now confronted me. As soon as marriage season arrived, friends and acquaintances began to approach me for marriage on behalf of guardians of marriageable girls. I once told them that I was going to marry a widow....."[114] When he finally married a widow, i.e. Anandibai he had to face a lot of criticism and opposition from the people, particularly the Brahmins.[115] Similar views were expressed by Dr. Gopalrao Joshi. In his own words he stated that "..... I wish to marry a widow, not necessarily a *Brahmin* widow, caste does not matter. It doesn't matter if the widow does not belong to a good family. A widow with a child will also do, what matter is that she should be woman and a widow....[116]" Also, Ranade expressed his desire to marry a widow when his first wife expired , though under parental pressure he did not do so. The pledges taken by the members of the Indian National Social Conference in 1889 also coincided with this method. Around 549 members pledged to abstain from alcohlic drinks, cessation of the practice of dowry, endorsement of widow remarriage, promised to give education to their daughters and assurance not to practice child marriage. Ranade was among others who took the oath[117].

The fourth was the method of compromise. The follower of this school also believed in the necessity of reform although at the same time they were not themselves prepared, either from moral cowardice or because of the cumulative influence of tradition to act upon their honest belief, e.g. Gopal Hari Deshmukh, despite the vigour of his attack against the *Brahmin* priests, submitted to their demands that he go through a penance ceremony, including taking *prayascitta* for having attended the re-marriage of Hindu widow. Deshmukh's reason for doing penance illustrate the problem; his daughter's mother-in-law threatened to obtain a new wife for her son if the reformer did not submit to social and religious requirements.[118] Similarly, Justice Ranade propagated in favour of widow marriage but when the opportunity arrived to translate his opinions into practice, he married a virgin. Justice Telang though vociferously supported the age of consent for girls to be married, but when the time came he married off his own daughter at the age of ten.[119] However, the most significant example regarding this method was a debate organized by Shankaracharya on whether widow marriage was sanctioned by *Shastra's* or not. This was held in Poona in 1871. A debate was arranged between the orthodox and the reform parties. Five *Shastries* were nominated by the orthodox and five by the reform party. However, the outcome of the debate, went against widow-remarriage. It was alleged that the fifth nominee of the reform party was really in favour of widow marriage, as far as his opinion was concerned, but voted against it owing to the undue influence that was brought to bear upon him.[120]

The last or the fifth method laid emplasis on state compulsion, which in other words seeks to involve the assistance of the legislature. Many of the reformers, particularly Ishwar Chand Vidyasagar and Malabari encouraged the state to pass legislation on Widow Remarriage, Age of Consent and so on, as result of which we find that Widow Remarriage Act was passed in 1856 and the Age of Consent Bill was passed in 1891, which raised the age of marriage of girls from ten to twelve.[121]

Therefore, various methods were advocated by the reformers in bringing about a change in the existing social institutions. Despite, the methods being varied, there was a common underlying current, i.e. the desire of bringing change or reforms into the state of the society already in existence. Existing *status quo* was not accepted to them. Reformer's like Ranade did not believe in anyone of the above methods, but believed in adapting anyone that suited the purpose.[122]

Also during our period there arose a controversy regarding whether social reform should be given precedence over political reform. By and large two significant schools of thought had developed or emerged during this period. One school of thought felt that social reform should be given preference over political reform. Reformers belonging to this school of thought believed that without social reform, political reform would have no meaning. Infact, Raja Ram Mohun Roy felt that both religious and social reform were prerequisites to any enchancement of India's political stature.[123] Reformers like Ranade, on the other hand, believed in the interdependence of social, economic and political reforms. In his address to the first Provincial Social Conference at Satara, he stated that "you cannot have a good social system when you find yourself low in the scale of political rights nor can you be fit to exercise political rights and privileges unless your social system is based on reason and justice. You cannot have a good economic system when your social arrangements are imperfect.If your religious ideas are low and grovelling you cannot succeed in social, economic and political spheres. This interdependence is not accidental but is the law of our nature".[124]

Malabari, like Ranade, also stated that if Indians wanted to acquire the political institution of the West they would first have to assimilate to some extent atleast western "moral and social usages".[125] Similar thoughts were upheld by R.G. Bhandarkar and Vireasalingam Pantulu.

On the other hand, the most important Reformer who preferred political to social reform was Balgangadhar Tilak. Though Tilak was not against social reform[126] he, however, did not agree with the precedence accorded to it, by few reformers. He was against all kinds of social legislation. He asserted that a foreign government should not be trusted with the power of making social changes. In his view social conditions could not be improved until political conditions were bettered. He held that slow and spontaneous action by society would bring about the desired result; education and consciousness of social evils would eradicate the defects.[127]

Despite, the existence of various methods and controversies, we find that the reformer's in their individual capacity or through various *samaje's* established by them, focussed on social and educational issues. On the social front, the major issues tackled by the reformers were caste system, customs effecting status of women, i.e. *purdah,* child-marriage and enforced widowhood and so on. In the field of education, they promoted primary, secondary and even to some extent vocational education. This they did by establishing formal institutions of learning; encouraging women's education in their roles as fathers, brothers, and husbands and by writing educational journals and pamphlets.

It is significant to note that though the intelligentsia constantly took up social issues, and even succeeded in getting social legislation passed, it was female education which they mainly emphasised. There was a gradual realization on their part that no amount of legislation would bring about a drastic change in the customs and traditions established in society. Also, status of women would not significantly improve unless awareness was created amongst women. Infact, it was felt that no amount of reform would be meaningful unless women realized its significance. Therefore, instead of imposing the reform from above a better course would be one where women themselves would come foward and demand reform. This would only be possible if women were educated and were aware of their rights and duties as individuals. Perhaps, education would enable a woman to perform her varied roles as mothers, sisters, wives and daughters in a better way. As B. M. Malabari stated "......The solution of Indian problems was in the lap of the women of India. The future of India, he argued was bound up with the problem of women; it was because they are ignorant and shut off from life that we have no real home life, and consequently we are deprived of those silent but all powerful influences, which mould the child's character and fit men to be heroes. It is in the development of women's true nature, that we must seek the future greatness of our people. In the moral and spiritual education of men, in the refinement of life, and improvement of home, in the up bringing of children, and in the implanting of a true faith in the hearts of men, the sphere of women is absolutely boundless; who but the women can inspire men with a high minded resolve for noble deeds? Who but the women can help the organization of charity, and provide comfort for the desolate, the ignorant and the friendless, and bring to the sick and the weary the love of a mother?...... If we think education and freedom is good for women, we must not think of personal inconveniences".[128] He further added that "...... Unless the women are eduated and emancipated from the bonds of ignoble customs, there can be little hope for the future.....".[129]

Vithaldas Thackersey felt that the index of a progressive nation lay in the education of women. He was a strong advocator of women's education. According to him, "..... Progressive womanhood is a sure symbol of a progressive nation; enslaved, illiterate and ignorant womanhood is no less a sure symbol of a degenerate, backward or a dependent country".[130]

Similar views were expressed by Karamaveer V.R. Shinde. He felt that unless the condition of women in society was improved there would be no social progress.[131] Indeed Shinde believed that progress of women was basic to all progress. Like Phule he was a champion of the lower castes and therefore felt that if education was given to the girls of the lower castes they would be released from the shackles of superstition and slavery. They would also improve their families and bring about a general elevation of their caste to higher culture.[132]

Thus, the reformers realized that only by educating women could culture and value like rationalism, liberalism be effectively transmitted to society. Also women could perform their role as prime agents of socialization effectively.

This line of thinking was also true of the Gujarati intelligentsia. A well-known poet Dalpatram wrote that if one wanted to improve society, one should give education to women. According to him, there were many advantages in educating one's daughter, even mentioning such things as the prevention of petty quarrels and petty obstecies among women. He added that "if a father gives dowry to his daughter, the husband would usurp it, if education is given to her no power on earth could deprive her of her wealth".[133]

The poet Narmada was also in favour of women's education. He urged the girls "to study, study and study". He argued that women should be educated as they were in no way inferior to men or their slaves...... "By educating a woman, the man will be able to talk to her and share his joys and sorrows...... An educated man cannot share his life with an illiterate wife. Education will make a woman a better wife, a better daughter-in-law and a better mother".[134]

Also, reformers like Karve found that propagation of widow marriage could not become popular among the people because it was difficult for them to break away from the established tradition so easily. Since these customs were legitimized by religion, people were reluctant to ignore it completely, and follow the sayings of the reformers.[135] In the case of widow remarriage it was found that though the Act was passed in 1856, it remained a dead letter for thirty years. A story was current at the time of a young reformer who announced to the cheer of his audience that he would marry a widow and none other.... The marriage never took place. Social ostracism at the hands of the orthodox he was ready to face, but to be shut out from the group that had approved and indeed inspired his action , was too much to be borne.[136]

Therefore, Karve and others realized that the better course of reform would be to lay emphasis on education. Perhaps, the opposition against education would be less severe than widow marriage. He felt that a good many widows who would not give thought to a proposal to marry again would heartily come forward to avail themselves of opportunities to receive the benefits of education. In his own words he stated that "why not then take up the work of providing educational facilities for the widow?

After all, the object was to enable them to have a new and happy life".[137] He further added that education would make them (widow's)self-supporting and would enable them to think for themselves.[138]

It was the Bengal Presidency which took a lead in tackling social and educational issues regarding women in the early 19th century. The prominent reformers were Raja Ram Mohun Roy and Ishwar Chand Vidyasagar. The former was a crusader of *Sati*. According to him this custom was inhuman and barbarous and was not prevalent in the Vedic period. Infact, *Sati* was a modern encroachment on the ancient right of females. He saw a direct connection between inheritance rights and the practice of *Sati*.[139] It is this connection which made him state that the custom existed where widow's had a right to inherit. In his journal *Sambad Kaumudi* he wrote in detail against this custom. As mentioned earlier it was because of his efforts that *Sati* was abolished in 1829. He also laid the foundation of *Brahmo-Samaj* which later played a prominent role in tacking social and religious issues.

On the other hand, Ishwar Chand Vidyasagar was a crusader of widow-marriage. He was the chief instrument in getting Widow Remarriage Act Passed in 1856.

Regarding women's education, though Raja Ram Mohun Roy spoke in favour of it, in practice he did not establish any formal school for girls. It was Ishwar Chand Vidyasagar who not only established schools for girls but also became Inspector of Girls Schools in Bengal.

It is interesting to note that some of the British officials in their private capacities promoted women's education. In the Bengal Presidency a lead in this direction was taken by J.E.D. Bethune who was the law member of the Executive Council of the Governor-General and the President of the Council of Education from 1848 to 1851. He opened a school for girls in 1849 and within a short-time it attracted a fairly large number of girl's.[140] The success of the institution lay in the fact that gradually it promoted higher education of women. A similar movement was started in the Bombay Presidency also. The earliest to voice concern regarding women was Vishnu Shastri Pandit. He took up the cause of widows and propagated extensively about re-marriage of widows. Infact, he was known as the Ishwar Chand Vidyasagar of Maharashtra. He founded the *"Vidhava-Vivahottejak Mandal* (Society for Encouragement of Widow Remarriage).[141] As a result of his efforts re-marriage of two *Brahmin* widows took place at Belgaum in 1842.[142]

Similar kind of work was undertaken by Dadoba Pandurang who founded the *Paramahans Mandali* (Divine Society) in 1840 with the object of abolishing caste and idolatry and fostering widow remarriage.

The printed media also played a role in popularising the cause of both the orthodoxy and the reformers. For instance, Gopal Hari Deshmukh, who wrote under the pen-name of *Lokahitwadi* made scathingly attacks on the monstrous and outdated customs and usages in Hindu society and the in human treatment of women, particularly widows in his *Shatapatre* (Hundred Letters)[143] Jambhekar through the monthly reform journal *Digdarshan* (show the way) and weekly journal *Bombay Durpan* supported widow remarriage and liberalization of caste formalities, and the readmission to Hindu society of persons who had been baptized Christians.[144]

In Gujarat too the earliest social reform activity did not lag far behind. One of the earliest and prominent social reformer was Mehtaji Durgaram Mancharam. He organized the *Manay Dharma Sabha* in 1844 (Universal Religious Society) to discuss social problems like treatment meted to widows, caste sytem and so on.[145] The thread of his activity was picked up by the poet Narmada who also took up the cause of women's education and urged widow remarriage. Most of the Gujarati reformers were associated with the Gujarat Vernacular Society in Ahmedabad which was founded in 1848 under the inspiration of Alexander Forbes. The society's main work was in the field of women's education and its Journal *Buddi Prakash* carried articles on women's education.[146]

One of the most prominent and organized efforts in the social and educational field was undertaken by the Students Literary and Scientific Society in 1848. It was founded at the Elphinstone Institution, with the support of the Elphinstone professors and under the leadership of four distinguished Elphnistonian's; Dadabhai Naoroji, Naoroji Furdunji, Sorabji Shapeerji Bengali and Bhau Daji. The members had in common the same school and education. To begin with, the society merely acted as a sort of evening class for those who had left the institution, to which they could come to hear papers read on scientific subjects such as metallurgy, social questions such as education, customs and traditions effecting the status of women in society, women's education and so on.[147] It was obvious that few of these discussions could be made attractive to a wider circle of society unless existing linguistic and social divisions were taken into account. Hence, the society very quickly split on linguistic and communal lines and resolved itself into the *Gujarati Dnyan Prasarak Mandali*, chiefly for the Parsis, the *Marathi Dnyan Prasarak Sabha* and from April 1851, the *Gujarati Hindu Buddhi Vardhak Sabha.* Each Society published its own journals, the frequency of which was a good indication of the strength of the parent body and attempted to produce cheap pamphlets on scientific and the other subjects in their respective language.

The members of the three branch societies faced different problems in relation to their own communities. These differences can be highlighted by reference to the fate of each branch society in the one practical cause they espoused in common. Articles and essays on the position of women in society, written by members of the Students Literary and Scientific Society, led to a project to provide schools for girls under the Society's auspices, at a time when only missionaries were showing interest in female education. The lead was taken by the members of the *Gujarati Dnyan Prasark Mandali*. In 1849 it started morning classes for women and by 1854 the society successfully conducted nine schools for girls. One of its members Jagannath Shankarset also housed one of its Marathi Schools in his own compund and sent his daughter to it.

Regarding education, it was the Parsis who were the first to realize the importance of female education and social reform in the Bombay Presidency. Few Parsis like Cursetjee Nucserwanjee Cama and Sir Jamsetjee Jeejeebjoy actively contributed in laying the foundation of girls school. Infact, the earliest school owed its foundation to them.[148]

The Maharashtrian intelligentsia did not lag behind in supporting female education. As mentioned earlier, they not only established a society which took up educational work but, in their private capacities, established schools for girls. In this connection the contribution of Jotiba Govind Phule stands out. Though he belonged to a lower caste, i.e. gardener, he established a school for girls in 1851.[149] By 1852 he had already opened three schools for girls and one for the untouchables.

The success of Jyotiba's school became evident when the female pupils of his school were publicly examined on 12th February 1853. According to the Annual Report, read by Bapurao Mande, the performance of girl's was better than the boys.[150]

Thus, we find that by 1854 the intelligentsia in Bengal and Bombay Presidency succeeded in getting social legislations passed and established educational institutions which promoted women's education.

In the post 1857 period also these two Presidencies led the way. In Bengal, Brahmo Marriage Act was passed in 1872. This Act made child marriage illegal, sanctioned inter-caste widow marriage among the *Brahmins* and forbade polygamy. This remained confined to the reformed groups only and could not acquire a wide base.[151] Also *Brahmins* themselves were split over this Act and, therefore, it could not become popular.

Regarding education, the contribution of Sasipada Banerjee came into prominence. Like his predecessor, he established schools for girls in

1865 and in 1871.[152] However, his greatest contribution lay in the fact that he established an institution for higher education of women.

Bombay also did not lag behind. The Parsis who were the pioneers of female education continued with their efforts by establishing the Parsi Girls' School Association in 1865.[153] This Association looked into all aspects of school edcuation for women. The Parsis also successfully passed the special Parsi Marriage and Divorce Act in 1865. This Act made bigamy a criminal offence and helped in emancipating Parsi women by giving them a legal status in society.[154]

It is interesting to note that there was a realization amongst the reformers that a national platform was essential to promote social and educational issues amongst women. Therefore, at the instance of Mahadev Govind Ranade, the Indian Social Conference came into being in 1887. Just as the Indian National Congress took up political issues, the conference took up social questions that were of national dimensions.[155] Debates were held on social evils prevalent in society: like child marriage, enforced widowhood and so on, and methods to ameliorate it were diffused amongst people.

The period also witnessed the passing of the Age of Consent Act in 1891. It shows that the Government was not totally against social reform. By this Act the marriageable age of girls increased from 10 to 12. Infact, it was Malabari who was the chief instrument in getting the law passed, despite stiff opposition.[156]

In the field of education the period saw the establishment of educational institutions for women under Maharshi Karve. The various institutions that were established by him shows the gradual evolution of his ideas on this subject — from *Anath Balikashram* founded in 1896, which was purely meant for widows he went on to establish the first Women's University in the Bombay Presidency in 1916[157] the door of which were open to all women. There was a strong realization of his part that education was the effective means of making women critically examine society and realize the evil effect of custom and traditions that had assigned her a secondary place in society. It would also enable them to become economically self-sufficient. Infact, Karve owes the credit of laying firmly the roots of higher education of women in Bombay Presidency.

Apart from the establishment of various associations and schools, some members of the intelligentsia, usually high caste, at home educated their daughters, wives and sisters. It is interesting to note that ina typical patriarchal society only a few saw the need for this. Ananta Shastri, who was a *Chitpavan Brahmin* along with his wife educated their daughter

Ramabai, who later because of her learning of the sacred texts in Sanskrit was conferred the title of "Pandita" and "Saraswati" by the learned *Brahmins* of Calcutta.[158]

Muslim women did not lag behind. Badruddin Tyabji was the first Muslim in Bombay Presidency to send his daughter to the girls' school opened in Bomaby at Mazagaon under the auspices of the *Zenana* Bible Medical Mission in 1876. His daughters continued to have their schooling till they were fifteen or sixteen. They rode horses in the outskirts of city. They had partially discarded their cloaks covering their face outside the busy locality. Infact, their family had the distinction of being the first to discard *purdah.*[159] In 1894, one of his nieces Mrs. Abbas. S. Tyabji went to England, where she completely gave up *Purdah.* In 1904 Badruddin sent his two daughters to a boarding school in England (Haslemere) for their education. Similar example was followed by the Parsi reformer. Maneckji Cursetji, gave his daughter thorough knowledge of English.[160] The example set by Maneckji was followed by Framji Cowasjee Banajee and Jamesetjee Jeejeebhoy.

As mentioned earlier, Anata Shastri not only educated his daughter but also educated his wife. He had made up his mind that knowledge was an excellent thing for women as well as for a men, his wife should also be taught to read.[161] Social persecution did not discourage him even though he had to take shelter in the forest of Gungamal in the Western Ghats.

Similarly, Ranade educated his second wife. As Ramabai Ranade in her autobiography clearly mentions. . . . "He asked whether I could read and write. I could do neither. So that very night I was given a slate and a pencil and the first lesson of seven syllabus, *Shriganeshyanamah* was taught. It was my first chance to handle a slate and a pencil and my first glimpse of the alphabet. It took nearly two hours for me to be able to read and write those seven letters. . . . I was taught the alphabet and *barakhadis* (alphabets in Devnagari) and after about a fortnight, I read the first lesson of the first reader with some help. . . . "[162]

Gopalrao Joshi, the husband of Anandibai Joshi, who was the first women to receive a degree of medicine from Philadelphia was initially encouraged by her husband. Before his marriage to Anandibai, Gopalrao had certain expectations from his marriage proposals ". . . . I have certain expectations from this marriage, I will educate my wife after marriage. I will also teach her English. She will be required to study the whole day."[163]

After his marriage to Anandibai, Gopalrao bought two books one was of Marathi Class I which consisted of simple short stories and the other of Maths which contained tables from two onwards. It also contained fraction tables. Gopalrao also gave her some books on Grammar, Sanskrit and English with a comment that from now onwards she must not ask "why this and why that?" Infact, she should go on studying; she should make proper use of her intelligence and should become more knowledgeable than him. She must study subjects that no man had ever studied before. A quest for knowledge was kindled within her and she felt like grasping all that was offered to her immediately.[164]

Kashibai Kanitkar who later on became part of the female intelligentsia during our period was educated by her husband. She gives a vivid account of how her education began. In her own words she said .... "My husband did not approve of my ordinary looks but I was to spend my whole life with him . . . . She once heard her husband telling somebody that if she educates herself then somehow it will be possible to live with her . . . ."[165]

It is interesting to note that though the imparting of knowledge to their wives remained confined to the upper castes, in few cases the lower caste males also educated their wives, e.g. Jotiba Phule educated his wife Savitribai Phule. After being educated by her husband, she assisted him in teaching. Though she had to face sever social persecution she was not discouraged and carried out her work, i.e. teaching with determination.[166]

In their roles as brothers also, the reformers promoted female education. Mr. Joshi, a friend of Karve, encouraged his sister Godhubai later Anandibai Karve to take up education. It was at his initiative that Godhubai joined the *Sharda-Sadan* where her initial education began.[167] Also, Venubai Namjoshi, a cousin of Principal G.G. Agarkar was motivated by him to undertake her education at the *Sadan.*[168] Infact, she did her matriculation and assisted Karve when he founded the *Anath-Balikashram.*[169]

Thus, the formal institutions established by the intelligentsia and their private efforts in promoting women's education succeeded in instilling among a tiny section of women desire for education. Journals and magazines founded by the male intelligentsia also provided such a stimulus. Most of the journals and magazines took up social and educational issues. The aim was to create an awareness among women; a desire to acquire education and not submit to irrational customs. In the Bengal Presidency, the earliest move in this direction was taken by Sasipada Banerjee who founded the first women's journal in Bengali. This journal was conducted by his two daughters and was exclusively run by women. In the Bombay Presidency, on the other hand, the significant journal that carried similar kind of message was *Stri-Bodh* and *Rast Goftar.* The former was started in 1857 at the munificence of Cursetjee Nursserwanjee Cama. The latter was begun by Dadabhai Naoroji in 1851.

Therefore, during our period, we find that women intelligentsia not only took to education but also established various *Samaj* and society which undertook similar kind of work A detailed account of their activity is discussed in the fourth chapter.

GOVERNMENT'S SOCIAL AND EDUCATIONAL POLICY

It is significant to note that the government was the last important agency which took up the cause of women's education. Prior to 1857, certain social legislation was passed by the East India Company such as abolition of *Sati,* Female Infanticide and Widow Remarriage Act as stated earlier. These Acts aimed at removing the long standing abuse prevailing in society. However, as far as female education was concerned, there was no specific policy prior to 1854.

As mentioned earlier it was the Christian missionaries and the male intelligentsia who took up the issue of women's eduation prior to mid 19th century. Interestingly though, the Charter Act of 1813 took the responsibility of educating the people it made no mention of female eduation. The Act stated that "...... It shall be lawful for the Governor-General in Council to direct that out of any surplus which may remain of the rent, revenue, and profits arising from the said territorial acquisitions, after defraying the expenses of the military, civil and commercial establishements and paying the interest of the debt, in manner herein after provided, a sum of not less than one lac of repees in each year shall be set apart and applied to the revival and improvement of literature and the encouragement of the learned natives of India, and for the introduction and promotion of knowledge of science among the inhabitants of the British territories in India."[170]

Gradually subsequent Acts were passed to give effect to the educational clause laid in the Charter. However, once again these Acts made no reference to women's education. This was because the British officials, particularly the conservatives, refused to have anything to do with the subject. They pointed out that the policy of the company was one of strict social and religious neutrality; that the prejudice against the education of women which prevailed among the people were so strongly rooted in their social and religious life that any attempt to educate women would create a very great commotion; and that the first attempt of the company should be restricted to the education of men who would themselves, at a later date, undertake the education of their womenfolk.

Perhaps another contributing factor which was responsible for the neglect of women's education was its absence in the various educational surveys conducted in all the Presidencies, i.e. Bombay, Bengal and Madras in the early 19th century. In the Bombay Presidency, Mountstuart Elphinstone stated that there was no female scholar attending any of the common schools of the Province. Infact, the common schools were meant for boys only.[171] Similar views were portrayed by William Adam for the Bengal Presidency. According to him the literacy census depicted a dismal picture. There were only four women literate as against 21, 907 men in a total population of 496,974.[172] However, conditions were apparently better in Madras where Munro found that the "women of the Rajabundah and some other tribe of Hindu" were generally taught and the returns of the indigenous schools showed as many as 5, 480 girls in a total enrolment of 184,110.[173] For the rest of India, nothing was known except Punjab where the existence of special girls school incharge of women teachers was reported. However, by and large the female population of the country was deprived of formal education. Further M.S. Elphinstone, the Governor of Bombay in his long Minute of eight paragraph (1817-27) did not make any reference to female education.[174]

The credit for having brought about a change in the policy towards women's eduation goes to Bethune and Dalhousie. As mentioned earlier, J.E.D. Bethune, the law member of the Executive Council of the Governor-General and the President of the Council of Education (1848 to 1851) established the first school for girls in Bengal Presidency in 1849. This he did in his own private capacity and bore all its expenses. After his death Lord Dalhousie not only took over the management of the institution but for few years paid from his own pocket for the upkeep of the institution. This was clearly stated in the news item published in *The Hindu Intelligence* of February 6, 1854.

> "His Lordship has signified his desire that the school may be kept open at his sole charge so long as he remains in India; his anxiety being that he might be assured that it may not fall to the ground whenever he retires from his present office."[175]

His support for female education is also reflected in his orders dated 11th April, 1850, which gives an indication of his views on the subject —

> "It is the opinion of the Governor-General-in-Council that no single change in the habits of the people is likely to lead to more important and beneficial consequence than the introduction of

> education for their female children. The general practice is to allow them to grow up in absolute ignorance but this custom is not required or even sanctioned by their religion, and in fact a certain degree of education is now given to the female relatives of those who can afford the expense of entertaining special instructors at their own house ..."

The Governor-General-in-Council requests that the Council of Education may be informed that it is henceforth to consider its function as comprising the superintendence of native female education, and wherever any disposition is shown by the natives to establish female schools it will be its duty to give them all possible encouragement and further their plans in every way that is not inconsistent with the efficiency of the institution already under their management. It is the wish also of the Governor-General-in-Council that intimation to the same effect should be given to the Chief Civil Officers of the Mofussil calling their attention to the growing disposition among the natives to establish female schools, and directing them to use all means at their disposal for encouraging those institutions and for making it generally known that the government views them with great approbation."[176]

It is interesting to note that the encouragement given to female education by Dalhousie found reflection in the Educational Despatch of 1854, which for the first time stressed on the promotion of women's education. It stated that --- "The importance of female education in India cannot be over-rated; and we have now afforded of an increased desire on the part of many of the natives of India togive a good education to their daughters. By this means a far greater proportional impulse is imparted to the educational and moral tone of the people than by the education of men. We have already observed that schools for females are incuded among those to which grant-in-aid may be given; and we cannot refrain from expressing our cordial sympathy with the efforts which are being made in this direction. Our Governor-in-Council has declared, in a communication to the Govenment of Bengal, that the Govenment ought to give to the native female education in India its frank and cordial support; and in this we heartily concur and we especially approve of the bestowal of marks of honour upon such natives gentlemen as Rao Bahadur Magahunbai Karamchand who donated Rs. 20,000 to the foundation of two native female schools in Ahmedabad, as by such means our desire for the extension of female education becomes generally known".[177]

In order to give effect to the contents of the Despatch in the Bombay

Presidency, particularly, 65 girl's schools was founded. It recorded a total attendance of about 3,5000 pupils. There were also 593 girls attending boys schools. A significant step was taken by the government to encourage women's education in 1857 by assigning small annual rewards to those school masters who would form girls classes in their schools, with the result that in 1864-65 there were 639 girls in such schools.

Thus between 1854, and 1882, female education in Bombay Presidency gradually expanded.

Table 2.3 : Government and Other Institutions Aided and Unaided

	Government Institutions			*Other Institutions, aided and unaided (under inspection)*					
	Normal Schools	*Sec. Schools*	*Primary Schools*	*Normal Schools*	*Sec. Schools*	*Primary Schools*	*Mix Schools*	*Total*	*Total Exp. Rs.*
No. of Institution	2	—	181	0	9	151	—	343	178,707
No. of Pupils	73	—	11,238	—	538	10,621	4,296	26,766	—

Source : Report of the Indian Education Commission — Appointed by the Resolution of the Government of India dated 3rd February 1882, p. 523.

Table 2.3 shows that though female education gradually expanded, it was primary education which really increased between 1854 and 1882. This was true not only for the Bombay Presidency but also for the other Presidency as well as mentioned in Table 2.4.

Table 2.4 : Government Aided and Unaided Schools

	No. of Institution for girls				*Total No. of scholars*
	Govt.	*Aided*	*Unaided but inspected*	*Unaided and not inspected*	
Collegiate schools	1	—	—	—	6
Secondary schools	6	50	25	—	2,054
Primary schools	605	1,591	398	6	82,420
Mixed schools primary	—	—	—	—	42,071
Normal schools	4	11	—	—	515
Total	616	1,652	423	6	1,27,066

Source : S. Nurulla and J.P. Naik, *Op.Cit.*, p. 388.

The concentration of the pupils at the primary stage was mainly due to the fact that the public had by now come to accept the necessity of elementary education only in the case of girls, and was still oposed to any higher education being given to them. Higher education at this period meant English education which was pursued with the exclusive object of seeking service under the government. As the idea of women serving in Government offices was considered unthinkable at this period, the demand for the secondary or collegiate education of girls did not arise at all. The average parent continued to be against all education of women, as in the year before 1854. But a few enlightened parents, mainly living in cities and belonging to the more advanced sections of society, felt that there would be no harm (and probably a little gain) if their daughters learned to read and write. After all, parents could afford to send their daughters to schools only until her marriage and as the age of marriage was low-anything between 8 and 12 for the classes who were now seeking education – the schooling of a girl beyond the primary stage was virtually impossible.

Perhaps a crucial feature of the period was the complete absence of collegiate education among women and the extremely small attendance of girls in the secondary schools. In the whole of India, there was only one institution, the Bethune School at Calcutta which had six girls in its college department.[178] Secondary education, on the other hand, could hardly be said to have advanced to any appreciable extent. The total number of girls in secondary schools for India as a whole was 2, 054 of which Bengal had 1,051; Madras 389, Bombay 538, N.W.P.8, and Punjab 8. Most of the girls who went in for secondary education belonged to the Anglo-Indians, Indian Christians and Parsi community. It may, therefore, be said that by 1882 the necessity of the elementary education of girls had come to be generally accepted but that their education beyond that stage had hardly begun.[179]

An important development of the period from 1854 to 1882 was the growing demand for a differentiation of curricula. As girls had hardly entered the secondary schools or colleges, this problem mainly affected the primary stage.The demand for a differentiation of curricula even at this early age was made on two grounds. Firstly, it was argued that a different syllabus was necessary for girls' school because the average school-life of a girls was very much shorter than that of a boy, and secondly, it was pointed out that subjects like needle-work which had special utility for women ought to be included in the syllabus for girls' school in preference to other subjects. But the attempt to carry out these demands were not very successful as the following review of the provincial syllabuses showed "As the subject of instruction laid down by the Department for girls do not in general differ much from those for boys it does not seem necessary to present a detailed account of them. They comprehended the usual amount of reading, writing and arithmetic, with some grammar, geography and history. In Madras, the standards are nearly the same as for boys, with needle work added and with singing as an optional subject... In the Central Provinces, while the scheme of studies is the same as for boys, an equal amount of attention is not infact given to geography and grammar, while it is found that girls' do not make so much progress in arithmetic as boys. Singing is occasionally attempted, and needle work in several branches is attended to .... In Bombay there are special standards of instruction for girls school which are lower than those for boys but include work in addition...."[180]

Thus, we find that even though the period witnessed a very gradual growth regarding higher education of women, it did lay down the seeds for its further development.

It was the recommendation of the Indian Education Commission appointed in 1882-83 which formed the second significant move of the government regarding the promotion of female education. The recommendation of the Commission studied the problems concerning women's education and made certain suggestions that emphasised on —

Support from Public Funds

Before enumerating our special recommendations with regard to girl's schools, we desire to briefly review the situation as disclosed in the forgoing paragraphs. It will have been seen that female education is still in an elementary backward condition and that it needs to be fostered in every legitimate way. In some provinces, the sympathies of the people do not yet run sufficiently in this direction to induce local bodies to devote to female education any of the funds at their disposal. Hence we think it expedient to recommend that public funds of all kinds — local, municipal, and provincial should be chargeable in an equitable proportion for the support of girls school as well as boys school; that the former, being in an earlier stage of development should receive even something more than what might appear to be a strictly impartial share of encouragement. Public opinion in this matter cannot yet be accepted as the standard of what ought to be done.

Grant-in-aid

We do not think it necessary to define the classes of girl's schools which should receive encouragement. The principle of religious neutrality prevents aid from being given for religious teaching as such, but we see no reason why such secular teaching as is actually given, if only incidentally, in schools intended mainly for religious teaching, should not be pro tanto rewarded. If a girl, learning to read religious book, acquires the power of reading the vernacular, it is atleast something accomplished, and may serve as a basis for something more. There are so many obstacles to the progress of female education that we think the conditions on which aid is granted to it should be made as easy as possible. It is, moreover, right that more liberal aid should be given for the education of those classes who cannot pay for it themselves, and whose children are often required to help in household work. For these, rules requiring regular attendance should be easy, lest they defeat their own object. Generally, the maintenance of a girl's school is more expensive than that of a boys school! Servants have to bring the children from their homes, and the number that can be expected to attend is smaller. Hence it is sometimes found that rates of aid even 50 per cent higher than those for boys, fail to cover the additional expenditure required. Again the short time that girls are allowed to remain at school leads to a very large percentage of the pupils being in the lowest stages of instruction. As these need as much attention as those more advanced, it is only just that allowance should in some way be made for them.

Differentiation of Curricula and Books

One great objection made by the native public to the instruction of girl's, is that it is of no practical use ot them. Too much stress should not be laid on this, as the value of education to a woman must of necessity be unknown to those who have no experience of it. But it ought not to be taken for granted that the instruction which is suitable for boy must necessarily be good for an Indian girl. In purely literary subjects, girl's need not go so far as boys, and there are subjects of a practical kind to which girl's might at least be introduced during their school course. It does not appear that much attention has hitherto been given to the production of books suitable for girls, and in some cases the book used have not been selected with sufficient care.

Fees and Scholarship

We approve of the principle that education should to some extent be paid for by the recipient. But the desire for girl's education has at present to be fostered, and in many parts of the country it has yet to be created. Hence, we would not make the taking of fees an essential condition of obtaining grants, although we would guard against unfair competition in this respect between rival schools. To extend the period given to the education of girls is obviously desirable, and we think that one important means of attaining this object will be the offer of scholarship. If some of these be reserved for girl's beyond the usual age to which school attendance extends, there may gradually arise a desire for more knowledge than can be attained within that narrow period.

Secondary Education

This points in the direction of secondary education for girls, in which a beginning has scarcely been made. We propose that the opportunities for such instruction should be judiciously extended, but only where private efforts indicate that the desire for its exists.

Hostels

There are many difficulties in the way of young women attending a school at any distance from their homes. For this reason we think that in special cases it might be well to encourge school-managers to make provision for boarders.

Transfer of Girl's School to Local Bodies

It may perhaps be found that Municipal and Local Boards are not in all cases prepared to undertake the management of girls' schools; to force it upon unwilling persons would not be likely to lead to satisfactory results. But where a Board does undertake the management, we think its authority ought to be real and effective. It ought to be able to appoint any mistress it selects, provided, of course, that she is in the judgement of the Educaion Department qualified for the work. Nor would we deprive the Board of the power of promoting or removing its own teachers, although to check arbitrary or hasty action the Department ought to have a veto in such cases. It should also be borne in mind that as the available funds are limited and as results are greater and more capable of being tested in girl's schools than in *zenanas*, the former have higher claims than the latter on State Aid.

Women Teachers

We have seen that one of the principal obstacles to the extension of female education is the difficulty of obtaining suitable teachers. There can be no doubt that women are preferable for this purpose to men; and while we would not altogether exclude male teachers from girls' schools, we believe that female teachers should be gradually and cautiously substituted for them. In order to induce girls' to look forward to teaching as a profession, it seems desirable to encourage pupil-teachers wherever the system is practicable. The pupil teacher should furnish materials for Normal schools and for Normal classes in connection with ordinary schools where there is sufficient teaching power. The careful and sympathetic management required for such classes, renders them peculiarly suitable for private agency to superintend; and when established by this means they should be liberally aided. Among other ways of assisting them, the grant of a bonus for each pupil finishing the course, commends itself. At the sametime the aid given to them should not depend too largely on such success at the final examination. There does not seem to be good reason for confining certificates for teachers to those who have been trained in Normal Schools. Fitness to teach should be recognized wherever and in whatever way it may have been acquired, although a Normal school training will always have a special value of its own. The number of young women qualified to teach is so small, that it seems necessary to recruit it by special inducements offered both to the pupil and to those who may instruct them. In some places the wives of school masters are almost the only class available as school mistresses and it is expedient to attract as many of them as possible to the work. In other places young women of mixed parentage may be largely employed, if only they can be persuaded to qualify themselves by a sufficient knowledge of the vernacular. By the different plans here indicated, something may be done gradually in the way of raising up a class of women fitted to educate the girls of another generation.

Appointment of Women Inspectors

Associations have arisen in some places, aiming at the extension and improvement of female education. These also might be encouraged so far as they produce secular results. In order that these results may be fairly estimated, it seems necessary that the services of sympathetic and well qualified inspectresses should be more largely made use of. In the present condition of female education in India, the visit of Inspectors are some-time not only futile, but a positive hindrance to progress. And even where this is not so, a women is generally much better able to deal with little girl's than any man can be.

Non-Official Co-operation

With respect to the management also of girl's, schools, it seems most desireable to obtain the help, wherever possible, of ladies who take an interest in the subject, whether Native or European. Nor is the object likely to be attained unless interest is promoted among Native gentlemen by giving them a share in the supervision of the the schools. Those who show their sympathy, by sending their own daughters to school are most likely to assist in directing the movement and in rendering it popular among their neighbours.[181]

Thus the Indian Education Commission made recommendations covering almost every aspect of female education. However, none of the recommendation spelt out were radical in nature. The Commission did not recommend compulsion for girl's. It also did not advocate a rapid expansion of girl's schools under the direct control of the Government. It merely recommended that the education of women should be expanded on a vountary basis. This could not have worked satisfactorily because, as admitted by the Commission itself, public opinion of this period was not much in favour of education of women. Again, the Commission did not make specific recommendation on the all too important subject of finance and could not secure larger resources to women's education.

On the whole, therefore, it may be said that the Indian Education Commission did nothing more than recommend slight alterations in line of policy which had already been developed. These altérations, though were an improvement over the then existing position did not go far enough and were not calculated to do anything but touch the fringes of the problem. For these and other reasons, the education of women did not expand very rapidly between 1882 and 1902 although most of the recommendations of the Commission were accepted by the Provincial governments.

In the period of twenty years between the Report of the Indian Education Commission and the beginning of Curzon's drive for educational reform, the education of women made slow but steady progress.

Collegiate Education

The most significant achievement of the period was the entry of women into the portals of the universities. A lead in this direction was taken in the Bengal Presidency where the first women to be graduated were Kadambini and Chandramukhi Bose of the Bethune College. Similarly, in the Bombay Presidency the first women graduate of Bombay University was Cornelia Sorabji. She graduated in 1888. It is significant to note that women of India did not have to struggle in anyway to obtain admission to university degree — this was a pleasant contrast to England where women could get *degrees by degrees* only. Infact, when the question of admitting women to the Bombay University arose, the authority merely passed a general resolution to the effect "that the words in the masculine in the rules of the University shall for the future include also the feminine" and thereby recognized the equal right of either sex to receive the honour and distinctions which it conferred.[183]

It was in 1883 that the Senate of Bombay University resolved to admit women to all degrees in arts, medicine, civil engineering and law on the same terms as men. Sir James Fergusson, the Chancellor of the University, in course of his convocation address paid a compliment to the fair sex in the following words, "Their intellects are as acute, their power of assimilating knowledge as great and means of usefulness open to them by the acquisition of knowledge not inferior to those of men".[184]

It is interesting to note that unlike the Bombay University, London University was late in overcoming its prejudices against the fair sex, and to throw its degree open to women, in 1878. The Scottish University followed suit in 1892. Oxford and Cambridge took a long time to get over their prejudices. It admitted women to its tripos examination in 1872, and it was not until the end of the first world-war that they were admitted to its titular degree. Oxford University, on the other hand, admitted women to its examination in 1883.[185]

Therefore, with the portals of University being open to women, we find that their was a significant expansion regarding this stage of education. By 1901-02 the number of women students of the Indian Universities rose from 6 in 1881-82 to 264-177 in Art college, 76 in Medical Colleges and 11 in College of Education. The caste composition of the students were as follows — of these 264 students, 148 were Anglo-Indians, 49 were Indian Christians, 38 were Parsis and only 28 were Hindus one belonged to the other group. Muslims girls, however, did not take to University education.

Perhaps a very important development during the period was starting of a separate college for women. The Presidency of Bengal again took a lead in this direction. In 1882, the Bethune College was the only institution in India which was exclusivey meant for girls' and which prepared them for university examination. In 1901-02 there were twelve colleges for women in the whole of India. Three of these were in Madras, three in Bengal and 6 in United Provinces. Bombay, however, did not have a separate college for women.

Secondary Education

The total number of girls studying in secondary schools in 1902 was 41,582 as against 2.054 in 1882. This was distributed as shown in Table 2.5. The table clearly depicts that the Anglo-Indians, Christians and Parsis dominated the field. It also reveals that the necessity of secondary education for women came to be recognized by the Indian society. By 1882 public opinion in India was prepared to concede that girls' may be permitted to receive education at the primary level. Gradually the selfless work of the intelligentsia (male and female) in the Victorian Era (1854-1902) were responsible in encouraging women to go in for higher education. Thus, secondary schools of government and those managed by the intelligentsia witnessed a significant growth.

Table 2.5 : Anglo-Indian, Christians and Parsis Schools

	Anglo-Indian	*Indian Christians*	*Hindus*	*Muslims*	*Parsis*	*Other*	*Total*
High School for Boys	270	112	47	1	1	139	570
High School for Girls	5,239	1,466	1,040	75	642	242	8,704
Middle School (English) for Boys	967	852	631	19	73	281	2,823
Middle School (English) for Girls	4,165	3,490	482	39	341	237	8,754
Middle School for (Vernacular) Boys	—	538	741	82	—	2,646	4,007
Middle School (Vernacular) for Girls	13	4,525	10,982	649	—	555	16,724

Source : H. W. Orange, *Fifth Quinquennial Review — Progress of Education in India 1902-1907*, p. 6.

As a corollary to the increase in the number of girls reading in secondary schools, the demand for the differentiation of curricula now began to be put forward at the secondary level as well and some attempts to meet the demand had already begun to be made. The Quinquennial Review of the Progress of Education in India, 1897-1902, shows the general nature of the differentiations attempted

> "The course of studies in girls' schools are modelled on those in schools for boys, with some variations in the middle school courses, and to lesser extent in the matriculation courses of the Universities. As regards the matriculation courses, there is no difference in the subjects for boys and girls at Calcutta, Madras and Bombay.... At Allahabad and Lahore, a classical language is compulsory for boys, but girls are given the option of a modern Indian or European language. In the Madras upper secondary course, girls' are given the option of variety of subjects in place of algebra and geometry, but hardly any girls follow this course. In the Madras lower secondary (middle) course the compulsory subjects for boys and girls are the same, but the optional subjects include needlework and domestic economy for girls. In the Bombay middle English stage, girls may substitute, for Euclid and algebra, any portion of science or domestic economy treated in a popular way, equal in extent and difficulty to one of Macmillan's Science Primers. In the new Bengal Regulation for vernacuar schools, needle work for girls takes the place of agriculture or science and geometry for boys... Manual training may be substituted for needle work in mixed schools which have no facilities for teaching needle work. In the reading books for girls, lessons or domestic economy are substituted for the lessons on hygiene contained in the boy's books.....[186]

Regarding primary education the progress was still greater. In 1901-02, the total number of girls at school was 348,510 (160,164 in Boy's Schools and 188, 346 in Girls' Schools) as against 124491 in 1881-82.

An interesting development during the period was the gradual growth of professional education. Despite, its progress, being slow it indicated that women were slowly coming out of the four walls of their household to become economically self-reliant. This however, was of a limited nature. According to the statistics of 1901-02, the profession women took to were given below.

Table 2.6 : Teaching Profession of Women

	Schools	*No. of women students in 1901-02*
1.	Training schools	1,412
2.	School of Art	40
3.	Medical schools	166
4.	Technical or industrial schools	468
5.	Commercial schools	26
6.	Other schools	695
	Total	2,807

Source : S. Nurulla and J.P. Naik *Op. Cit.*, p. 399.

The above Table 2.6 clearly shows that of all the careers open to women, teaching was obviously the most popular. In order to encourage women to take up teaching profession, a proposal was submitted by the Government of Bombay on 26th September 1910. It stated that in order to encourage married women to take up the profession of teaching female teachers should be eligible for leave on full pay for two months, extensible to three months in exceptional cases, about the time of confinement. The letter mentions that .... "regarding a proposal submitted by the government of Bombay that a school mistress should be granted, for the purpose of confinement and on the certificate of a competent medical officer, the privilege leave which may be due to her plus such special leave on full pay as may bring the total period of absence from duty to two or, in exceptional cases, three months.

In view of the great derth of qualified female teachers in this country at the present time, we concur in the opinion expressed by the Governor-in-Council that it is very desirable to consider favourably any proposal which is calculated to popularize the teaching profession among Indian women....... "We suggest, as an alternative proposal that the special leave contemplated should be classed as hospital leave under Articale 288, Civil Service Regulation and that a Subsidiary rule should be added to that Article permitting the authority who may be nominated by the local government for the purpose to grant school mistresses leave of absence from duty, on full pay, for 2 or, in exceptional cases, three months to meet the exegencies of child birth......"[187]

Apart from teaching, which the Government wanted to encourage, medical career, nursing, midwifery and medicine came next in order of popularity so far as profession of women was concerned. A detailed account of the professional education of women will be taken up in the next chapter.

Thus, taken in all, the education of women in 1901-02 inspite of all advances recorded since 1854, cannot be said to have been satisfactory... "Though some advances has been made, said Lord Curzon in 1904, "female education as a whole is still in a backward condition. The number of female scholars in public schools in the year 1901-02 was 444,470 or less than a ninth of the number of male scholars. The percentage of girls in public schools to the total female population of the school going age has risen from 1.58 in the year 1886-87 to 2.49 in 1901-02."[188]

Though Curzon had pointed out drawbacks and slow progress of female eduation, he had nothing new to suggest beyond the appointement of suitable teachers, organization of model schools, and provision of larger funds :

> "...... Here the figures exhibit a relatively very backward state of affairs. Indeed, Mr. Cotton in the last Quinquennial Review described it as "the most conspicuous blot on the education system of India". In the past year there were only 425,000 girls' attending all classes of schools out of the entire population, and of these nearly one-third were in Madras, where the native Christian and Eurasian population are usually large. Moderate as I have shown the number of boys to be who go to school, only one girls attends for every ten of the male sex; and the total expenditure upon Female education in Primary and Secondary Schools from all public funds (I exclude fees subscription and endowments) was last year only 11 lakhs as compared with 80 lakhs on boys. Female education has to suffer from many drawbacks in this country. It is contrary to the traditions and prejudices of the people. Their native customs, particularly that of ealy marriage and the idea that women ought not be trained up to remunerative employment are unfavourable to it. In so far as it is practised, it is almost entirely confined to girls of the lower classes who go to the Primary Schools to pick up the three R's. Parents in the higher classes will not send their girls to schools, they prefer to have them educated in the *Zenana* at home. It is too much, with these obstacles in the way, to expect that Female Education in India will make any sudden or rapid strides. But I think that we might do more to foster its growth by providing suitable teachers, and, perhaps by encouraging the formation of a few model schools.[189]

The Simla Conference of 1911 also emphasised views similar to those upheld by Lord Curzon, i.e. it advocated the institution of model primary schools, the provisions of more training schools where necessary and the strengthening of the staff of inspectress. It further provided certain statistical account which stated that "out of a female population of more than 119 million only 830,000 are at school and of the total direct expenditure upon Education in India, only 11 per cent represents expenditure upon the education of girls. In the last 5 years, however, there has been an increase of 200,000 in the number of girls scholars and a demand for female eduation may be expected to grow rapidly in many parts of India".[190]

The Government of India keeping the demand in anticipation drew certain schemes to meet it. This was also stated in the Conference --- "The scheme will conveniently take the form of a 10 year programme for (1) the expansion of girls education by means of the allocation of educational funds whether destined for the maintenance of Board schools or as subsidies to aided schools, (2) the improvement of facilities for the training of mistresses, (3) the amelioration of the condition of service in the case of mistresses and members of the inspecting staff such as the granting of free quarters of a suitable kind, of carriage allowances, and of special facilities during journey, etc....."[191]

Further, the Government Resolution on Education Policy (1913) carried the same line of thinking upheld by Lord Curzon and those upheld at the Simla conference 1911. It observed that —

> "The education of girls remains to be organized. In 1904 the Government of India remarked that peculiar difficulties were encountered in this branch of education owing to social customs of the people but that as a far greater proportional impulse is imparted to the educational and moral tone of the people by the education of women than by the education of men; liberal treatment had been accorded for girl's in respect of scholarship and fees. This policy has been continued. Efforts have been also made, not without success, to bring education, through the agency of governesses, within the reach of *purdha* ladies, to increase the number of ladies on the inspecting staff and to replace male by female teachers in government aided schools. The number of girls' under instruction has risen from 444,470 in 1901-02 to 864,363 in 1901-11. But the total number still remains insignificant in proportion to the female population. The Government of India believes, however, that in certain areas there are indication of a swiftly growing demand for a more extensive education of girls.

The immediate problem in the education of girls is one of social development. The existing customs and ideas opposed to the education of girls will acquire different handling in different parts of India. The Governor-General-in-Council accordingly hesitates to lay down general lines of policy which might hamper local government and Administration and has preferred to call for schemes from each provinces, but he recommends the following principle for general considerations :

(a) The education of girls should be practical with reference to the position which they will fill in social life;
(b) It should not seek to imitate the education suitable for boys nor should it be dominated by examinations;
(c) Special attention should be paid to hygiene and the surroundings of schools life;
(d) The services of women should be more freely enlisted for instruction and inspection; and
(e) Continuity in inspection and control should be specially aimed at.

The difficulty in obtaining competent school mistresses is felt acutely in many parts of the country. In this connection it has been suggested that there is a large opening for women of a domiciled community, who have a knowledge of the vernacular and who might be specially trained for the purpose.[192]

Thus broadly the Educational Policy (1913) approves of the line laid down by Lord Curzon and the Simla Conference of 1911. But it also goes a good deal further. It emphasises the social aspect of the problems and pointed out that any great advance in the education of women would not be possible unless social prejudices against it are overcome. Moreover, a general dissatisfaction depicted in the Report regarding the system of education and pointed out that the then system of women's education was not related to the practical and social needs of women; that it was dominated too much by examinations and that it was based on a mechanical imitation of the education system for boys. Consequently, this Resolution led to some changes in the education of girls' and also to a more rapid expansion than the earlier period.

Thus, the period between 1905 to 1921 witnessed steady and comparatively rapid expansion in the education of women at all stages. Regarding collegiate education of women which had made a beginning in 1882 and 1902 was now rapidly expanding. In 1921-22, there were as many as 1,263 girls reading in Arts Colleges as against 6 in 1882 or 177 in 1902. Moreover, Hindu girls now began to enter colleges in far larger number than ever before, and Muslim girls also made their first entry. Out of the 1,263 girls in Art Colleges, 382 were Europeans, 402 were Indian Christians, 398 were Hindus 25 were Muslims and 35 were Parsis.[193]

Perhaps a very significant development during the period was the establishment of a Women's University in our Presidency i.e. the S.N.D.T. Indian Women University by Karve.[194]

Secondary Education

The number of girls' reading in High and Middle Schools in 1921-22 was 36,698 and 92,466 respectively as against 9,274 and 32,308 in 1901-02. The main cause of this were — firstly, there was a great expansion in the primary educaiton of girls which naturally resulted in directing a far larger number of girls than hitherto to the secondary schools; secondly the changing social conditions led to an increase in the age of marriage, a factor which materially assisted the spread of secondary education among women; thirdly the earlier practice of sending girl's to schools for a short time at the pre-marital stage on the ground that such education did them no harm gave place to a practice of keeping them longer at schools, sometimes even after marriage, because it was now gradually realized that education did a lot of good to women; lastly, the earlier prejudice against the teaching of English to girls began to die out rapidly and Indians, particularly the higher caste amongst the Hindus realized the economic advantages of giving secondary education to their daughters. However, this expansion was of limited nature. In the first place it was generally restricted to towns and cities. Secondly, it continued to be largely confined to Anglo-Indians, Indian Christians, Parsis and the higher castes among the Hindus.

Primary Education

There was an unexpected expansion. The number of girls attending primary school rose from 348,510 in 1901-02 to 1,198, 550 in 1921-22.

Therefore, the various Acts and Resolutions passed by the Government since 1854 led to the overall expansion of women's education during our period. However, it was primary education that the greatest expansion took place by 1921-22. A detailed account of the growth of various institutions regarding women's education and government's expenditure on it will be taken up in the next chapter.

REFERENCES

1. Quoted in *Manu, IX,* p 137 in Pandita Ramabai Sarasvati, *The High-Caste Hindu Women,* p 40.
2. R.M. Das, *Woman in Manu and his Seven Commentators,* p. 43.
3. Pandita Ramabai Sarasvati, *op. cit,* pp. 43-44.
4. Neera Desai, *Social Change in Gujarat,* pp. 64-65.
5. *Ibid.,* p. 65.
6. *Ibid.,* p. 65.
7. Pandita Ramabai Sarasvati, *op. cit,* p. 60-61.
8. The position of the wife in the Vedic Age was, therefore, very high. A man offers oblations to the gods jointly in a pair; they are like a pair of horses-yoked to a Chariot. C.P. Ramaswami Aiyar, *The Cultural Heritage of India,* Vol. 11, p. 572.
9. *B.C. Editorial* May 25, 1925, p. 6.
10. V.S. Kadam, "The Institution of Marriage and Position of Woman in Eighteenth Century Maharashtra" *in the Indian Economic and Social History Review,* 25-3-1988,
11. Padmaja Fatak, *Tarabai Modak,* p. 2.
12. Parvatibai Athavale, *My Story,* p.4.
13. Pandita Ramabai Sarasvati, *op.cit,* p. 67.
14. M. Malabari, *Infant Marriage and Enforced Widowhood in India,* p. 1.
15. *Ibid.,* p.1, In 1901 70 per cent of girls under the age of fifteen were married and the number of child brides at the beginning of 19th century must have been the same if not more.
16. Parvatibai Athavale, *op. cit,* p. 8.
17. Quoted in Neera Desai, *op. cit,* p. 66.
18. *Ibid,* p. 67.
19. Quoted in Manu IX, pp. 88-89 in Pandita Ramabai Sarasvati, *op. cit.,* p. 60.
20. D. N. Jha, *Ancient India : An Introductory Outline* , p. 16.
21. *ISR, May 1921, Madras, Vol. IX, No. 28,* p. 297.
22. Tarabai Sathe, *Aparajita Rama,* p. 59, Neera Desai, *op.cit.,* p. 344.
23. M. Malabari, *op.cit,* p. 1.
24. Pandita Ramabai Sarasvati, *op.cit.,* p. 72.
25. *Ibid.,* p. 72.
26. *ISR, June 18, 1899, Vo, IX, No. 42,* p. 330.
27. M.G. Mardi, *Krantijyoti Savitribai Jyotirao Phule,* p. 8.
28. Sow. Anandibai Karve, *My Story,* pp. 23-25.
29. *Ibid.,* p. 27, *op.cit.,* pp. 25-26.
30. *Ibid.,* p. 27.
31. Pandita Ramabai Saraswati, *op. cit,* p. 107, see Aparna Basu, "A Century's Journey : Women's Education in Western India 1820 - 1920" in *Socialization, Education and Women : Explorations in Gender Identity.* Ed. Karuna Chanana,

N.M.M.L. New Delhi, April 1985, p. 34; E.F. Chapman, *Notable Indian Women of the 19th Century,* p. 1-6, B.M. Malabari : *Rambles with the Piligrim Reforms,* p. 112.

32. Quoted in Pandita Ramabai Saraswati *op. cit,* p. 99.
33. *Ibid.*
34. Throughout India, widowhood is regarded as the punishment, for a horrible crime or crimes committed by the women in her former existence upon the earth... Disobedience and disloyalty to the husband or murdering him in an earlier existence are the chief crimes punished in the present birth by widowhood, *Ibid,* p. 95.
35. Neera Desai, *op. cit,* pp. 65-68.
36. Ganesh Prabhakar Pradhan, *Agarkar Lekh Sangrah,* p. 174.
37. S. Natarajan, *A Century of Social Reform in India,* p. 26.
38. Tarabai Sathe *op.cit,* p. 62; Pandita Ramabai Sarasvati, *op.cit,* p. 107.
39. Pandita Ramabai Sarasvati, *op.cit,* p. 80.
40. *B.C. Editorial, May 13, 1913,* p. 9.
41. Cited in S.A. Wolpert, *Tilak and Gokhale, Revoluion and Reform in the Making of Modern India,* p. 36.
42. Quoted from G.K. Gokhale's *Introduction to Ramabai Ranade,* mentioned in Aparna Basu, *op. cit,* p. 5.
43. A. Basu, *op. cit,* pp. 5-6.
44. *Ibid.,* p. 6
45. Quoted from Narmadashankar L. Daves, *Streedharma 1857, in Narmad gain Bombay, 1874,* pp. 20-217; *Ibid.,*pp. 6.
46. *B. C, 17th July, 1933,* p. 6.
47. J.A. Richey (ed), *Selections from Educational Record, pt. II, 1840-1859,* p. 33.
48. *ISR, January 8, 1989,* p. 145.
49. *Kesari, 28th September 1887, 25th October, 1887.*
50. Quoted from *Fishers Memoirs in Bengal Past and Present,* p 135, in K.K. Datta's *A Social History of Modern India,* p. 109.
51. William Adam, *Report on the State of Education in Bengal, 1835-38,* pp. 188-189.
52. *ISR, August 26, 1900, Vol X, 52,* p. 415.
53. Swami Madhavananda and Ramesh Chandra Majumdar, *Great Women of India;* p. 5; see also *ISR,* p. 314, 1899, *Vol. IX, No. 42.* Durgabai Deshmukh (Chairman) --- *Report of the National Committee on Women's Education* (May 1958 to January 1959), Ministry of Education, p. 13.
54. In a very Large Extent Female Education is indebted to the missionary societies for systematic support and fostering care. In this Presidency, indeed, as well as in other parts of India, the missionaries have been the pioneers of female education... For details see *ISR Sunday, May 7, 1888, No. IX,* p. 282.
55. Geraldine, H. Forbes, "Missionary Women in 19th Century India" in *Economic and Political Weekly, April 26,* 1986, pp. 735.

56. M.D. David, *John Wilson and his Institution*,. pp. 31-32.
57. S.R. Shirgaonkar, "The Education of Girls in Maharashtra", in *Maratha History Seminar, May 28-32, 1970*, p. 353.
58. Geraldline. H. Forbes, *op.cit.*, p. 742.
59. H. Sharp, *Selections from Educational Records*, Part1, p. 16.
60. J.A.Richter, *A'History of Missions in India*, pp. 150-51.
61. William Adam, *op.cit*, pp. 46-47. J.A. Richey (ed.) *op.cit.*, pp. 34-36.
62. *Ibid.*, p. 450.
63. *Ibid.*, p. 50. *A Review of Education in Bombay State 1855-1955*, p. 387. T. Albquerque, *Urbs Prima in India : An Epoch in the History of Bombay 1840-1850*, p. 131-132.
64. Rev. John Wilson, *Memoirs of Mrs. M. Wilson*, p. 228.
65. J.A. Richey *op.cit.*, pp.38-41. S. Mookerjee (ed.) *The Wilsonian 1832-1957*, p. 20.
66. Mrs. Wilson also translated the History of Egypt, Persia and Greece. For details see --- H.V. Mote, *Vishab Sharada, Vol. 1*, 1897-1947, p. 176.
67. M. Weitbrecht, *The Women of India and the Christian Work in the Zenana*, p. 176.
68. Anna and Hay Bayne were the sisters of Margaret Wilson.
69. M. Weitbrecht, *op.cit*, p. 32.
70. J.A. Richter, *op.cit*, p. 183-84.
71. Minna, G. Cowan, *The Education of the Women of India*, p. 199.
72. *B.C., March 10th, 1914*, p. 7.
73. H. V. Mote, *op.cit*,p. 51-53.
74. *B.C., March 10th 1914*, p. 7.
75. These castes were the lowest in the social heirarchy in Bengal. For details see William Adam, *op.cit*, p. 304.
76. In Ray Wilson's Schools girls belonged to Gujarati and Marathi families. In Gujarat, on the other hand, a large portion of the converts where Gujarati women. They also formed a large number in formal institutions of learning. For details see H.V. Mote, *op.cit*, p. 52, *ISR, February 12, 1899, Vol. IX*, p. 128.
77. Mary Carpenter, *Six Month's in India Vol. 1*, p. 113. M.D. David, *op.cit*, p. 32.
78. Rev. John Wilson, *op.cit*, p. 235.
79. *Ibid.*, p. 334.
80. *ISR, Bombay June 19, 1904, Vol. XIV*, p. 505. *Directory of Women's Instruction in Bombay Presidency Social Section. Bombay and Suburbs*, p. 1.
81 *India Calling - The Memoires of Cornelia Sorabji*, p.. 1, Kusoom Vadgama, *India in Britain - The Indian Contributions to the British Way of Life*, p. 201.
82. S.J. Joshi Anandi-Gopal pp. 139-51.
83. John S. Chandler, *A History of the Missions in South India Under the American Board of Commissioners for Foreign Mission*, p. 58.
84. William Adam, *op.cit*,p. 108.
85. K.K. Datta, *op.cit*, p. 129.

86. Sheerings, *The History of Protestant Missions in India,* pp. 442-47.
87. S.Nurullah and J. P. Naik, *A History of Education in India,* 178-179.
88. *Ibid.,* p. 135.
89. J.A. Richter, *op.cit,* pp. 308.
90. H. Sharp, *Progress of Education in India 1912-1917, Seventh Quinquennial Review Vols. 1 & 2,* p. 51-52.
91. Literary, *zenana* was a Persian word which meant both women and women apartments. Education given in this apartment came to be know as *zenana* system of education. Earlier it was conducted by guardians and later through hired tutors, particularly the missionaries. See Malavika Karlekar, *Voices form Within,* p. 6.
92. In the beginning of 20th Century increasing number of girls began to go to primary schools, however, their participation at higher levels was limited; at the sametime *zenana* education gained in popularity. There were number of reasons for this uneven growth in girl's education. To start with early marriage meant the girl's left schools well as insufficient numbers of women teachers meant that in society where women's seclusion was not uncommon, families were under social pressure to take their girl's out of co-education institutions... Malvika, Karlekar, "Women's Nature and Access to Education", in a Symposium on *Socialization, Education of Women,* April 18, 1985, p. 23.
93. Geraldine H. Forbes, *op.cit,* p. 740.

    Malavika, Karlekar "Kadambini and the Bhadralok-Early Debate over Women's Education in Bengal" *Economic and Political Weekly* Vol. XXI, No. 17, April 26, 1986.
94. M. Weitbrecht, *op.cit.,* p. 135.
95. N. L. Basak, *History of Vernacular Education in Bengal 1800-1854,* pp. 145-46.
96. *Ibid.,* p.146
97. Mary Carpenter was the daughter of a British priest. She devoted her whole life for promoting women's education. At the request of Rammohan Roy and Dr. Joseph Tukeram who appealed to her to visit India and give education to Indian women. She reached India on 5th February 1867. She toured the whole of Bombay Presidency in six months and gave her account in her book entitled *Six Months in India.* In this book an in-depth account of the condition of women in the Presidency is given. It is she who brought out clearly in her work that lack of female teachers was an important reason in hindering women's education. She therefore suggested the opening of training schools for women teachers. Mary Carpenters, *op.cit,* pp. 64-47.,
98. Lakshmi Misra, *Education of Women in India 1921-66,* p. 36.
99. Margaret I., Balfouri Ruth Young, *The Work of the Medical Women in India,* p. 3.
100. *Ibid.,* p. 16.
101. *Ibid.,* p. 111.
102. *Report of the Indian Education Commission,* pp. 542-43.
103. An in-depth discussion of the organizations established by them will be taken up in the fourth Chapter.
104. Swami Madhavananda and Majumdar, R.C., *op.cit,* p. 405.

105. Devdutt Narayan Tilak, *The Brilliant Lady of Maharashtra : Pandita Ramabai*, p. 231.
106. The intelligentsia of the period may be defined as all those in Bombay who received English education in the collegiate classes of the Elphinstone Institution before the founding of the University and those who gained University degree after that date. The term also comprises those who attended professional institution, such as the Grant Medical College and the Government Law classes, both before and after the instituting of degree.... See Christine Dobbin, *Urban Leadership in Western India --- Politics and Communities in Bombay City*, 1840-1885, p. 28.
107. Neera Desai, *op.cit.*, pp. 55-57.
108. S. Nurulla and J.P. Naik, *op.cit.*,p. 194.
109. H.V. Derozio and his followers felt that rapid changes in the existing social institution would not only reform society but would lead to all round progress.
110. K.K. Datta, *op.cit.*,pp. 264-265.
111. *A vivid account of the life of Reformers mentioned in the Chapter is given in the Appendix.* Also, a brief note of widow re-marriage in the Presidency is given.
112. Ishwarchandra Vidyasagar, *Marriage of Hindu Widows* pp. 8, 15-16.
113. S. Natarajan *op.cit.*,p. ix.
114. D.K. Karve, *Looking Back*, p. 47.

     D.K. Karve, *Atamvirith-Va-Charit*, pp. 7, 50-51.
115. *Ibid.*, pp. 50-51.
116. Shri J. Joshi, *op.cit.*,pp. 23-25.
117. N. Desai, *op.cit.*,pp. 82-83.
118. Charles H. Heimasath, *Indian Nationalism and Hindu Social Reform*, pp. 23-24.
119. A.K. Bhagwat, *Maharashtra --- A Profile*, p. 336.
120. D.K. Karve, *op.cit.*,pp. 43-44.
121. R.P. Karkaria, *India: Forty Years of Progress and Reform Being A Sketch of the Life and Time of Behramji, N. Malabari*, p. 129.
122. *Indian Worthies Vol. 1*, (Bombay : Manoranjak Grantha Prasarak Mandali 1906), p. 57.
123. Raja Ram Mohan Roy when he first met Bentinck opposed legislation on *Sati* on the ground that the British, a foreign power, should not interfere with Hindu Customs. He felt that reform should come from within Hindu Society through education and persuasion. For details see V.N. Datta, *Sati : A Historical, Social and Philosophical Enquiry into the Hindu Rite of Widow Burning*, pp. 119, 129-132.
124. S. Natarajan, *op.cit.*,p. 66.
125. Charles H. Heimsath, *op.cit.*,p. 217.
126. Tilak had been one of the first five to sign a pledge in 1889 by which he bound himself to educate his daughters and not to get them married below the age of 10. For details see S. Natrajan, *op.cit.*, pp. 66-67.
127. D. Keer, *Lokamanaya Tilak, Father of Our Freedom Struggle*, p. 56.
128. Sirdar Jogendra Singh, *B.M. Malabari - Rambles with the Pilgrim Reformer*, pp. 122-23.

129. R.P. Karkaria, *op.cit.*,pp. 118.
130. Hiralal Lallubhai Kaji, *Life and Speeches of Sir Vithaldas Thackersey,* p. 195. *ISR,* July 20, 1902, Vol. XII, No. 47, p. 381
131. Karamveer V.R. Shinde, *Reñaissance in Western India (1873-1944),* p. 141.
132. *Ibid.,* p. 141.
133. Aparna Basu, *op.cit.*,p. 13.
134. *Ibid.*
135. Ganesh L. Chandavarkar, *Maharshi Karve,* p. 80.
136. S.K. Nehur (ed.), *Our Cause,* pp. 8-9.
137. Ganesh L. Chandavarkar, *op.cit.*,p. 85.
138. Dhondo Keshav Karve, *op.cit.*,p. 59.
139. S. Natarajan, *op.cit.*,p. 33.
140. Jogesh C. Bagal, *History of the Bethune School and College (1849-1949),* pp. 12-13.
141. Stanley A. Wolpert, *op.cit.*,p. 6-7.
    Ganesh. L. Chandavarkar, *op.cit.*,p. 54.
    D.Keer, *Mahatma Jotirao Phooley : Father of our Social Revolution,* p. 83.
142. D. Keer, *op.cit.*,p. 83.
143. A.K. Bhagwat, *op.cit.*,p. 335.
    Charles H. Heimsath, *op.cit.*,pp. 99-100.
144. Stanley A. Wolpert, *op.cit.,* p. 6.
    Charles H. Heimsath, *op.cit.*,p. 100.
145 *Ibid,* p. 100.
146. *Ibid.,* p. 101.
147. S. Natarajan, *op.cit.*,pp. 54-55
    Charles H. Heimsath, *op.cit.*,p. 100.
    S. Nurulla and J.P. Naik, *op.cit.*,p. 189.
    Christine Dobbin, *op.cit.*,pp. 55-56.
148. *Famous Parsis : Biographical and Critical Sketches of Patriots, Philanthropists, Politicians, Reformers, Scholars and Captains of Industry,* pp. 16, 186.
149. D. Keer, *op.cit.*,pp. 62-63.
150. *Ibid.,* pp. 62-63.
151. Charles H. Heimsath, *op.cit.*,pp. 92-95.
    S. Natarajan, *op.cit.*,p. 51.
152. *Ibid.,* p. 55.
153. *Ibid.*
154. *Ibid.,* p. 55.
155. *Ibid.,* p. 66
156. Charles H. Heimsath, *op.cit.*,pp. 160-61.
157. A detailed account of the growth and development of various institutions established by Karve is given in the Appendix.
158. Pandita Ramabai Sarasvati, *op.cit.*,pp. 8-11.

159. Husain, B. Tyabji, *Badruddin Tyabji, a Biography,* pp. 71-79.
Jyotis Chandra Dasgupta, *A National Biography for India,* p. 9.
160. Faredun Hormusji Bana, *History of Institution Supported by Parsi Philanthropy and Enterprise in Education,* p. 150.
161. Helen S. Dyer, *Pandita Ramabai : the Story of Her Life,* p. 10. Pandita Ramabai Sarasvati, *op.cit.,*pp. 8-10.
162. Kusumvati Deshpande, Ranade - *His Wifes Reminiscences,* pp. 3-7.
163. Shri J. Joshi *op.cit.,*pp. 49-50.
164. *Ibid.,* pp. 123-124.
165. Sarojini Vaid, *Shrimati Kashibai Kanitkar, Atmachairt Anicharit,* pp. 74.
166. *Jyotiba Phule Samagrah Granth,* p. 294.
167. A detailed account of *Sharda Sadan* which was founded by Pandita Ramabai is discussed in the fourth chapter.
168. *Agarkar letter, Poona, Dated 25th November, 1890.* N.M.M.L., New Delhi
169. Mahadev Patwardhan, *Autobiography and Character of D.D. Karve,* pp. 187-88.
170. H. Sharp, *op.cit.,*p. 22.
171. R.V. Parulekar, *A Source - Book of History of Education in the Bombay Province, Part 1, Survey of Indigenous Education* (1820-30), p. ix.
172. William Adam, *op. cit,* pp. 219-20.
173. *Selections from the Records of the Government of Madras, No. II, Appendix E.*
174. *A Review of Education in Bombay State 1855-1955,* p. 388.
175. Kalidas Nag (ed)., *op.cit.,* pp. 21-23.
176. *Dalhousie Muniments Sec. 6 No. 258, Home Department - A statement of the most important measures carried out during the administration of the Government of India by the most Noble the Marquis of Dalhousie 1848 to 1855 both inclusive.*
Selections from Educational Record, Vol. 11, pp. 59-60.
177. J.A. Richey (ed.) *op.cit.,*pp. 338.
Report of the Indian Education Commission - Appointed by the Resolution of the Government of India dated 3rd February 1882, p. 523.
178. Sir Alfred Croft, *Review of Education of India in 1886,* p. 43-44.
179. S. Nurulla and J.P. Naik, *op.cit.,*p. 389.
180. *Report of the Indian Education Commission,* p. 533.
181. *Ibid.,* pp. 545-548.
182. Alfred Croft, *op.cit.,*p. 44.
183. *A Review of Education in Bombay State 1855,* pp. 390-91.
184. S.R Dongerbery, *Bombay 1857-1957,* p. 26.
185. *Ibid.,* p. 27.
186. S. Nurulla and J.P. Naik, *op.cit.,*p. 399.
187. *No. 94 of 1911 Government of India Finance Department Leave and Leave Allowance,* p. 11.
It is significant to note that it was only in 1935 that the Maternity Benefit Act

was passed by which working women were allowed Maternity leave with full pay.

188. *Government Resolution on Education Policy (1904)*, Para 27.
189. Sir Thomas Raligh, *Lord Curzon in India : Being a selection from his Speeches as Viceroy and Governor General of India 1898-1905*, p. 53.
190. *Simla Record 3-1911, Government of India, Department of Education, Education -A Proceedings, July, 1911*, No. 70. pp. 5.
191. *Ibid*, p. 5.
192. S. Nurulla and J.P. Naik, *op.cit.*,pp. 572-73.
193. *Progress of Education in India 1917-1922*, p. 14.
194. A detailed account of the University is given in the appendix.

3

GROWTH, DEVELOPMENT AND SOME ECONOMIC ASPECTS OF WOMEN'S EDUCATION

GROWTH OF COLLEGES, PROFESSIONAL AND TRAINING INSTITUTIONS

The initiative taken by the Christian missionaries, male intelligentsia and later by the government towards women's education saw a gradual growth of institutions promoting higher education of women in our Presidency. As mentioned in chapter one, it was Lord Dalhousie, the then Governor-General of India, who was responsible in directing the Council, "to consider its functions as comprising the superintendance of native female education"[1] and further the Education Despatch of 1854 approved of these orders and thus the responsibility of educating women was taken up by the Government directly: Infact, the direct involvement of Government not only led to the expansion in primary education but secondary, collegiate and professional education made a steady advancement. Also, there was a positive increase in government's expenditure on women's education. This encouraged the private agencies to establish separate colleges for women. An in-depth statistical and graphical account of the expansion and expenditure on women's education is taken:in,this Chapter.

It is a lesson of the history of education in India the education of women followed that of men at a respectable distance. As stated in the previous chapter, as far as men were concerned the government took the responsibility of their education as early as 1813 but regarding women it took twenty seven years for the government to assume direct responsibility in 1854. In that year, there were 2,875 schools for the education of men all over India, with 10,6040 pupils but at the sametime girl's schools numbered only 65 with an enrolement of about 3,500 pupils. This was a modest beginning no doubt but its promises were great and it ultimately exercised a very salutory influence on the creation of a new social order in the country. Following the Despatch of 1854, Government offered in 1857, small annual rewards to those primary teachers who could form girls classes in their schools. But the progress of this scheme was slow and even in 1864-65 the government schools contained only 639 girls. In that year, the proceeds of the local funds also became'available and it was possible for the department to start more girls schools in all the Presidencies. In 1870-71, there were as many as 218 girls school (against 23 in 1864-65) with 9190 pupils and the government expenditure on the education of women which was Rs. 341 only in 1864-65 increased to Rs. 39,337 in 1870-71. The two training Colleges for Women, one in Poona (1870) and the other in Ahmedabad (1871) were established. The difficulties of these early institutions may easily be imagined because of the eight women who first entered the Poona College some did not know even the alphabets.[2] Also, the absence of adequate numbers of feeder schools which would train teachers to a prescribed minimum standard further aggravated the problem. Infact, the training Colleges of this period had to admit women without paying attention to their educational attainments. The cart had to be put before the horse and a training college had to do the work of a school in the first instance, in order that primary schools for girls could be placed under competent teachers a little later. No entrance standard was, therefore, prescribed till 1878 and then the passing of the third primary standard was declared to be enough to qualify a student for admission to the college. Upto 1882; this college sent out 34 women teachers which works out to an average of about 3 per years, the largest number sent out in any year being 6 in 1882. Of these 34 students, six were *Brahmins,* eighteen *Marathas,* one *Sonar,* one *Wani,* one Jew and one Muslim. Further 19 were married, 11 were widows and 4 were unmarried.[3] The largest proportion of married women deserves notice. At this time it was the policy of the Department to encourage primary teachers under training in the Male Training College in Poona to send their wives to the Female Training College. Thus, husband and wife both became teachers and were appointed in the same place.

The story of the Ahmedabad College is almost similar and till 1882, it sent out 38 women teachers. Between 1882 and 1921, both these training institutions made considerable progress. Besides, eight additional training institutions[4] for women were also established so that the total number of women under training increased to 234 in 1901-02. However, as there was no common examination (like the Primary school certificate) on the basis of which girl's could be admitted to the College, each training College for women had its own code, held its own entrance exams, and even had its own curriculum which, however, had to be approved by the Department. It may, therefore, be said that by 1920-21, the training of women teachers had already been placed on a permanent basis although the progress was not very satisfactory.

The period 1857-1921 also witnessed the introduction of special courses in primary schools for girls'. The prevailing opinion in the 19th century was to have an absolutely separate system of education for girls with separate schools, separate syllabus and even separate textbooks, not to speak of women teachers and women inspectors. As soon as the condition became favourable, each one of these measures was being brought into practice. Separate schools and women teachers had already become a reality by 1875. The principle of appointing women inspecting officers was also recognized because the lady superintendents of the training colleges at Poona and Ahmedabad were required to supervise the working of the girls schools in the neighbourhood. In 1877-78, therefore, it was felt that the time was ripe for the introduction of separate courses for girls schools. Separate textbooks for girls was long felt to be necessary but they were introduced only as late as 1906.

Another development during the period (1857-1921) which was even more significant in the long run than the establishment of training colleges for women primary teachers was the entry of women in secondary schools and colleges. A lead in this matter was taken by advanced communities like the Europeans, Anglo-Indians, Indian Christians and Parsis. But a typical event was the establishment of a High School for Indian girls in Poona in 1884. So, the movement had started and not only were more secondary schools established for girls in different centers but girls began to attend boys secondary schools in fairly large numbers.

The expansion of the Secondary Education of girls' was naturally followed by their entry into Colleges. By 1921-22 there were 179 girls' in Colleges .[5]

As already stated, the profession of teaching was thrown open to them by the establishment of training colleges at Poona, Ahmedabad, Rajkot, Kolhapur and Hyderabad.[6]

Next to teaching in popularity, came the medical careers-nursing, midwifery and medicine. In the first two of these, women have always had a monopoly. But what deserves special notice is that women were now taking quickly to a career in medicine and becoming physicians and surgeons. The necessity of women doctors began to be felt very early because Indian women were naturally averse to consulting male doctors; *Vaidyas* and *Hakims* were gradually dying out and thanks to the allopathic hospitals and dispensaries established by Government and missionaries in several parts of the country. The Western System of. medicine was becoming more and more popular. This created a demand for trained women doctors, and it was, therefore, natural that the medical education of women should get a great fillip in this period.

An important event which contributed in the development of medical education of women was the establishment of the Countess of Dufferin Fund in 1885. The main object of this Fund was to establish hospitals. and maternity homes for women; to train women as nurses and midwives; to give scholarships to such women as desired professional education in medicine; to promote child-welfare and ante-natal care and to take such steps as may be necessary to reduce infant mortality and death rate among women during child-birth. A large amount was collected and it was utilized to give scholarships to women undergoing some type of education in medicine.[7]

In Bombay Presidency, Midwifery classes were started in the Grant Medical College (1875-76) and women students also began to be admitted to the degree course in Medicine. In 1883, there were 74 women students in Grant Medical College when it was first opened to women. On the date of the last report, the number of students in attendance was 29, and this increased to 35 by the admission of 6 new students--- of this total 6 left, one obtained the L.M.S. degree, and 2 qualified as certificated practitioners, leaving 26 on the college rolls. In the matriculated class eight and three female students respectively, presented themselves for the lst and 2nd University examinations in medicine but only 3 of the former and one of the latter were successful.[8] Miss Grahams, the successful student at the second examination in medicine was awarded the Sir James Ferguson scholarship ofRs 20, tenable for one year. Miss A. Dunn passed brilliantly for the degree of L.M.S., obtaining from the University the Lady Reay gold medal, the Cama gold medal, and the scholarship of the Medical women of India Fund. Six students appeared for the final examination in the non-matriculated class, and 2 qualified, viz. Miss Smith and Miss Browne, the former being recommended for the Viceroy's silver medal. The remaining four students were allowed to continue their studies till the end of April. The general conduct and attendance of all the students was well reported upon.[9]

Art Courses in the J.J. School of Art, Bombay attracted several women students and the missionaries as mentioned in the former chapter had started industrial training of girls in some of their institutions. It is true that the number of girls attending institutions of professional education was small even in 1920-21 and that a large percentage of them belonged to the four advanced communities mentioned above. But the achievement of the period was that the professional education of women did make a beginning, however, humble and that some careers outside the home were thrown open to women for the first time.

Taken all in all, therefore, the education of women had made but little progress by 1920-21 The total female population of the State, according to the census of 1921, was 12,792,611 but the total number of girls at schools was only 1,87,265 and the percentage of literacy among women was just about 2.35. Most of the girls under instruction were reading in primary schools and the higher education of women had just begun and still mostly confined to the four minor but progressive communities i.e. Europeans, Anglo-Indians, Parsis and Indian Christians. Quantitatively, this is a very disappointing picture. But it would hardly be fair to the administrators and social scientists of this period to judge their achievements from modern standards. A better and more equitable method would be to compare the condition in 1920-21 with those that existed at the advent of the British rule. At the beginning of the 19th century, no girl attended public schools and an extremely small number were educated at home. As against this dark picture, there were over 1,87,265 girls under instruction in 1921-22. A statistical and graphical account of the growth of Colleges of General Education, Professional and Training schools for women is discussed in detail in this chapter.

Growth of Colleges of General Education and Scholars

In Bombay upto 1921, there was no separate college for general education of women but women had started studying in the colleges for men. Upto 1884-85 no girls had passed the entrance examination of the University nor was there any institution in which they could be taught to that standard. In his Report, for that year, the Director of Public Instructions, Bombay Mr. H.B.Grigg observed with reference to the absence of any provision for training female students to the entrance examinations, "This defect is much to be regretted, and if not remedied, will probably result in natives of India being supplanted in the advanced institutions by mistresses imported from Europe having higher qualifications. The introduction of French and German into the subjects at the entrance examinations

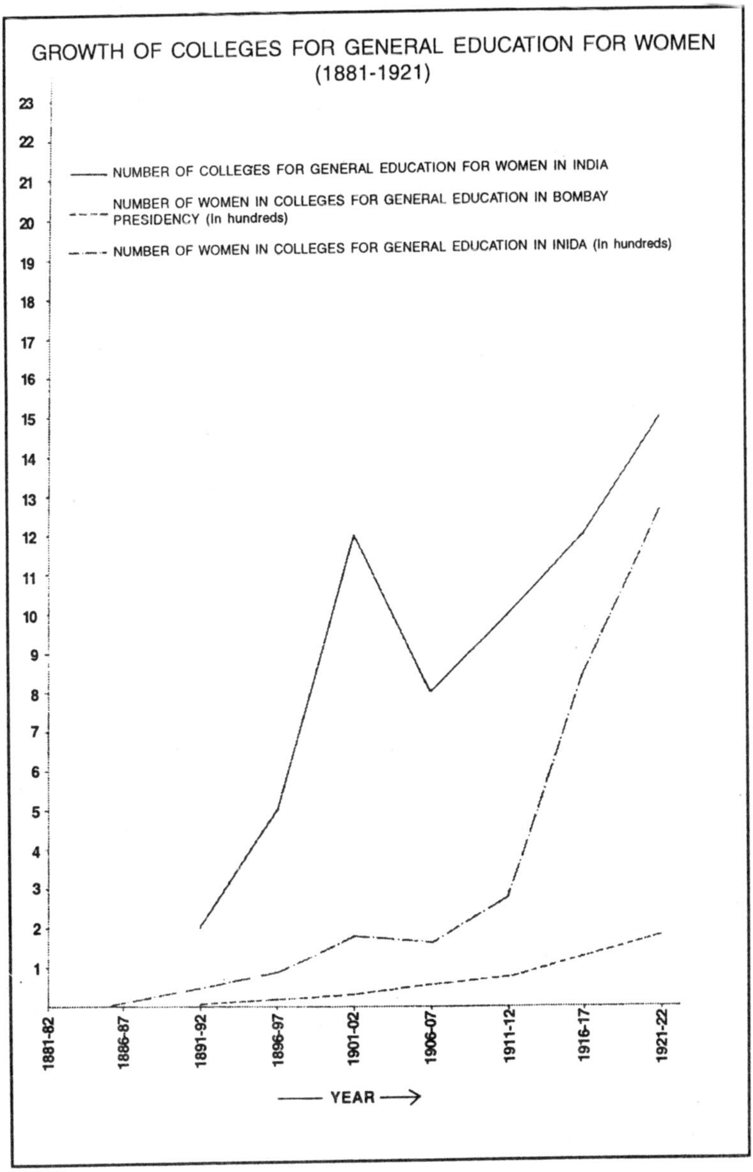

Figure 3.1 : Growth of Colleges for General Education for Women 1981-1922

remove the language difficulty, and there is no good reason why girls should not be taught mathematics and physical sciences upto the required standard."[10]

Table 3.1 shows the number of Colleges, number of women in colleges and percentage of women to the total number of scholars for the period under study. From the table we see that though there were no colleges for women, even for. men the growth in number of colleges was not encouraging. In 1881-82 there were six colleges for men and the number grew to ten by the year 1921-22 — an increase of only four colleges over a period of 40 years. So far as the growth in number of women is concerned, we see that in 1891-92 there was only one woman studying in the college and the number increased to 179 in the Year 1921-22.

Table 3.1 : Growth of College for General Education in Bombay Presidency

Year	*No. of Colleges*	*No. of Colleges for Women*	*Total No. of scholars*	*No. of Women*	*Percentage of women scholars*
1881-82	6	—	475	not ava.	—
1886-87	9	—	955	not ava.	—
1891-92	10	—	1,332	1	0.08
1896-97	10	—	1,064	18	1.69
1901-02	10	—	1,941	30	1.55
1906-07	10	—	2,747	57	2.08
1911-12	11	—	3,719	76	2.04
1916-17	8	—	4,888	125	2.56
1921-22	10	—	4,829	179	3.71

Source : A Review of Education in Bombay State, p.270.

This increase was 178 times while in case of male scholars the number increased from 1331 to 4650 over the same period — an increase of 2.5 times. If we look at the percentage of female to the total number of scholars, the last column of the table shows that in 1891-92 the percentage was only 0.08 which increased to 3.71 by the end of the period. For a comparative study, we present in Table 3.2, the growth of colleges for general education for the country as a whole (Fig. 3.1). We see that in 1891-92, the number of colleges for women was two and in 1921-22 it was 15. The number of women scholars increased from 45 in 1891-92 to 1263 in 1921-22. The graph on the previous page shows the trend in growth of colleges and women scholars in the Bombay Presidency and India. It is evident from the graph that the numbers of women scholars grew at a faster rate at All India basis, particularly in the Bengal Presidency than in

Bombay. In other words more women were registered for collegiate education in other provinces of India.

Table 3.2 : Growth of Colleges for General Education in India

Year	*No. of Colleges for women*	*No. of Colleges for men*	*Total of women scholars*	*Total No. of scholars*
1885-86	—	86	8	8127
1891-92	2	102	45	12985
1896-97	5	115	87	14420
1901-02	12	133	177	17651
1906-07	8	128	160	18918
1911-12	10	130	279	29648
1916-17	12	122	842	47135
1921-22	15	152	1263	45933

Source : *Progress of Education in India Quinquiennial Review for 1886, 1891, 1901, 1911.*

Professional Colleges

Again upto 1921 there was no separate college for professional education for women in the Bombay Presidency and the women scholars were admitted in the college for men. (Fig. 3.2)

Table 3.3 : Growth of Professional Colleges in Bombay Presidency

Year	*No. of Colleges*	*No. of Colleges for women*	*No. of Women*	*Total No.*	*Percentage of women*
1881-82	3	—	Not Available	570	—
1886-87	4	—	-do-	678	—
1891-92	4	—	8	495	1.62
1896-97	4	—	20	760	2.63
1901-02	5	—	45	1064	4.23
1906-07	5	—	39	1450	2.69
1911-12	4	—	29	1239	2.34
1916-17	6	—	52	1841	2.83
1921-22	7	—	79	2595	3.04

Source : *A Review of Education in Bombav State 1855-1955,* p. 265.

Table 3.3 shows the number of colleges, number of women in the colleges, total number of scholars and percentage of women scholars to

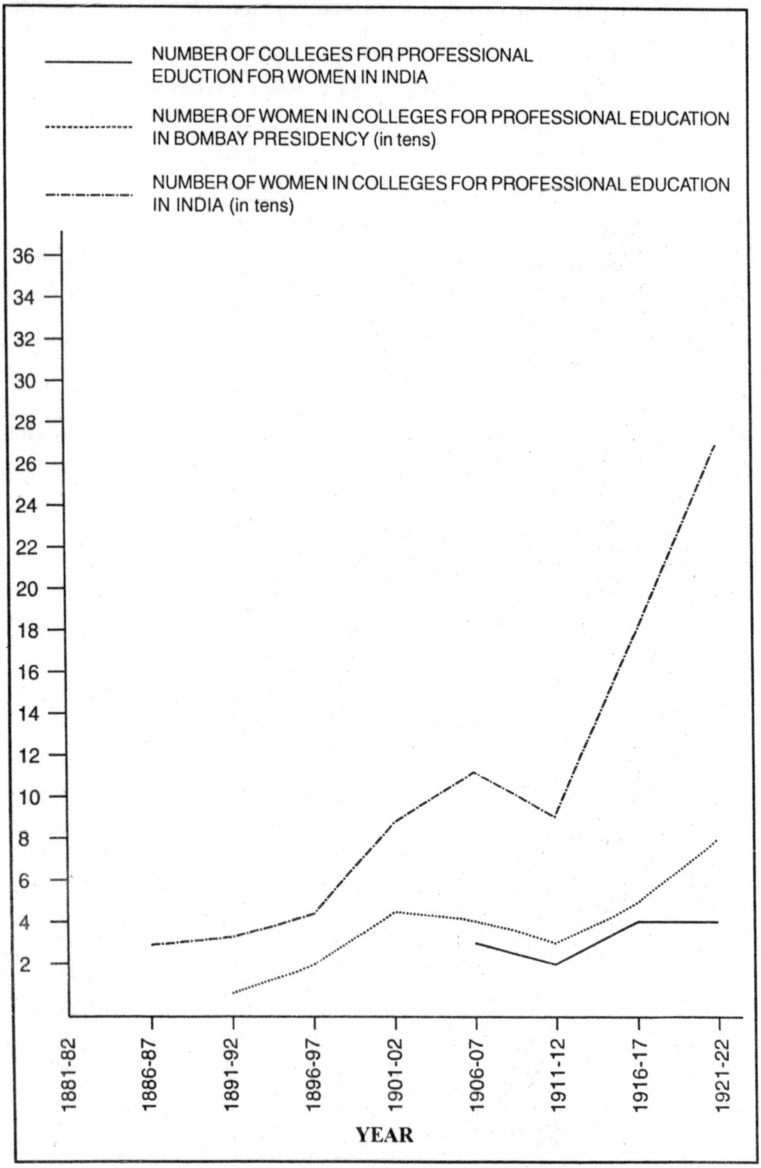

Figure 3.2 : Growth of Colleges for Professional Education for Women (1881-1921)

total number of scholars. We see from the table that though during the period no separate colleges for women were established but even for men there was not much growth in the colleges. In 1981-82 there were three colleges which increased to 7 in 1921-22 an increase by two times over a long period of 40 years. The number of women was 8 in 1891-92 which increased to 79 in 1991-92 an increase by 9 times in 30 years.

Thus, we find that the growth in professional education of women was very slow. This was because women's education was not linked to employment and as is well known more women opted for general education (Table 3.1) than professional education. A comparative analysis of women scholars in the whole of India vis-a-vis number of women professional colleges clearly shows that there were only three colleges for women and they increased to four in 1921-22 (Table 3.4). Similarly, the number of women scholars increased from 27 in 1885-86 to 266 in 1921-22. The number of women in Professional Colleges in India increased at a faster rate than in the Bombay Presidency as is clear from the graph in Fig. 3.2

Table 3.4 : Growth of Professional Colleges in India

Year	*No. of Colleges for women*	*No. of Colleges for men*	*No. of women scholars*	*Total No. of scholars*
1885-86	—	24	27	2411
1891-92	—	37	31	3292
1896-97	—	40	43	4363
1901-02	—	46	87	5358
1906-07	3	43	113	6250
1911-12	2	44	90	4636
1916-17	4	57	180	11504
1921-22	4	60	266	13662

Source : Progress of Education in India - Quinqennial Review for 1886, 1891, 1896, 1901, 1906, 1911, 1916, 1921.

Growth of Training Schools for Women

Though no separate Colleges for women existed or were started in the Bombay Presidency during the period under study, the Government and the private agencies had shown keen interest in preparing teachers for primary and secondary schools, even in the early years, of the period. Table 3.5 gives the number of schools for women, and number of schools in the Presidency. We see that there were two schools in 1869-70 and the number increased to 21 in 1920-21. The number of women scholars increased from 17 in 1860-70 to 929 in 1920-21 — an increase by about 55 times over a period of 50 years. Though the growth was not very impressive, it was better than growth in general and professional education of women. This was basically because the Government and the private agencies had realized the importance of preparing school teachers which forms the background for a good college education. Table 3.6 exhibits the growth of Training Schools for Women at All India Level. In the year 1885-86 the number of College for women was 27 which increased to 146 in the year 1921-22. The number of female scholars grew from 660 in 1885-86 to 26931 in 1921-22. The trend in growth of training schools for women in the Bombay Presidency and India is shown on the graph (Figure 3.3). Once again it clearly shows that the number of women in Training Schools in India increased at a much faster rate than that in the Presidency under study.

Table 3.5 : Growth of Training Schools in Bombay Presidency

Year	No. of schools for women	No. of Women Scholars
1859-60	—	—
1869-70	2	17
1879-80	2	62
1889-90	8	178
1899-1900	10	238
1909-10	13	347
1920-21	21	927

Source : Report on Public Instruction in Bombay Presidency for the Years mentiond.

Table 3.6 : Growth of Training Schools for Women in India

Year	No. of schools for women	No. of Women Scholars
1885-86	27	660
1891-92	37	819
1896-97	45	1170
1901-02	46	1412
1906-07	63	1420
1911-12	85	1578
1916-17	111	2757
1921-22	146	4391

Source : Progress of Education in India - Quinqennial Reviews for the years mentioned 1885-86 to 1921-22.

EXTENT OF CO-EDUCATION

It is interesting to note that the public opinion in the Bombay Presidency

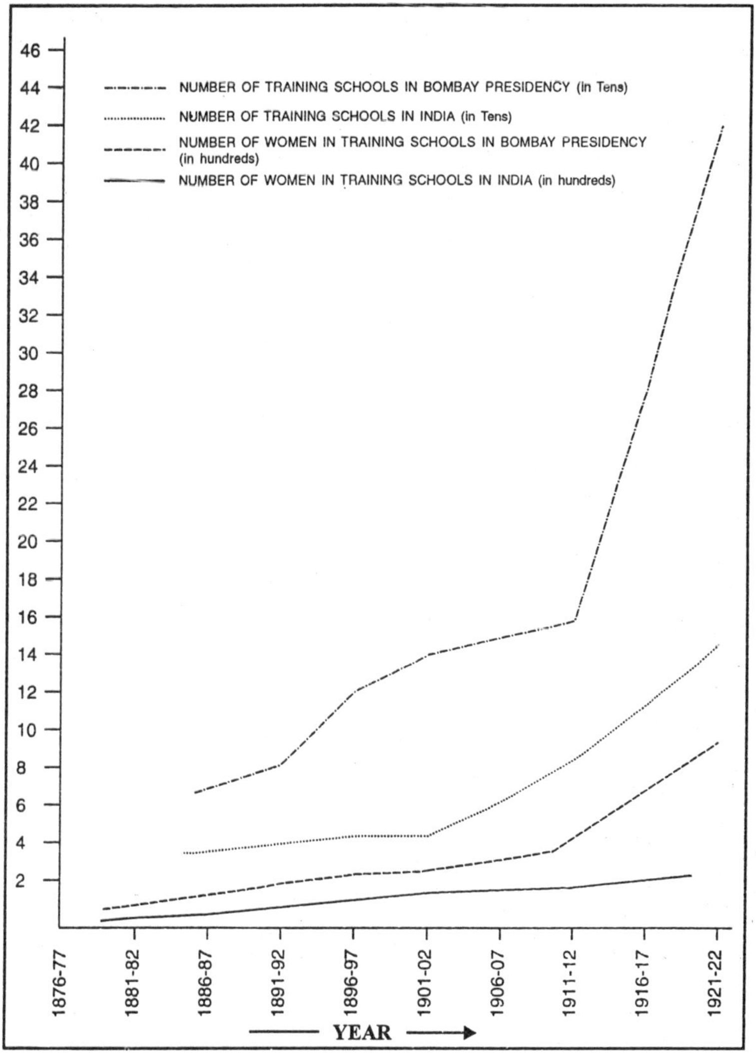

Figure 3.3 : Growth of Training Schools for Women (1881-1921)

was never hostile to co-education at collegiate level or stage. In most other parts of India people were opposed to sending their grown up daughters to men's colleges and consequently separate colleges for women were started there at an early date. Even in 1901-02 there were as many as 12 colleges for women in the whole of India — in Madras, 3 in Bengal and 6 in United

Province. But no separate colleges for women were started in Bombay until 1916 when the S.N.D.T. Indian Women's University was established. The colleges started by this institution were naturally attended by girls only, but they had not been largely attended even after the University has been placed on a statutory basis. It may, therefore, be stated that the general public opinion in the State was in favour of co-education at the collegiate stage. The positive attitude of the public opinion towards co-education can also be seen at the levels of secondary and primary schools.

The education statistics shows that the percentage of girls in boys secondary schools increased from 15.4 in 1901-02 to 17.8 in 1921-22. In the terms of number there were 664 girls in the boys schools in 1901-02 and 1716 girls in 1921-22. The extent of co-education was even more marked in primary schools and this was also encouraged by the Government. In the year 1901-02 there were 22438 girls' in boys schools which formed 56.4 per cent of total number of girls in primary schools. The number increased to 60070 in the year 1921-22 and it was 59.5 per cent of the total number.

Thus, as a result of expansion of higher institutions of learning, girls under instruction in all institutions (including those for boys) for Bombay Presidency and the whole of British India increased. We see from the Table 3.7 that in 1886-87 there were 52941 girls under instruction and this number increased to 187265 in the year 1921-22. This amounts to an increase by about 3.5 times. At All-India level there were 227736 girls under instruction in 1886-87 which grew to 1418422 in the year 1921-22.. This comes to an increase of about 63 times. This trend in the growth in number of girls under instruction in Bombay Presidency and in India is shown in the graph. It can be concluded that the growth at the All India level was much faster than that in the Bombay Presidency.

Table 3.7 : Total Number of Girls under-Instruction in All Institutions

Year	*In Bombay Presidency*	*In India*
1886-87	52941	227736
1891-92	73017	834031
1896-97	82153	402158
1901-02	93063	444470
1906-07	108716	645028
1911-12	153096	952911
1916-17	144621	1230419
1921-22	187265	1418422

Source : Report of Public Instruction in Bombay Presidency and Progress of Education in India -Quinauennial Review for Corresponding years 1886-87, 1922.

Therefore, during our period there was an expansion in primary, secondary and professional education. Though it remained generally confined to four major communities,i.e. Europeans, Anglo-Indian, Indian-Christian and Parsis, a beginning had been made. Professions that became common during our period were teaching, midwifery, nursing and so on. Art courses also became popular. Infact, it depicts that the profession which women opted for was a mere extension of their household work. They failed to take to technical and engineering professions.

A comparative analysis from various tables and graphs depicted in this chapter clearly portrays that as compared to Bombay Presidency the number of scholars in general colleges, training in professional institutions on all India basis expanded at a greater rate. This reveals an overall consciousness in all Presidencies regarding higher education of women. The next part of the chapter is devoted on an in-depth examination on government expenditure on higher institutions of learning. Also, the result of the expenditure is analysed by examining the number of successful candidates in all the examinations.

GOVERNMENT'S EXPENDITURE ON HIGHER INSTITUTIONS OF LEARNING

This section examines in detail some economic aspects of the growth and development of- higher education of women in the Bombay Presidency. For this, we have attempted to analyse the trend in growth in expenditure on colleges for general education, professional education and training schools for women in the Presidency. An account of the annual cost of educating a pupil in each class of the institution is also undertaken. The result of the expenditure can be judged from the final results or pass out of women candidates in different prescribed examinations. This aspect has also been analysed for selected years during the period.

Expenditure on Colleges for General Education of Women

As mentioned in the earlier section, upto 1921 no separate colleges for the general education of women existed in Bombay Presidency. Most of the women were studying in colleges for men. In 1891-92 there was only one woman studying at the college level and the number increased to only 179 by the end of the period, i.e. 1921. Since there was no separate colleges for women, it is not possible to make any accurate estimate of the full amount spent on the higher education of women.

But a rough estimate can be made from the available data. If we assume that the total expenditure per student (boy or girl) was the same (and which is not unreasonable), then column 11 of Table 3.8 gives the estimated annual expenditure on education of women in the colleges. We see that in the year 1891-92 the expenditure on women was only Rs. 235.96 but it grew to Rs.4630.54 in the year 1921-22. The trend was encouraging and positive and led the government and private agencies to establish separate colleges for women in later years. From the table we can also conclude that the expenditure on general education was largely met by the provincial government. In 1891-92 the provincial share on expenditure was Rs. 137353— which increased to Rs.521023 by the year 1921-22 — an increase by about two times. Detailed statistical account regarding expenditure on women' education is taken in the chapter.

Expendiure on College for Professional Education of Women

Again upto 1921, there was no separate colleges for professional education of women and it is not possible tc make any accurate estimate of the expenditure but a rough estimate has been made as done in the previous section, Table 3.9 shows the numbers of colleges; number of boys and girls and total expenditure incurred on their professional education. In the year 1891-92 the expenditure was Rs. 1079 on women which increased to Rs. 30876.2 in 1921-22 fifteen fold increase over a period of thirty years. Again the expenditure was largely met by the provincial government.

Expenditure on Training Schools for Women

Though no separate colleges for women existed for general and professional education in the Bombay Presidency upto 1921, the Government had realized the importance of preparing teachers for primary and secondary schools early in the period and two training schools for female were established — one at Poona in 1870 and the other at Ahmedabad in 1871. By the end of 1921 there were 21 Training Schools for women. Table 3.10 shows the actual expenditure or Training Schools for women. It can be seen that Training Schools received fairly good attention of the government as well as private agencies throughout the period. In 1901-02 the Government share of total expenditure was

Table 3.8 : Expenditure on General Education of Women

Year	Number of Colleges	Number of Students			Expenditure from			Other sources Rs.	Total Rs.	Expenditure on Girls Education (Estimated) (Rs.)
		Boys	Girls	Total	State Funds Rs.	Local Funds Rs.	Fees Rs.			
(1)	(2)	(3)	(4)	(5)	(6)	(7)	(8)	(9)	(10)	(11)
1881-82	6	—	—	475	90567	3000	34845	56415	184827	—
1886-87	9	—	—	955	120895	4494	57698	66247	249334	—
1991-92	9	1331	1	1332	137353	13524	87281	76142	314300	235.96
1996-97	10	1046	18	1064	166598	16675	98009	88252	369534	6251.52
1901-02	10	1911	30	1941	128906	14625	132561	76732	352824	5453.23
1906-07	10	2690	57	2747	149038	14300	179137	124127	466602	9681.95
1911-12	11	3643	76	3719	146911	24249	248585	114588	534333	10919.42
1916-17	8	4763	125	4888	293828	19150	394549	68189	775716	19837.25
1921-22	10	4650	179	4829	521023	16225	452379	259507	1249134	46302.54

Source : *A Review of Education in Bombay State 1855-1955*, published by the Director, Govt. Printing Press, Bombay, p. 270.

Table 3.9 : Expenditure on Professional Education of Women

Year	*Number of Colleges*	*Number of Students*			*Expenditure from*			*Other sources Rs.*	*Total Rs.*	*Expenditure on Women Education (Estimated) (Rs.)*
		Boys	*Girls*	*Total*	*State Funds Rs.*	*Local Funds Rs.*	*Fees Rs.*			
1881-82	3	—	—	570	62541	—	24017	2028	88586	—
1886-87	4	—	—	678	51119	—	38878	3795	93792	—
1891-92	4	487	8	495	70361	—	41276	4626	116263	1879.00
1896-97	4	740	20	760	37864	—	57462	5267	100593	2647.18
1901-02	5	1019	45	1064	66900	—	110496	5312	182708	7727.31
1906-07	5	1411	39	1450	215201	—	56171	5929	277301	7458.44
1911-12	4	1210	29	1239	270100	250	142195	6567	419112	9809.72
1916-17	6	1789	52	1841	345699	—	236846	4801	587346	16589.89
1921-22	7	2516	79	2595	649430	—	341883	22912	1014225	30876.21

Source : *A Review of Education in Bombay state 1855-1955*, published by the Director, Govt. Printing Press, Bombay, p. 274.

about 45 per cent which increased to about 68 per cent in the year 1921-22. Infact, the actual government expenditure made a five fold growth over the period.

Expenditure on Hostels or Boarding Houses for Women

It is significant to note that hostel and boarding establishments which was initially opened by the missionaries gradually began to be established by the government and private agencies. Perhaps its importance was realized because it was felt that girls staying at far of places, particularly in rural areas could not take the advantage of education. Therefore, hostels and boarding houses for women were established. Table 3.11 shows the expenditure from various sources on girls hostels for the year 1899-1900, 1901-1910, and 1920-21 for which statistics are available.

This Table 3.11 shows that government and private agencies were also concerned about the accommodation of outstationed students. By 1921, local cess was also used for the maintenance of boarding houses and hostel.

Table 3.10 : Expenditure on Training Schools for Women

Year	*Govt funds Rs.*	*Local funds Rs.*	*Fees Rs.*	*Other source Rs.*	*Total Rs.*
1881-82	13841	30	1160	773	15804
1886-87	20436	3778	4	1664	25862
1891-92	21197	8175	1050	13661	44083
1896-97	26876	11818	2270	17842	58806
1901-02	25955	8688	3182	19593	57412
1906-07	24790	16073	4553	24277	69693
1911-12	47970	10757	4760	26232	89719
1916-17	95691	13336	4919	39119	153065
1921-22	183858	25904	7204	5394	270560

Source : Report of Public Instruction in Bombay Presidency for Corresponding Year 1881-82 to 1921-22.

Table 3.11 : Expenditure on Girls Hostels or Boarding Houses

Year	*State funds. Rs*	*Local cess Rs*	*Fees Rs*	*Other Sources Rs*	*Total Rs*
1899-1900	10061	—	9856	8054	28115
1909-1910	20564	—	25901	40246	86711
1920-1921	2604	3048	7773	18090	31515

Source : Report of Public Instruction in Bombav Presidency for Corresponding Year 1899-1900 to 1921-22.

Thus, we find that as far as expenditure on college for General Education and Professional education of women was concerned, it was largely met by various provinces. In the former case the provincial share on expenditure increased from Rs. 137353 in 1891-92 to Rs. 521023 in 1921-22 — an increase by two times. In the latter case there was a fifteen fold increase of expenditure over a period of 30 years, i.e. in the year 1891-92 the expenditure was Rs. 1079 and in 1921-22 it was Rs. 3087.

It is interesting to note that as far as expenditure or training schools for women was concerned it was largely met by the Government. In 1901-02 Government share of total expenditure was about 45 per cent and this increased to 68 per cent in 1921-22. Regarding hostels and boarding establishments, the expenditure from the State fund: gradually declined as expenditure was met from local cess, Fees and other sources by 1921-22.

The gradual increase in Government's expenditure point to the fact that it was interested in promoting women' education for which it tried to promote certain essential services like establishing hostels and boarding houses for women.

COST OF EDUCATION

Apart from the expenditure on women's education an in-depth examination of unit cost of education at school as well as college level is important in the study of educational finance. Infact, this has become more pertinent in the realm of higher education. It acts as an indicator to the government to determine the amount of allocation of funds to the educational institutions. If the unit cost of education shows an increasing trend, the government could provide more funds towards the education sector.

Tables 3.12, 3.13 and 3.14, give the annual cost of educating each pupil in college for general education, professional education and training schools for women, respectively. Total cost and cost to Government are shown for every ten years from 1859-60. Though for all the three classes of institutions the total cost and cost to government have been fluctuating throughout the period yet it can be said that the cost of government forms a. major part of the total cost showing that the expenditure on these classes of institutions was mostly borne by the government.

Table 3.12 : Annual Cost for General Education

Year	*Total Cost*			*Cost to Government*		
	Rs.	*a.*	*p.*	*Rs.*	*a.*	*p.*
1859-60	643	8	1	456	7	9
1869-70	399	8	—	320	8	6
1879-80	481	12	6	205	9	17
1889-90	244	15	0	98	12	10
1899-1900	199	7	4	76	13	5
1909-1910	183	5	4	55	7	1
1920-1921	232	—	—	91	—	—

Source : *Report of Public Instruction in Bombay Presidency for Corresponding Year 1859-60, 1920-21.*

Table 3.13 : Annual Cost for Professional Education

Year	*Total Cost*			*Cost to Government*		
	Rs.	*a.*	*p.*	*Rs.*	*a.*	*p.*
1859-60	348	0	6	322	14	11
1869-70	Not avaiable			Not available		
1879-80	Not available			Not available		
1889-90	181	5	2	90	3	9
1899-1900	134	6	6	43	3	7
1909-1910	335	9	8	213	13	7
1920-1921	385	—	—	237	—	—

Source : *Report of Public Instruction in Bombay Presidency for Corresponding Year 1859-60, to 1921.*

Table 3.14 : Annual Cost for Training Schools

Year	*Total Cost*			*Cost to Government*		
	Rs.	*a.*	*p.*	*Rs.*	*a.*	*p.*
1859-60	Not available			Not available		
1869-70	545	5	0	540	10	—
1879-80	382	12	0	309	10	—
1889-90	202	3	2	108	2	1
1899-1900	250	12	7	106	0	9
1909-1910	186	6	5	135	12	5
1920-1921	276	6	0	180	10	0

Source : *Report of Public Instruction in Bombay Presidency for Corresponding Year 1859-60, 1920-21.*

EFFECTIVENESS OF THE SYSTEM OF EDUCATION

The examinations of costs are only one side of the coin. The other side is the effectiveness of the system. Given these costs we have to see how effective the system is; more failures results in the wastage of funds and also make the system as an ineffective one. Separate data for passouts of women candidates in various prescribed examinations are not available for best part of the period. Therefore, an in-depth analysis of the result for the last five years of the period is undertaken.

An analysis of the result of the various courses during the period reveals the fact that Intermediate (Arts) courses were popular among the women students. Referring to Table 3.15 we see that in 1916-17, 22 women appeared in I.A. examination and 17 of them passed out the course (77.27%) only; in 1917-18 the passout percentage declined but throughout the period the percentage has been more than 70. But the Intermediate in Science (I.Sc) course was not popular among the women candidates of the Presidency. In 1920-21 for the first time three women appeared at the I.Sc examination and all of them were successful — a hundred per cent result.

Table 3.15 : Passouts in Intermediate Examinations (Women)

Year	*Intermediate in Arts*			*Intermediate in Science*		
	No. appeared	*No. passed*	*Per cent*	*No. appeared*	*No. passed*	*Per cent*
1916-17	22	17	77.27	—	—	—
1917-18	44	27	61.36	—	—	—
1918-19	28	20	71.43	—	—	—
1919-20	30	21	70.00	—	—	—
1920-21	31	23	74.19	3	3	100

Source : Report of Public Instruction in Bombay Presidency for Corresponding Year 1916-17 to 1920-21.

Table 3.16 reveals the comparative performance of female and male scholars in I.A. and I.Sc examinations. It can be said that the pass percentage of female students was always higher than that of male students and we can conclude that the system of education was more effective and the expenditure on women's education was better utilized wastage of fund was less.

In the case of B.A. (pass) course (Table 3.17) the pass percentage for women was not encouraging.

Table 3.16 : A Comparative Statement of Pass Percentage of Men and Women in the Intermediate Examinations

Year	*Intermediate in Arts*		*Intermediate in Science*	
	Female	*Male*	*Female*	*Male*
1916-17	77.27	64.97	—	46.50
1917-18	61.36	53.29	—	44.89
1918-19	71.43	64.79	—	67.44
1919-20	70.00	62.48	—	54.88
1920-21	74.19	51.89	100	51.40

Source : Percentage has been calculated from data taken from *Report of Public Instruction in Bombay Presidency for corresponding year 1916-17 to 1920-21.*

Table 3.17 : Percentage of Passouts for B.A. (Pass) Course

Year	*Male Scholars*	*Female Scholars*
1916-17	58.33	47.38
1917-18	50.00	48.20
1918-19	72.73	54.48
1919-20	53.85	39.00
1920-21	73.33	57.95

Source : Percentage has been calculated from data taken from *Report of Public Instruction in Bombay Presidency for Corresponding Year 1916-17 to 1920-21.*

A comparative study of the performance of male and female scholars reveals that the performance of women was not better that men. In 1916-17 the percentage of passouts was 47.38 for women and 53.33 for men. In 1920-21, it was 57.95 for women and 73.33 for men.

Table 3.18 : Percentage of Passouts for B.A. (Hons.) Course

Year	*Male Scholars*	*Female Scholars*
1916-17	76.51	100
1917-18	77.12	100
1918-19	81.20	90.9
1919-20	75.66	82.35
1920-21	87.97	78.57

Source : Percentage has been calculated from data taken from *Report of Public Instruction in Bombay Presidency for Corresponding Year 1916-17 to 1920-21.*

Table 3.18 shows the percentage of passouts in B.A.(Hons) course for men and women. Though the number of female examinees was always much less than that of male, yet their performance was always better than men except in 1920-21. In 1916-17 and 1917-18 nine and four women appeared for the examination and all passed out — this was a matter of credit. Though quantatively their number increased, qualitatively the percentage declined, i.e. pass percentage. The B.Sc (Pass) course was not popular among the women. In 1916-17 only one women appeared in the examination and she could not pass out. In 1917-18 and 1920-21 one women appeared in the examination and passed out (Table 3.19).

Table 3.19 : Percentage of Passouts for B.Sc. (Pass) Course

Year	*Male Scholars*	*Female Scholars*
1916-17	50.73	zero
1917-18	70.59	100
1918-19	61.90	—
1919-20	56.12	100
1920-21	51.43	—

Source : Percentage has been calculated from data taken from *Report of Public Instruction in Bombay Presidency for Corresponding Years 1916-17 to 1920-21.*

A comparative study of the performance of male and female scholars in the Master of Arts examination shows that there were only one, two or three women candidates in 1917-18, 1918-19 and 1919-20 and their pass percentage was 100 but in 1916-17 and 1920-21 it was 66.67. In case of male scholars it was more than 50 per cent in 1916-17, 1918-19 and 1919-20 except in 1917-18 and 1920-21 when it was less than 50 per cent.

Table 3.20 : Percentage of Passouts for M.A. Course

Year	*Male Scholars*	*Female Scholars*
1916-17	55.33	66.70
1917-18	43.48	100
1918-19	53.66	100
1919-20	53.13	100
1920-21	47.13	66.67

Source : Percentage has been calculated from data taken from *Report of Public Instruction in Bombay Presidency for Corresponding years 1916-17 to 1920-21.*

Table 3.21 shows the statistics of pass percentage in Master in Science courses for women and men. We see that though there were no women in M.Sc. course except 1919-20 when one woman appeared and passed out successfully. There were also not many male candidates. The maximum number being 11 in 1919-20 out of which 9 passed out. For other years it was 100 per cent.

Table 3.21 : Percentage of Passouts for M.Sc. Course

Year	*Male Scholars*	*Female Scholars*
1916-17	100	—
1917-18	100	—
1918-19	100	—
1919-20	81.82	100
1920-21	100	—

Source : Percentage has been calculated from data taken from *Report of Public Instruction in Bombay Presidency for Corresponding Years 1916-17 to 1920-21.*

Therefore, we can say that at the post-graduate level the educational system was quite effective with least failures. This was because for these courses admission were done purely on merit basis and the enrolment of students was also limited for these courses and it was possible for the teachers to bestow personal attention on the progress of the students. Moreover, post-graduate studies would be undertaken by students with good academic background and aptitude and aspiration for a position in life and hence the wastage was negligible.

Medical education received attention of intelligent students from the beginning of this period. In 1916-17 four women appeared for the Bachelor of Medicine and Surgery examinations and all passed.out. Afterwards, the number of female examinees fluctuated and the passout percentage also declined but was also better than that of male scholars (see Table 3.22).

Table 3.22 : Percentage of Passouts for M.B.B.S. Course

Year	*Male Scholars*	*Female Scholars*
1916-17	57.34	100.00
1917-18	43.22	60.00
1918-19	39.09	66.67
1919-20	46.70	53.85
1920-21	46.77	40.00

Source : Percentage has been calculated from data taken from *Report of Public Instruction in Bombay Presidency for Corresponding years 1916-17 to 1920-21.*

The expansion of primary and secondary education for girls increased the demand for trained teachers which in turn increased the desire for women students to get a degree in teaching so as to get into this noble profession, i.e. teaching. Table 3.23 shows the percentage of passouts in Training Schools for male and female both. It is encouraging to note that both male and female students faired well in the examination resulting in high percentage of passouts, but the performance of male students was always better than female students.

Table 3.23 : Percentage of Passouts for Training Schools

Year	*Male Scholars*	*Female Scholars*
1916-17	87.26	75.83
1917-18	89.88	70.21
1918-19	86.11	75.80
1919-20	87.15	77.05
1920-21	90.69	79.01

Source : Percentage has been calculated from data taken from *Report of Public Instruction in Bombay Presidency for Correspondincg years 1916-17 to 1920-21.*

Thus, from the foregoing analysis we can conclude that intermediate courses were most popular among women. There were few women in undergraduate and postgraduate courses. Further few women opted for science courses but their performance in examinations was good and infact, on many courses better than their counterparts.

Thus, during out period there was expansion in higher education of women, and government's expenditure on it was also increasing, though it was gradual. . However, a beginning was made. The result of various examinations undertaken by women was also encouraging. As a result of which a few women in their own capacity started organizations which promoted social and educational activity. Some even participated in the national movement. A detailed account of this is taken in the next chapter.

REFERENCES

1. *Report of Director of Public Instruction in Bombay Presidency 1879-80.*
2. *A Review of Education in Bombay State 1855-1955,* p. 389.
3. S. Nurulla and J.P. Naik, *op.cit.,* p. 391.
4. Of these 3 Institutions with an enrolment of 30 women were meant for European and Anglo-Indians.
5. *Bombay University Calendar (1888),* p. 140.
6. *Ibid.*
7. *The Counters of Dufferin's Fund, Ninth Annual Report of the National Association for supplying Female Medical Aid to the Women of India : For the year 1893,* pp. 7-13.
8. *Ibid.,* p.14.
9. *Ibid,* p.14.
10. *Report of the Director of Public Instruction,* Bombay, 1879-80.

4

POLITICAL ASPECTS

THE WOMEN INTELLIGENTSIA — THEIR ACTIVITIES IN PROMOTING EDUCATION, SOCIAL AND POLITICAL CONSCIOUSNESS AMONGST WOMEN

During our period the women intelligentsia played a crucial role in promoting social, educational and political consciousness among women. By women intelligentsia, we mean those who were formally educated in schools and colleges and also those who received some education at home from their fathers, husbands or brothers. Numerically this was a very small group. It consisted of women belonging to the higher castes, e.g. the Chitpavan Brahmins, Gujaratis, Nagar Brahmins, Parsis, Jains and to some extent the Muslim community. They were largely urban based and belonged to the social reformist families.[1]

The ideas and intentions of the emergent women intelligentsia remained closely integrated with those of the social reformers. Like the social reformers, they wanted no widespread changes in the social role of women and sought social change through extension of educational facilities, social welfare work and greater legal protection to provide better conditions and a wider world outlook for women of the household. The women sought gradual reform from within not any kind of social revolution. Infact they acted as a bridge between the world of the household and the world of public affairs. We shall examine in this chapter :

(a) Women who went in for higher education, e.g. Pandita Ramabai Saraswati, Kashibai Kanitkar, Anandibai Joshi, Cornelia Sorabji, Vidyagauri Nilkanth and Sharda Mehta.

(b) Organizations founded by them and its purpose.
(c) The section of society that had the benefits of their activity.
(d) The social reactions faced by them.
(e) The impact of their activity on society, particularly with regard to the status of women vis-a-vis family and society in general.

In the Bombay Presidency the women who went in for higher and professional education, as stated earlier belonged to the higher caste, i.e. Chitpavan Brahmins, Gujaratis, Nagar Brahmins, Parsis and Jains. Some Muslim women also took to education.

Initially women were educated at home. Some of them did receive formal instruction[2], but by and large education was home centered. Despite, this, most of them were able to adjust to the curriculum laid for higher and professional courses. However, the percentage who went in for such courses was limited.

Pandita Ramabai Sarasvati who was a pioneer in the education of women, as stated earlier was educated at home. She attained proficiency in Sanskrit as a very early age. Infact, at the age of twelve she had committed to memory 18,000 verses from *Puranas*[3] She was thoroughly conversant with *Shastras, Bhagvats* and so on. Her detailed knowledge of scriptures made the *Pundits* of Calcutta confer on her the highest title i.e., *Saraswati* (goddess of learning). It is interesting to note that the in-depth knowledge of the sacred literatures acquired by her can be compared to those received by men in higher institutions of learning i.e., the *Tols* and the *Chatuspathis.* In other words, she was in the receipt of traditional higher learning at an early age.

It was because of her knowledge of scriptures, that she was appointed as Professor of Sanskrit in the Chettenhom Female College in England. To further increase her qualifications she studied natural sciences, higher mathematics, English literature and Greek. Also the knowledge of History Geography, and Physics was acquired by her.[4]

The education of Kashibai Kanitkar, like Pandita Ramabai was home centered. She acquired in-depth knowledge of Marathi language. Inspite of not receiving any formal instruction in English literature, she could read George Elliot, Marie Correlli, Miss. K. Henry Wood, Lord Lytton, Maria Aeworth, *at el.* She went through the stories of Arabian Nights also. Her detailed knowledge of literature made her select those which she liked to read and those she did not, e.g. she liked to read Lord Lytton's 'Night and Morning' and was extremely fond of George Elliot. Without any formal acqaintance with English literature, she could read books, generally prescribed for higher classes.[5]

Similarly, Anandibai Joshi, after having acquired most of her education domestically, finally succeeded in getting her doctorate degree in Medicine from Philadelphia. It is ironical to note that though Anandibai had to face a lot of hardships while pursuing her education in India, her success in America was widely felicitated. Her achievement was reported in the *Bombay Times* of 24th June 1884 :

> "We hear that Mrs. Anandibai Joshi, the Maharatta lady who proceeded to America for the purpose of studying medicine, passed the matriculation examination at the Women's Medical College at Philadelphia. Mr. Joshi will be joined in America by her husband...."[6]

Similarly, Ramabai Ranade, acquired knowledge of Marathi and Sanskrit at home. Though she was helped by Sagunabai Deo from the Women's Training College, it was entirely her hard work that saw her through fifth standard in 1875. In other words, she studied informally upto the fifth standard. She continued studying and could complete the first, Haward Reader. Simultaneously, an in-depth knowledge of Sanskrit was also acquired by her. As she mentions in her autobiography, ".... sometimes he would himself begin chanting a sanskrit *shloka* (versa) or hymns and explain the meaning to me and get me to learn it by heart. He would ask me to repeat *shlokas* learnt earlier and test how much of the meaning I could remember. This continued till the day break....."[7]

Therefore, some of the educated women, during out period received education, particulary higher education without going to school or college. Few who joined formal educational institutions like Ramabai Sarasvati or Anandibai Joshi could adjust and fulfil the demands made by these institutions. Infact, their perseverance and hard labour in the acquisition of knowledge became a source of inspiration for many women of our Presidency.

In certain cases even though women joined educational institution or professional institution of learning at a later stage, as mentioned earlier, they successfully passed the respective courses they had joined. Parvatibai Athavale joined the school in Hujurpag at a ripe age of twenty-six. After passing the examination successfully, she joined the Teachers Training College and received a Teacher's Certificate of the highest grade.[8] Anandibai Karve who had joined the *Sharada-Sadan* at the age of twenty-four, i.e. prior to her marriage, later on, joined the Duffrein's hospital at Nagpur to undergo a course in nursing and midwifery. Despite being senior in age, like Parvatibai, she was successful.

In a period, when close relationship existed between educational attainments and age, most of these women could prove by their own personal examples that such one to one kind of relationship could be foregone by them. They achieved their desired goals despite age. This also reflects that domestic education during our period was very common.[9]

A few number of women pursued their education upto the collegiate stage, e.g., Cornelia Sorabji who after studying at Victoria High School, continued her education at Deccan College, Poona, where she was the ony girl student. Having performed well in each year of the college examinations, she won the Havelock prize and the Hinghlinge scholarship of the Bombay University.[10] This prize was generally awarded to those who achieved the highest distinction in the First Arts Examination. Though she was denied government scholarship, she managed to collect money on her own to pursue higher studies at Oxford. In the initial stage, she devoted herself to the study of literature but later on she took to law. Her performance in the examination was excellent and her achievement was commended by all. Infact, she became the first women graduate of the Bombay University in 1888.

Similar example was found in Gujarat where Vidyagauri Nilkanth and her sister Sharda Mehta went to school and later to college. Infact, the two sisters were the first lady graduates of Gujarat in 1901.[11]

It is interesting to note as a result of their learning , some of the women wrote their own biographical accounts, e.g. Pravatibai Athavale wrote *Mazi-Kahani* (My story), her sister wrote *Maze Puran* (My autobiography). Similarly, Ramabai Ranades *Amchya Ayushatil Kahi Attavani* not only give account of their own life but also mirrors the society in which they lived and wrote. Despitre having a subjective touch, these biographies give in-depth account of customs and traditions and social norms followed by society. In this connection the works of Pandita Ramabai Sarasvati are important. Her book, *The High Caste Hindu Women* and *Stree Dharma Neety* (Moral Rules for Women) carry similiar thoughts and ideas of sociey.

Apart from biographies, different types of literary works were written by the women which covered miscellaneous subjects, e.g. Pandita Ramabai Sarasvati compiled many Marathi school books after studying and taking a thorough course of kindergarden training in America.[12] Tarabai Modak, like Ramabai also wrote Marathi books for children; such as *Nadichi Gosht* (The story of the River), *Paropakari Raja Vikram* (The Selfless Ruler-Vikramaditya), *Ajabaicha Gosht Bhag I-II* (the story of Ajabai, Volume I and II). These books were noted for their simple language and style. She also wrote in Gujarati and is credited for having written an English accounts of Balwadis is rural areas.[13]

Among other books belonging to the period are collections of 41 poems, *Kavyaphule* (Poetry's Blossoms) written by Savitribai Phule. It was published in 1854. Many of the poems are nature poems, some depict about the wealth that comes with education, few advice the children to do away with the caste system. Her second book *Bavankashi Subodharatnakar* (The Ocean of Pure Gems), 1892, was a more ambitious book, and is a biography of her husband Jotiba Phule in verse.In addition to these two books, Savitribai edited for publication four of Jotiba's speeches on Indian History.[14] Infact, her works became a source of inspiration for many women in Bombay Presidency.

It is interesting to note that gradually women began to edit journals, e.g. Miss Rebacca Reuben edited a journal *Hind Mahila* in English. This was first published in Bombay in 1920. Similarly, *Stri Bodh* Gujarati Journal which was first edited by K.N. Kabraji was later edited by his daughters, Miss Sirin Kabraji and Miss Piroja Kabraji.[15] Books and Journals compiled by women received wide publicity during our period.[16]

The families from which the women intelligentsia came and the fact that education was not easily obtained, made them socially conscious and they held that in order to improve the century long degraded position of women, social and educational activity should be undertaken by them. As a result, many women during the period under study established various *Samajs* or Association which had the common goal of ameliorating the position of women.

The earlier effort of establishing an association for women goes to Mary Carpenter. Though she was not an Indian, she not only founded the Female Training Schools in the Presidency but also established in 1870 at Bristol the National Indian Association which was a secular forum mainly devoted for uplifting the position of women. Its main objectives were[17] :

1. To extend a knowledge of India in England and an interest in the people of this country.
2. To co-operate with all efforts made for advancing education and social reform in India.
3. To promote friendly intercourse between English people and the people of India.

In 1875 Mary Carpenter established the branches of this association in various parts of India. This association was responsible in conducting debates on social issues, particularly those which degraded the position of women, e.g. enforced widowhood and so on. Annual meetings were held to give a fresh impulse to the efforts undertaken by the Association. Infact, its philanthropic activity in the Presidency gradually came to be recognized. In November 1908 a very significant paper was read on, "... The Education of Women and Girls in India" at the Annual meeting of the National Indian Association. The paper emphasised on encouraging female education in India. Two practical suggestions were made in this connection.

(a) To train a batch of promising young girls (selected from all the provinces of India, and as far as possible from good orthodox families) in all the modern methods of teaching and equip them properly for doing efficient work as teachers.
(b) The second was the introduction of a sort of home examination scheme with scholarship attached to serve as an inducement or encouragement to study.[18]

The paper further added that the ladies branch of the association could begin translating the above mentioned suggestion into practice by forming themselves into small educational committees or examining bodies, and by prescribing curricula especially suited to orthodox Indian homes and conducting and supervising examinations and awarding scholarships. [19]

A similar association was founded by Pandita Ramabai Sarasvati called *Sharda Sadan* "Home of learning", which was considered to be pioneering effort of its kind. It was established on 11th March 1889 in a spacious rented house near Wilson College at Chaupati in Bombay, primarily for child widows. The first girl to be enrolled was the daughter of a child widow who had remarried. The name of the girl was Sharda Gadre and it is beiieved that the Sadan got its name after her.[20]

Th main objective of the *Sadan* was to make young widows economically self-reliant. Most of them were trained as teachers, house-keepers, nurses, midwives and so on.[21]

The curriculum in the *Sadan* laid emphasis on the Kindergarden educational system; Sanskrit, English , Gujarati and Marathi were also taught. The curriculum was comprehensive and included useful vocational training subjects like Geography, Astronomy, History, Mathematics, Chemistry, Botany, Zoology, Physiology and Hygiene were also taught.

Particular attention was given to moral education, good manners, home management , etc.[23]

The *Sadan* also trained its pupils in sewing, embroidery, knitting sketching, decorating Chinaware, Clay modelling and photography, wood carving making,things from bamboos, etc.... Many girls benefitted from such a kind of education. Anandibai Karve alias Baya, who was Pandita Ramabai's student believed that given freedom and a healthy environment; girls' could develop as expert house keepers and good social workers.[24]

The popularity of the *Sadan* can be ascertained from the fact that gradually unmarried girls began to be admitted to it. By 1890, the number of widow inmates was 18 and in the same year the *Sadan* was shifted to Poona, after shifting the *Sadan* to Poona the number of students of the *Sadan* increased to sixty-four. Amongst them Durgabai Kirloskar, Kashibai Deodhar, Venutai Joshi were prominent immates. All of them became social workers in their future life. Later on they worked for the *Anath-Balikashram* at Hingane.[25] It is interesting to note that Karve drew his inspiration from Ramabai's *Sharda Sadan* and decided to open a similar one to promote the cause of widows. His *Anath-Balikashram* was a culmination of this inspiration.

The cause of widows, particularly child widows whom Pandita Ramabai strongly upheld was translated into practice with establishment of the Sadan. Widows in her *ashram* not only got educated but also led a ralatively free and a causal life. This was in sharp contrast to what they used to experience at their in laws place, where they were treated as domestic servants after the death of their husbands. Describing the free atmosphere of the *Sharda Sadan,* Krishnabai Gadre says,

> "We were allowed to wander anywhere in the bunglow. We could even sit in the drawing room We could enjoy sitting on the soft luxurious coaches or we could collect scented flowers like Jasmine, etc. from the graden to adron our hair with them. Ramabai used to tell us about various plants, flowers, birds and taught us to examine them through a microscope. Any child-widow would naturally be eager to enter the *Sadan.* We had such a great collection of pictures and books....[26]

Apart from the *Sadan,* Pandita Ramabai, also established the *Arya Mahila Samaj* in 1882 at Bombay. Its aim was to uplift and enlighten women by brigning about social contacts and co-operation amongst them.

Weekly lectures and monthly "At Home" were arranged. Scholarships were also given to the deserving members. A hostel for women students was maintained. Badminton courts were also provided for members of the *Samaj*. In the initial stage, the membership consisted of approximately three hundred and twenty ladies who belonged to different castes.[27]

The main objective of the *Samaj* was to sponsor lectures on social and economic issues; to encourage women to come together and undertake social work, hold discussions, *kirtans* (devotional songs) and arrange trips. Gradually, branches of the *Samaj* were opened all over Maharashtra.

Pandita Ramabai Saraswati was thus a pioneer in opening associations for women during our period. In an age when women were unfamiliar with organizations or associations, Ramabai not only took the lead in establishing them but also encouraged women, particularly from amongst the higher castes to come together and undertake activities which would generate an awareness amongst women regarding social evils like the custom of shaving of a widows head, wearing coarse *saree* during widowhood and so on and also a determination and will to fight it. It is interesting to note that Godubai, an inmate of the *ashram* — later known as Anandibai Karve not only gave up the above mentioned customs but also married Karve. She was the chief instrument in helping her husband in his mission of educating women.[28] Therefore, the Samaj played a crucial role in raising the status of women.

Unlike the earlier association, the *Gujarati Hindu Stree Mandal* was established in 1903 at the initiative of Gujarati *shetias* and reformers like Sir Gokuldas Parekh, Sir Vijbhukandas Atmaram, Sir Narandas Purshotamdas, Sir Lallubhai Shamaldas and Karsondas Mulji. The first President of the organization was Jamnabai Nagindas Sakkai. It also included wives of men sponsoring the *Mandal,* e.g., Lady Dhunkoverbai Purshotamadas Thakurdas, Lady Parsanbaj Gokuldas Parekh, wives of the reforming *shetias.*[29] Its membership was thrown open to women belonging to *Brahmins, Banias, Jains, Bhatias, Lohanas* and *Kshatris.* The main object of the Mandal was to raise the "social, economic, moral and political status of women without offending the religious feelings of any section of the community. Its political activity came into prominence in 1917 when women of the *Mandal* sent a resolution to lord Willingdon that Gujarati women were prepared to help in the war effort; collected Rs. 918 for the war widows and orphan fund, and spoke at a propaganda meeting presided over by Lady Willingdon.[30]

This clearly reveals that women were not only gaining political consciousness but were actively associating themselves in the freedom struggle.

Ramabai Ranade, wife of Mahadev Govind Ranade, started the *Seva-Sadan* at Bombay in 1908. This *Sadan* was opened with the co-operation on Bayramji Malabari and Dayaram Giḍumal. Within a year a branch in Poona was opened with a class for girls above 14, who were taught reading, writing and arithmetic. Initially, the *Sadan* began with only 6 pupils. The underlying idea was to provide primary education and also give an opportunity to unmarried girls, widows and deserted married women to be self-reliant. She was assisted in this work by Gopal Krishna Gokhale, G.K. Devdhar, Annapurnabai Apte, D.N. Patvardhan Sitabai Dukale and Sitabai Phandarka. All of them were well known social reformers. Branches of the *Sadan* were opened at Satara, Sholapur, Ahmednagar and in different parts of the Bombay Presidency.[31]

The *Sadan* provided training in sewing knitting, embroidary, devotional music, English and Sanskrit, Lectures were given on practical subjects bearing on sanitation, nursing and right conduct and so on . Like the *Sharda-Sadan,* the aim was to make the widows self-sufficient and self reliant.[32]

The *Seva-Sadan* did a pioneering work in training women as nurses and as primary school teachers. The first Indian women nurse of western India was the product of *Seva-Sadan.* Ramabai devoted herself completely to the *Seva-sadan.* Infact, in 1909, she founded the branch of the *Sadan* in her own home. Also, industrial classes were attached to it. A high school and medical department was also added.

Married and unmarried girls and even adult women belonging to different communities, Hindu, Muslim and Parsis could join the *Sadan.* Women who volunteered for lecturing and training in the *Sadan* were mainly Parsis.[33]

The other significant Association established by Ramabai Ranade was the Hindu Ladies Social and Literary Club. This club was cosmopolitan in nature and was attended by the wives of ruling princess and ladies from the families of social reformers of different communities. Mrs. Ranade was the President of the association. Members of the club held discussions on social and educational issues concerning women. The club had a library attached to it. By 1899, the library consisted of two hundred books on various themes. Her highness Maharani Chimnabai Saheb of Baroda subscribed Rs. 500 for the purchase of additional books.[34] The annual meetings of the club not only took account of its earlier activities but effors were made to improve on mistakes committed earlier. Essays and debates were constantly held to further the cause of women's education.

Another important institution that was established during the period was *Vanita Vishrams.* The first one was started in Ahmedabad in 1907 by Sulochana Desai, a child widow, who was the daughter of Ambalal Sankarlal Desai, a reformer and an educationalist. The institution was meant primarily for widows who were taught sewing, embroidery knitting and were given religious instruction. Bajigauri Munshi and Shivagauri Gajjar, also child widows from respectable families, started similiar Vanita Vishram in Surat in 1907, "to ameliorate the social conditions of the suffering women's of Gujarat".[35] The Bombay city Vanita Vishram was started in 1915 by Zaveribai Bhagvandas Narottamdas with the help of Sir Vithaldas Thakardas and Sir Purshottamdas Thakurdas. In the first year, girls were trained in first aid and nursing. Its success became evident and gradually various branches were opened at Rajkot, Bhavnagar and other cities of Gujarat. In Ahmedabad, Vanita Vishram Mahila Vidyalaya was started at the initiative of Sharda Mehta. The school offered a year's course where girls were taught English, Gujarati. History Geography, Sanskrit, Hindi, Music Sewing and Drawing. Also debates and cultural activity were organized , e.g. *garba* (folk dances).[36]

About the Surat branch of Vanita Vishram, Miss Corbery reported, "The surat institution is now well housed, and is doing excellent work among widows and married women whose household duties do not permit of their joining a full time school. In addition to instruction in the Vernacular and English, Industrial work is also taught, dyeing and needlework (plain and embroidery) being the lines selected. The staff has been strengthened by volunteers from the Servants of India Society, prominent among whom is Mrs. Sharda Mehta (the second Gujarati lady to take the B.A. degree). With her little band of workers she is doing much to brighten the lives of women to whom the doors of learning were formally closed. At my last visit I found 200 names on the roll of the Vernacular and 150 of the Anglo-Vernacular school. There were very few absentees. The success of the Surat institution has prompted the beginners to start work in Bombay. A beautiful building has been erected at Sandhurst Road and the popularity of the movement is undoubted."[37]

The institution was aided by Sir Vithaldas Thackersey, who donated a sum of Rs. 1,00,000 to the institution in its initial stages. The purpose was to provide boarding , lodging and education to atleast 24 Gujarati Hindu ladies, Bhatia ladies and for maintaining a school to be named 'The S.N.D.T. Mooljee Vanita Boardig School. The Boarding had grown into flourishing school, where education was provided to day scholars. The Rajkot branch of Vanita Vishram also received an annual grant of Rs. 6000 for 3 years from Vithaldas.[38]

Therefore, the donations of Sir Vithaldas greatly helped in expanding the work of the organization which espoused the cause of women, particularly widows.

Similar kind of activity was undertaken by the ladies club in Ahmedabad, which was founded in 1887. It was a cosmopolitan club and had Hindu, Parsi, Muslim and Christian, members. It encouraged outdoor activities, e.g., tennis, badminton and so on which was never thought of earlier.[39]

An important Parsi Women's Organization, the *Stri Zorthosti Mandal* was founded on 7th August, 1903 and its aim was to promote physical, mental, moral and material welfare of poor Parsi women. It succeeded in providing education and employment to women at the Industrial Institute under its supervision.[40]

An All-India organization known as Bharat Mahila Parishad was established at the initiative of Ramabai Ranade. Infact, she was the President of the first session held in Bombay in 1904. Members of the organization met annually and discussed various social and economic issues concerning women. Efforts were made to solve each problem through consensus. Perhaps in a convention like this it was possible for women to see the magnitude of social and educational problem in a larger perspective. Steps were taken to arrive at certain measures that woul be effective in all the Presidencies. One of the famous women personalities who participated in the meetings of the organization was Vidgauri Nilkanth. It cut across caste and religious barriers as membership was not restricted to any community. The time and venue of the first meeting of the organization was important because it coincided with the meetings held by the Indian National Congress and the National Social Reform Conference which were also held at Bombay. As mentioned above the meeting was chaired by Ramabai Ranade.[41]

This All India organization was attached to the National Social Conference.[42] It coul not be completely independent because the prime requisite for a national organization was lacking i.e. a large base of educated and professional women. However, this organization succeeded in creating communal solidarity among women. Its activities gradually promoted national consciousness among women.

The Women's Indian Association was the second organization of an All India nature. It began in May 1917 at Adyar in Madras. Its initial president was Dr. Annie Besant who later on became the President of the Indian National Congress. The purpose of the association was to "advance the interest and further the progress of women in India...."[43] The fundamental sphere of activity was to promote women's education. Within a year it had 33 branches in as many towns as possible. By 1922 the association had 43 branches and 2,300 members. The most important work of the Association was in the field of education. Its official journal *Stri Dharm* (Women's Morals Standard) started as a quarterly and gradually became a regular journal after three years.

Unlike the other organizations, it did take up political issue in a significant way. Its activity came in sharper focus in 1919, particulraly when the Home Rule movement had spread throughout the country under Dr. Annie Besant. When Mrs. Besant was interned or imprisoned, it was the members of this organization who took active part in releasing her. Also, members of this organization were representatives in the All-India Women's Deputation to Montague, the Secretary of State for India in December 1917, when the first demand for the extension of the franchise to women in India was made. Since then, the Women Indian Association identified itself with the cause of women representation to governing bodies and removal of sex disqualification.[44]

The Bombay Branch of the Women's Indian Association was founded by Herabai Ardeshir Tata in 1919. Mrs. Jaiji Jehangir was its first President and Mrs. Tata, the Honorary Secretary.[45] Membership of this association was open to women belonging to different communities, e.g. Parsis and Maharashtrians, etc.[46] It is credited of haveing started classes for female dropouts who had left school at the age of thirteen and fourteen.

Thus, by 1920 womens association came to be firmly established in our Presidency. Through them women were not only encouraged to take to education but also became politically aware.

The section of society which benefited from the activities of associations begun by women were largely urban based, e.g. Parvatibai Athavale in her work states, ".... People in Poona and Bombay think that because schools are open to girls, the condition of widows must have been improved. But this is not so; schools for girls exist in larger cities, but elsewhere only ignorance is to be found."[47]

Also, most of the branches of various *Samajs* begun by women were located in urban areas. The branches of Sharda Sadan opened by Ramabai Saraswati was located in Bombay initially and later on it was shifted to Poona. Similarly the branches of Seva-Sadan which was opened at the initiative of Ranade were at Satara, Sholapur and Ahmednagar. These were all important cities of the Presidency. Also the branches of Vanita Vishram were located at Ahmedabad, Surat, Bombay, Rajkot and so on. As mentioned earlier, the two significant clubs established during the period, i.e. Hindu Ladies Social and Literary Club and the Ladies Club at Ahmedabad were by and large cosmopolitan in nature. Infact its membership was largely confined to wives of ruling princes and ladies belonging to the families of social reformers.

As far as caste composition of the *Samaj* goes, women generally belonged to higher castes — Hindu, Parsi, Nagar Brahmin and Mahommedan families. Among the Hindus, it was the Brahmins who had a large say in the activity of the *Samaj,* e.g. the prominent members of the Hindu Ladies Social and Literary club were Lakshmibai Candavarkar, a *Saraswat Brahmin;* Monekbai Kothare, a *Pathare Prabhu;* Lady Cowasji Jehangiri, a Parsi and Mrs Badruddin Tyabji, a Muslim.

It is significant to note that as far as higher education was concerned it once again remained confined to the higher caste, e.g. Pandita Ramabai Sarasvati, Anandibai Joshi belonged to the *Chitpavan Brahmin* community and Vidyagauri Nilkanth and Sharda Mehta were *Nagar Brahmins.*

Thus, the educational and social activity underaken by the intelligentsia largely remined confined to the upper caste, Hindus Parsis and the Muslims. As stated earlier, it was largely urban based. Within the traditional family, there arose a contradictory situation — While on the one hand, the men who had received western education wanted their women to come out of seclusion[48]; the older women belonging to the family resisted changes. They were not ready to break traditions. Ramabai Ranade in her autobiography clearly portrays the hardships she had to face in the family of her in-laws while pursuing her education. Very often she was in a state of dilemma, i.e. whether to obey her husband who wanted her to study or her mother-in-law and other women who were opposed to the idea. They wanted her to perform the traditional duty of a daughter-in-law. She finally decided to obey her husband and pursued her studies despite hardships at home. In her own words, ".... I continued my studies at home, but only as much as could be done at night and early in the morning. It was unthinkable for one to go downstairs, books in hand during the day. Even if the news that I sat reading a book reached the ears of the elderly women, it was enough to raise a lot of discussions. For days together it would be a source of amusement of them an opportunity for redicule and ironical laughter at my cost. I had to listen to all their remarks alone and suffer in silence. It was quite trying .... A secret order was circulated in the family that no one should talk to me more than was absolutely necessary."[49]

A similar kind of reaction was faced by Anandibai Joshi when her husband Gopalrao began to teach her. It was her grandomother-in-law who constantly opposed her education. There is mention in her biography that once Gopalrao gave two books to Anandibai's grand-mother asking her to give it to his wife. A week had passed and Gopalrao inquired about the books from his wife. Perhaps Anandibai knew where her books were and she started crying. Her father intervened and said, "We are still alive. There is no need to ask her about it," Gopalrao answered, "she is the one to study that is why I asked her"! The tension mounted and ultimately Anandibai's grand-mother triumphed and said, "I did not allow her even to touch the books. I threw the books in front of the cattle."[50]

Also Kashibai Kanitkar faced a similiar situation. She states that her husband became a graduate and therefore wanted his wife to learn, particulary English. In her family women were not allowed to pronounce names properly. Her mother-in law though a daughter of a *Shastri,* was not allowed to pronounce words properly, e.g., she used to pronounce *Mumai* (Bombay) instead of *Mumbai.* When she began her education, she was constantly abused and threatened by the members of her family.[51] In her biography she mentions that, "Once it so happened that Sadashiv Pandurang Kelkar asked the women present at one of the meetings of *Prarthana Samaj* to write an essay. No one had written, with the only exception of me. I had written on Earth's Power of Gravitation and Eclipse'. I t was read in the meeting and all the ladies present were asked to write on the simple subject - the women of old and the women of present. I wrote quite a lengthy one on the subject. It was also read in the meeting and was appreciated by Shadashivrao. Next morning In found my essay printed in *Subodh Patrika...* My father-in-law not only read it but asked one of his friends to also read it. I cannot describe my mental turmoil because of it. In the first place I had gone out without the permission of my father and mother-in-law and now this ! Kashibai was punished for this crime by loading her with heavy menial duties which led her to thin' of committing suicide."[52]

Savitribai Phule wife of Jotiba Phule faced reactions not only at home but also from society.After getting educated by her husband, she along with him taught in the girl's schools which they had opened. Many higher caste people used to throw stones at Savitribai when she went to school. To protect her a male servant had to be appointed. However, people continued to throw stones. They advised Jotiba's father to throw Jotiba along with his wife out of his home. They thought that by applying such pressures, Jotiba would close the newly opened school. His father discarded him along with his wife. However Jotiba never wavered. He vowed that even if he died, he would see the work taken in hand was finished and accordingly spent all his life for it. Savitribai also stuck to her rcutine.[53]

The efforts of Pandita Ramabai Sarasvati was also critically looked at by reformers like Tilak. In one of his newspaper *Kesari*, dated 8th August 1882, the *Arya Mahila* Samaj and the issue discussed at its meetings were criticized. The *Kesari* remarked, "We thought that in these meeting (of *Arya Mahil Samaj*) the subjects discussed would be mainly those which lead to the betterment and progress of our women .... in the last meeting (held on 31st March) the subject discussed were child marriage and hair removing of widows. When the discussion were over, a motion was moved to usher a joint application of women's societies to bring in law against these atrocities, but two other women opposed it no doubt, these customs are inhumane, to look after the pros and cons of these is the task of men; women cannot handle it for many years to come ...."[54]

Therefore, we find that despite social reactions faced by women they were not discouraged. As stated earlier they continued to pursue their educaional attainments and promote social activity, i.e. form organizations, opened clubs which encouraged outdoor activities, e.g. games.

Regarding the status of women vis-a-vis family and society there was a gradual change. As stated earlier this change became more evident in the case of the higher castes, i.e. the Parsis, the Prabhus and the Gujarati community. Women belonging to these communities came out of the "four walls", took to education and other activities. Most of them addressed public gathering's e.g. Ramabai Ranade often addressed the All India Women's Conference on social and educational themes, particularly when she was the President. Similarly, Pandita Ramabai Saraswati espoused the cause of widows throughout America in public gatherings. Her powerful speeches made deep impression on the people and as a result of their co-operation Ramabai Association was established in America. Some women even represented India in the International Conference, e.g. Parvatibai Athavale attended the International Workers Conference held in Washington in 1919.

It is significant to note that though women took to educational and social activities, their role within the family did not change drastically. They continued to perform their household work as before. Ramabai Ranade in her autobiography mentions that she had to study in the night and in the early morning because of household duties. Similarly, Anandibai Karve, despite receiving training in nursing and midwifery had to perform her household duties.

Also the kind of education emphasized by the women intelligentsia was not divorced from the roles expected from them in society. They infact, helped in training women as better mother, wives and sisters. In other words, education did not revolutionize the position of women. The kind of education they got continued to emphasise their existing position in society, i.e., women being the prime agent of socialization within the family. Though revolutionary changes could not be brought about as far as role of women was concerned, their activities generated political awareness amongst women. They not only participated in the freedom struggle but demanded franchise rights. An in-depth discussion of women's participation in the freedom struggle and their demand for franchise is taken up in the next section.

THE SUFFRAGE MOVENENT

To realize the full significance of the suffrage movement of women in India, it is necessary to give a brief survey of suffrage movement in England. England was a pioneer of Parliamentary democracy in Europe and its political experiments influenced the political thought of other countries, particularly India which had adopted this form of government.

The English ideal of parliamentary government based on universal suffrage was not achieved very easily. Infact, women had to go through a grim struggle before they could wrest this right from the parliament. The suffragist movement of England has been ridiculed for its violent tactics and heldup as an example of an unwomanly movement, but it must be remembered that it began as a purely constitutional agitation.[55] Women first organized themselves into numerous groups and started educating the public by means of sending petitions to the Parliament and asking staunch supporters in the parliament like Johan Stuart Mill, to advocate thier cause in the House of Commons. Lydia Baeckes, a leader with remarkable foresight decided to get the ruling of a Court of Law as to whether under the existing law of the land, women, were entitled to vote or not. The ruling was against her. Whereupon the suffragists started their agitation. The first result of this movement was that in 1869 women were granted Municipal franchise and were being elected to the Education Boards.[56] This however, did not mean that the country was prepared to give the vote to women. In 1870 Jacob Bright's bill to enfranchise women for parliament could not pass the third reading and so gave ample material for women's agitation to spread. Gladstone's persistent opposition to any concession being shown to these demands led to the strengthening of the suffragist movement. In 1903, they restored to direct action under the leadership of Mrs. Pankhurst through an organization known as the Women's Social and Political Union. With the spread of these activities the demand set forth by these women militant suffragists met with increased opposition. In 1911, Mr. Asquith firm refusal to consider their demand favourably and later in 1913, the failure of a move for conciliation between the opponents led to the strengthening of this novel campaign waged by women for the recognition of their political rights, and in 1913 just before the outbreak of the world war, the women suffragists organized their famous march on foot throughout England rousing public opinion in favour of their cause. This went a long way in the bitterness with which people generally vicwed their fight with the forces of conservatism. The great war of 1914 changed the entire trend of normal life throughout Europe and these militant women at once suspended their hostile activities and rallied all their forces for rendering service to the nation in hour of need. As many as 14,00 women's clubs sprang into existence, rendering every form of service, 40,000 women enrolled in the Emergency Corps and early in 1917, the Women's Land Army and the Women's Branch of the Ministry of Agriculture were formed. In 1918, a limited form of franchise was extended to householders, wives of householders, of thirty years of age and over, and later in 1918 it was widened by the passing of the Parliament qualification of Women Act entitling them to stand for the House of Commons, a town or country council, etc. on the same term as men. However, this limited form of franchise fell far short of the demand of representative women's organization. It was only in 1928 that Peoples Equal Citizenship Act was passed giving women complete equality with men voters.[57]

In India, the suffragist movement was not marked by any violence. Its question came into prominence in 1917 when the British government announced its policy of introducing responsible government in India in gradual stages. It sent Sir Edwin Montague, the Secretary of State for India, to conduct a detailed study and suggest his views regarding political changes. Margaret Cousins, who was the founder of the Irish Women's Suffrage movement and a leading member of Women's Indian Association, utilized the occasion and demanded franchise for women.

A women deputation consisting of fourteen woman leaders such as lady Abala Bose, Mrs. Mazural Huque, Mrs. Nehru, Mrs. Chandrasekhar Aiyar, Mrs. Lazarus, Mrs. Herabai Tata, Dr. (Miss) Joshi (later Rani

Rajwade), Mrs. Sanjiva Rao, Miss Gokhale, Annie Besant, Dorothy Jinaragadasa and Mrs. Cousins drawn from all over the country under the leadership of Sarojini Naidu, waited on Montague at Madras.[58] A memorandum was presented to the Secretary of State whch clearly stated that, "when the franchise is being brought up, women may be recognized as people and that it may be worded in such terms as will not disqualify our sex, but allow our women the same opportunities of representation as our men". The demand for expansion in education and increase in social welfare measures was also put forth by women.

Although the reply given to this deputation by the Secretary of State revealed a sympathetic attitude towards the political aspiration of Indian women, all hopes of women's enfranchisement for the legislature was dashed to the ground after the publication of the Montague Chelmsford Scheme of reforms. Although, one of the reforms suggested was a definite widening of the electorate, no mention of women's claim was made.[60]

Despite, the indifferent attitude of Montague, towards women's demands the Indian National Congress placed its seal of approval at its session in Calcutta in 1917. It is interesting to note that this session was presided over by Mrs. Annie Besant who strongly advocated the cause of franchise for women, suggesting that the denial would invite a powerful agitation from women. She argued that the sex disability was introduced by the West and was alien to the Indian spirit, for "in the elected councils which have marked Indian civilization from the dawn of history, women were not barred."[61]

Along with the Indian National Congress the Muslim League and the Social Reform Conference supported Women's franchise in 1918. At the special National Congress held in Bombay with the Muslim league in September, 1918, Sarojini Naidu moved a resolution that "women possessing the same qualification as are laid down for men in any part of the scheme shall not be disqualified on account of sex."[62] This was passed by a three quarters majority. She argued that franchise was the right of women as mother of the sons of the nation; that it would not destroy her role in the home; and that she would not wrench away the power belonging to men. The "separate destinies" of men and women would remain the same.

> "We ask for franchise, we ask for vote, not that we might interfere with you in your official functions, your civic duties, your public place and power; but rather that we might lay the foundation of national character in the souls of the childrens. We hold upon our laps and instil them with the ideas of nationality. We want the

> franchise for them; that we might glorify the dirt, the degeneration of civic life, that we might be able, by our own implacable ideas of moral purity, to cleanse our public life. We want the franchise to yield that power that says that our sons shall not be denationalized. We want the franchise to say that our education shall not be the imitation of unsuitable and alien things but rather that our nationality shall be enlightening for our national traditions and that our national characteristics shall be the outcome of our own needs and capacities."[63]

These views upheld by Sarojini Naidu clearly reflects that like men, most of the women desired to participate in the decision-making process as individuals.

Towards the end of 1918, the British Government appointed the Southborough Committee to make an in-depth study regarding a requisition signed by about eight hundred educated women of Bombay Presidency which was submitted to it.[64] Similar requests were made by the Women Graduate Union of Bombay as well as all the branches of the Indian Women's Association, the women's branch of the Home Rule League and other women's associations.[65] In 1919, the Committee reported that it had received numerous petitions from women of the educated class urging some form of female suffrage.[66]

It is ironical to note that despite receiving numerous petitions, the Committee members did nto recommend the extension of franchise to women on the ground that, in the prevailing social conditions in India, it was premature to do so.[67] Among many other reasons it stated that the *purdah* system among women would not allow the vote to be exercised properly and grave difficulties would be involved in the recording of votes. Moreover, they considered that the Congress party did not represent masses and that its demands were limited to the educated middle class. The members of Women's Indian Association which was pleading for the reform was undoubtedly an elite group of rich and educated women. The social condition of India, the Committee considered, would make it premature to extend franchise to women. However, they felt that extension of franchise to women being a domestic subject, it should be left to the Indian legislatures to decide.[68]

The decision of the Southborough Committee led to widespread discontentment and resentment amongst women. Several protest meetings were held throughout the country. In Bombay, women passed a resolution at a public meeting protesting against the Southborough Committee's recommendations.[69] They urged the Government of India and the British Parliament to reconsider the issued of votes for women and suggested that denial of suffrage would hinder the progress of women. Mrs. Margaret Cousins sent a cable to London protesting against the decision.

In the meantime the government appointed a Joint Select Committee of the House of Lords and the House of Commons to consider the Government of India Bill. It sat in London taking evidence from individuals representing different sections of Indian opinion and Association. Foremost among them were Mrs. Sarojini Naidu, Mr. Annie Besant and Mrs. Herabai Tata who gave evidence before the Committee as the All India representative of women. She once again stated that Indian women were not seeking office or powers but ony desired to have a say in the decision making process. It would also, according to her, raise the"prestige in the eye of other nations whose taunt to us is that our women have no place in the scheme of things."[70]

It is interesting to note that the deputation of the extremist wing of the Congerss and the Indian Home Rule League, both led by Mr. B. G. Tilak, the All India Home Rule League, led by Mr. C.P. Ramaswami Aiyar, the National Home Rule League led by Annie Besant, even the All India Muslim League led by Jinnah and the Moderate Wing of the Congress with the exception of Surendranath Banerjea and Srinivasa Sastri, all supported the notion that women possessing the necessary qualification should not be excluded from the franchise.[71]

Despite, the recommendation made by the above mentioned deputations, Lord Southborough reiterated his views that women's franchise was being advocated as a means to improve the status of women rather than any thing else and that little consideration had been given as to how women would use the vote or whether this would outrage conservative opinion.[72] When the advocates of women's franchise considered practicalities they spoke of women polling booths and election agents or collecting votes from women's houses. In Lords Southborough's opinion these arrangements would be neither desirable nor practical.

In their evidence, both Sarojini Naidu and V.J. Patel provided the answer to Southborough. They asked why should the *purdah* which is kept only among certain sections and in the north, result in the sex disqualifications for all Indian women. Sarojini Naidu stated that she had never known *purdah* to come in the way of anything a women wanted to do from examinations to sports.[73] V.J. Patel stated that in Bombay, women not ony exercised municipal votes but also exercised their right at the polling station along with men. Mrs. Sarojini Naidu suggested that even if it were not possible to have *purdah* polling booths at present they would be conceded in principle and set up when there would be sufficient demand from the *purdahnashins* themselves.[74] She along with Annie Besant and other supporters joined together in a deputation of both Indian men and women to the Secretary of State to put the case of vote for women.[75]

In Bombay the women actively demonstrated their displeasure at Southborough's inference that the women themselves did not want franchise. They heid a large meeting at the end of July 1919. In this meeting a resolution was passed clearly stating that women themselves wanted franchise rights. This was then cabled to the Secretary of State in the name of Mrs. Jaijiee Jehangir Petit. This was supported by a cable representing all forty-five branches of the Womens Indian Association. At this meeting it was decided to form a women's committee of twenty prominent ladies of different communities of Bombay Presidency. On August 1, a women's public meeting was held to send the representatives of this committee to England to work for women's franchise. On August 2, Mrs. Herabai Tata and her daughter Mithan Tata set sail for England accompanied by Sankaran Nair.[76]

However , by the time they reached England it was too late for them to give evidence before the Joint Select Committee but they were able to submit a statement to the Committee.[77] They stayed in England for sometime lobbying members of the Parliament, addressing women's associations and watching the progress of the Government of India Bill through the Houses of Parliament.[78]

The Government of India Act of 1919, left the responsibility of deciding the question of franchise for women to be settled by the provinces. It is of great significance to note that provincial legislature, one after another, began enfranchising women on the same term as men. Madras was the first province to remove sex disqualification and had also the distinction of having the first women legislator. Dr. S. Muthulakshmi Reddi, was chosen Deputy speaker of Madras Legislative Council. Infact, by 1926 women enjoyed franchise on the same term as men in all the provinces so far as elections to the provincial legislature was concerned. The Government of India Act of 1935 extended the franchise to more than six million women, this was a great improvement on the figure of 315,000 under the Act of 1919. Thus, women voters increased by no less than twenty-one times.[79]

PARTICIPATION OF WOMEN IN THE FRREDOM STRUGGLE

The activities of the male and female intelligentsia succeeded in encouraging women to take to education and motivated many of them to participate in the freedom struggle. There was a strong realization on their part that the struggle for *swaraj* would be meaningless without women's participation in it. It is interesting to note that A.O. Hume, who aided the foundation of the Indian National Congress in 1885, stressed the importance of women's participation. In his inaugural speech, he said that "the political reformers of all shades of opinion should never forget that unless the elevation of female element of the nation proceeds with equal pace with the work, all their labour for the political enfrachisement will prove vain.[80]

Right from the beginning women attended the annual sessions of the Congress. In 1889, around ten women attended the fourth session of the Congress held at Bombay.[81] The women participants were mainly from Calcutta and Bombay. From Bengal, Swarnakumari Devi, the sister of Rabindranath Tagore and Kadambini Ganguli attended the 1890 session. The former, not only discarded *purdah* but along with her husband edited the Bengali journal *Bharati* and thus earned the distinction of being the first women editor. The second delegate was a graduate of Calcutta University and the first women doctor of Bengal. Kadambini Ganguli spoke from the Congress platform and proposed a vote of thanks to the President Ferozshah Mehta.[82] From Bombay, Pandita Ramabai, Mrs. Shevantibai Trimbak, Mrs. Shantabai Nikambe, Mrs. Kashibai Kanitkar and Miss Manekjee Cursetjee, who were renowned educationalist and social reformers attended the 1889 session. In 1901 Sarladevi Chaudhurain, the daughter of Swarnakumari composed a song urging the people of different provinces of the country to participate in the freedom struggle. She trained a group of over fifty girls to sing the song in chorus at the Congress Session in 1901. Similarly, at Ahmedabad, the Congress proceedings of 1902 session commenced with the singing of the National Anthem by lady Vidyagauri Nilkanth and her sister Sharda Mehta.[83] Also, the Congress session at Surat was attended by Tarabai Modak in 1907. She attended the session instead of her mother, Umabai, who was not keeping good health.[84] In 1917, Annie Besant, the founder of the Home Rule League, became its president.[85]

Therefore, a small beginning had been made, of women from Bengal and Bombay Presidency taking interest in politics. The partition of Bengal in 1905 brought into sharper focus the involvement of women. In Bengal, where the movement had originated, women were infused with the spirit of patriotism. In September 1905, Rabindranath Tagore announced his plan for observing *raksha bandhan* on the partition day, i.e. 16th October 1905. Women took active part in it. Another rite observed was *arandhan;*

suggested by Ramendrasunder Trivedi, asking women not to light the hearth for cooking that day. Women not only co-operated but protest meetings were held and about five hundred of them came out of their homes and watched the laying of the foundation stone of the Federation Hall at Calcutta on 16th October 1905.[86] Women organized *Swadeshi Melas* (fair of indigenous goods) and also sold them. They gave up the use of foreign clothes and smashed their foreign *Churis* (bangles).[87] Bipin Chandra Pal addressed ladies meetings in course of his tour of Eastern Bengal in Februrary 1907 and the women of Tangail gave a great reception to S. Banerjea when he visited Mymensingh later that year. Two more significant event of this period are note worthy. First is that a number of women in Barisal gave up their savings to the *Swadeshi Bandhab Samiti* to promote the cause of partition. Secondly, most of the ladies organised a meeting in 1907 at the house of the famous physician and a *swadeshi* enthusiast, Dr. Nilratan Sircar to chalk out their course of action.

The intense impact of the movement which was felt in Bengal had its repercussions in the Bombay Presidency as well, where the *Bharat Stree Mahamandal* was established.[88]

Women's participation contributed to the success of the *swadeshi* (use of indigenous goods) and boycott movements. Infact, Mrs. Ramsay MacDonald who accompanied her husband in his tour of India, noted that the *swadeshi* movement, could not have succeeded without the help of women, some of whom "do not know how to read or write, but inspite of this, the *swadeshi* movement is spreading very much in the places where one would hardly, think there would be an opportunity for its growth."[89]

The growth of revolutionary terrorism during this period also saw th participation of women in it . Some of the women helped in circulating revolutionary leaflets and literature and maintained liason between different revolutionary leaders.[90] In this connection, the name of Madam Bhikaji Cama stands out. While staying in England, she came in contact with Indian revolutionaries like Vir Savarkar, Virendra Chattopadhyay, Mukund Desai and others. Along with them she started carrying on propaganda for India's liberation.[91] In 1906, she toured America and propagated the message of India's Independence. On 18th August 1907, she attended the World Socialist Congress at Stuttgart (Germany) where over a thousand delegates from various countries of the world had come. It was at this Congress that Madam Cama moved a resolution demanding complete independence for India. Also, it was here for the first time that India's National flag was unfurled by her with the following words :

> "This flag is of Indian independence — behold it is born — it is already sanctioned by the blood of martyred Indian youth. I call upon you gentlemen to rise and salute this flag of Indian independence."[92]

In 1909, Madam Cama left London for Paris where she associated herself with S.R. Rana, J.C. Shroff, Shyamji Krishna Verma and other nationalists. Here she was chiefly interested in preparing and forwarding to India seditious literature and in assisting the revolutionary propaganda with her advice and with her money. She was at that time one of the recognised leaders of the revolutionary movement in Paris and was regarded as an incarnation of some deity, presumably *Kali.*[93] During the first World War, she appealed to the Indian not to help the allies. This led to her internment and she was released only when the war was over.

Women's participation received further boost with the entry of Annie Besant in the Indian political arena in 1914. The Home Rule agitation begun by her in 1914-17 saw the involvement of women from all the Presidencies. Infact, her attitude regarding emancipation of women was quite unequivocal. Like most of the reformers, she felt that India's progress rested with the emancipation of women. She held the view that the time had come not only for women to understand, in an intelligent manner, what the men were fighting for, but also to participate in it.[94]

The membership of her Home Rule League was open to everyone above 18 years of age and it had a special section for women. Mrs. Besant's internment in June 1917 stinulated political consciousness among women in various parts of the country.[95]

In Bombay Presidency, particularly in the city of Bombay, the Home Rule League had a profound impact on the intelligentsia. This occurred through a process of informal politization and participation in political activities. In the initial stage only four women including Sarojini Naidu and Avantikabai Gokhale were members of the Home Rule League.[96] Gradually, many women who later became prominent nationalist were influenced by it. Ratanbehn Mehta, a widow was one of them. She was a member of various women's associations and was secretary of the *Gujarati Hindu Stree Mandal*. Her father was a solicitor and interested in Congerss politics. In the days of Tilak and the Home Rule League, the men of her family attended political meetings and the atmosphere of the household was such that men could discuss political questions with women. Ratanbehn did not participate actively at this stage but was to do so within two years.

Lilavati Banker was also actively associated with the freedom struggle. She writes about herself that it was thorough Annie Besant, whom she met in 1918, that she received the inspiration to join the movement. From 1917 onward, she participated in the national movement. She was the first Jain women graduate and after her marriage she became deeply involved in social work. She joined the *Bhagini Samaj*[98] and worked as honorary treasurer collecting funds for the franchise committed.

This phase in the growth of nationalist consciousness among women saw the creation of new association as discussed in the earlier chapter. In the Bombay Presidency, the Bombay branch of the Women's Indian Association was established in 1917. Although it was not explicitly connected with Mrs. Besant's Home Rule League, it was financed by Home Rulers and the Theosophists.[99] Hirabai Tata, a Theosophist, acted as the secretary of the association in Bombay, and represented it on the Central Committee in Madras. She was helped in her work by some Parsi ladies among whom were Mrs. Jaijee Petit, wife of J.B. Petit and her daughter Miss Hilla Petit and Dinshaw Mullan.[100] Herabai was sent to England as one of the members of the franchise committee.

The participation of women in the anti-partition movement of Bengal and the Home Rule movement reveals that along with the men, women were also inspired by patriotic feelings and nationalist sentiments. However, in the beginning this awareness was limited to a few educated and reformed families and it was only when Mahatma Gandhi took the reigns of the freedom struggle that this awareness was extended to a larger section of women. An in-depth discussion of women's participation in the struggle for independence is taken up in the last section of the chapter.

In July 1920, women belonging to different associations in Bombay met together under the Presidentship of Mrs. Jaijee Petit and passed a resolution condemning the Hunter Commission white-wash of the Jallianwallah bagh massacre and advocating that Sir Michael O' Dwyer and the Viceroy should be held responsible for what had occurred. They demanded that the military officers involved should be dismissed and that the money levied against innocent people should be returned. This incidence revealed the gradual politization of women and their anguish over colonial repression. Similary, in November 1921, when the Prince of Wales was scheduled to visit Bombay, women gathered in large numbers under the Presidentship of Sarojini Naidu and condemned the Prince's visit because of certain unfortunate incidents that had occurred that year. They were, as mentioned earlier, the Jallianwallah bagh massacre, and famine conditions in Malabar. Therefore, women urged the boycott of all functions connected with the Prince's visit. They especially condemned the action of the Bombay Municipal Corporation in voting an address of welcome to the Prince. This occasion was briefly described in the Bombay Chronicle. Thus :

> "The meeting was unique in this. Never before in this city was there a procession of women, all high born and cultured ladies belonging to various communities to offer prayers for the speedy attainment of *Swaraj*"[102]

Also, the same year is significant from the point of view that the Congress declared April 6th to 13th as National or *Satyagraha* week. It was during this week that Sarojini Naidu addressed[103] meetings and presided over a meeting of five hundred ladies at the Marwari Vidyalaya Hall on Sandhurst Road. At the meeting it was decided to establish the *Rashtriya Hind Samaj.* This new organization though independent, was closely allied to the Congress. Most of the ladies agreed to become members of the District Congress Committee and volunteered to collect money for the Tilak Swaraj Fund and assist in the introduction of the *Charkha* into all Bombay houses.[104]

By June 1921, the women had collected Rs. 5,340 for the Tilak Swaraj Fund.[105] Some of the fund's money was collected through the sale of jewellary. Funds raised by women were treated ceremoniously and were handed over to the Congress with great fanfare.

In the non-cooperation movement women from different walks of life participated in the propogation of *Charkha* use of *Khadi* and boycott of schools and colleges. A detailed discussion of their participation in the non-cooperation movement under Gandhiji will be discussed in the following section of the chapter.

THE GANDHIAN ERA AND WOMEN'S ROLE IN THE STRUGGLE

The coming of Gandhiji on the Indian scene, saw increased participation of women in politics. Earlier only educated elite women took part in political activity, but gradually women belonging to less affluent and non-elite backgrounds and even rural areas came out.

Like most of the 18th century social reformers, Gandhiji also had great faith in women.[106] He felt that child-marriage leading to enforced widowhood, *purdah* dowry and other social evils, which women were subjected to can best be removed if women took initiative on their own and educated themselves to resist such evils. In his speech at *Bhagini*

Samaj at Bombay on February 20, 1918 he said :

> ".....Your President, I really feel, should be a women, though you may seek men's help or advice in your work. The *Samaj* is dedicated to the nobel aim of women's regeneration and, in the same way that another's *tapas charya* does not help one to ascend to heaven, men cannot bring about the regeneration of women.... The *Samaj* will come into its own when it elects its office-bearers from among its women members, and gives a better account of itself than it does today. I have a close association , as you know, with both men and women, but I find that I can do nothing in the way of service to women without help from women workers. That is why I take every occasion to protest in no uncertain terms that so long as women in India remain ever so little suppressed or do not have the same right (as men), India will not make real progress...."[107]

> "..... The Mahatma ... made them realize that the righting of the wrongs of women could never be complete unless women themselves took the task of emancipation into their own hand."[108]

Similarly, Gandhiji felt that in order to win *Swaraj,* the two important techniques i.e. *Satyagraha* and non-violence could be effectivey used by women. According to him.... "The women of India should have as much share in winning *Swaraj* as men. Probably in this peaceful struggle, women can out distance men by many a mile. We know that she is any day superior to man in her religious devotion. Silent and dignified suffering is the badge of her sex........"[109]

In another place, he stated that.....

> "I would love to find that my future army contained a vast preponderance of women over men. If the fight came, I should then approach it with much greater confidence than if men predominated. I would dread the latter's violence. Women would be my guarantee against such an outbreak...."[110]

He also felt that picketing of liquor and foreign cloth shops could be effectively carried by women. This is because, according to Gandhiji, picketing could never be a matter of coercion but moral persuasion and women were more effective in this task. He further stated that prohibition of intoxicating liquors and drugs and boycott of foreign cloth had ultimately to be by law. But the law could become effective only if women's support could be got.

> "Let the women of India take up these two activities, specialize in them; they would have an access of power and self-confidence to which they have hitherto been strangers....."[111]

It was in South Africa that Gandhiji realized the significance of involving women against the racist regime. It is interesting to note that his *Satyagraha* "army" consisted of women.[112] A large number of Gujarati women along with their Tamilian sisters on their own initiative persuaded Gandhiji to involve them in his struggle against the oppressive *Immigration Regulation Bill* and the *Three Pound Tax.* Women violated prohibitory laws of trespass, inspired Indian miners to go on strike and even court arrested themselves. Generally, women who went to prison included mothers of babies who were a few months old. This incident, Gandhiji wrote, "stirred the hearts of Indians not only in South Africa, but also in the motherland."[113] Phirozeshah Mehta, a veteran Congress leader, declared that his blood boiled at the thought of these women lying in jails, herded with ordinary criminals, and that India could not sleep over the matter any longer.[114]

On his arrival from South Africa, Gandhiji established his *ashram* at Kochrab, a suburb of Ahmedabad. Here he got the support of two women, i.e. Sharda Mehta and Champabehn Mehta. Sharda Mehta, as mentioned in the earlier chapter was the first graduate of Gujarat. In 1919 she helped Indulal Yagnik in editing Gandhiji's *Navjivan.*[115]

To enhance and widen women's involvement in the struggle for *Swaraj,* Gandhiji felt that the mediation of the female intelligentsia and their support was crucial and therefore, from 1917 onwards, he set about acquiring the loyalty of key individuals.

The first issue on which he received the support from the female intelligentsia was the question of indentured labour. This issues aroused the support of women throughout the country who viewed it as a social welfare issue.[116] Most of the women belonging to the upper class were moved by the plight of the female labourers who through sex disparity in recruitment were often pressed into a form of prostitution in serving the needs of the numerous male labourers. In Bombay, Gandhiji got the support from Mr. Jehangir Petit and his wife Jaijee Petit.[117] He also gained support from few distinguished women, e.g. Lady Phirozeshah Mehta,

Laxmibai Jugmohandas, Surajaben Dalal and so on. These women represented a cross section of the female intelligentsia from different communities and different ladies association including *Arya Mahila Samaj, Gujarati Hindu Stree Mandal* and the *Bhajini Samaj*.[118] A detailed account of the activity of the samaj is mentioned in the earlier section of the chapter.

On the same issue Kasturba addressed a women's meeting organized by Mrs. Hamid Ali, a grand daughter of Sir Badruddin Tyabji and the wife of the Assistant Collector of Baroda. It is interesting to note that nearly 300 women attended this meeting This incidence took place in Godhra in February 1917, when Kasturba along with Gandhiji went to preside over a meeting on the occasion of Gokhale's second death anniversary. At this meeting, a resolution was passed urging lady Chelmsford to secure the abolition of indentured labour.[119]

Another occasion which also portrays the support Gandhi got from women also occurred in the same year in the month of November. Here he presided over the First Gujarat Political Conference at Godhra. He addressed a meeting of untouchables.[120] The audience not only consisted of women but also those belonging to Abbas Tyabji's and Ambalal Sarabhai's families. Ambalal Sarabhai was a leading millowner of Ahmedabad.

However, the most significant event which saw women's involvement was the Ahmedabad mill workers strike where Gandhiji not only used the technique of non-violence to solve the millworkers problem but also got the support of Ansuya Sarabhai, sister of Ambalal Sarabhai. She was influenced by the Fabian Socialist like Sydney and Beatrice Webb during her stay in England and on her return in 1913 she started various social welfare projects. These projects mainly catered for female workers and their children in the premises of the Calico Mill, owned by her family. She also wrote a brilliant pamphlet, called *Strio ane Temna Rajakiya Ahdusaro* (women and their Political Rights).[121]

During the textile workers strike which lasted for four weeks in February and March 1918 and involved 16,000 weavers, Ansuya Sarbhai assumed the leadership.[122] She along with Gandhi's nephew Chhaganlal spent every morning and evening visiting the workers home, questioning and admiring them, sending medical help and bringing back to Gandhi daily reports of their hardships and rumours. In the evening, often until midnight Ansuyabehn's house would be open to any worker with problems.

On the name of Ansuya, Gandhiji daily issued leaflets to the workers and every evening he and Ansuyabehn addressed the workers. When the strike finally ended,[123] Gandhiji and Ansuyabehn were driven through the city in a Victoria, heading a triumphant procession.[124]

Also, the Kheda *Satyagraha* of March-April 1918, saw increasing involvement of women under Gandhi. The reason why Gandhiji took up the issue was that in this particular district of Gujarat, crops had sustained serious damage owing to floods. Most of the peasants were not in a position to pay revenue. They demanded partial or whole remission of revenue. The Government, however, was unresponsive to the situation Gandhiji surveyed the entire problem and decided to take up the issue.[125]

It is of significance to note in this struggle he tried to establish an emotional rapport between the citybred women and women inhabiting the rural areas of Kheda district. He took along with him Ansuyabehn Sarabhai, Miraben (Madeline Slade), Anandibai and Maniben Patel (Vallabhai's daughter) and his wife Kasturba. Infact, Kasturba and Ansuyabehn organized women's meetings in order to carry out the propaganda work.[126] Their speeches which were in Gujarati and their *khadi* clothes inspired the rural women to follow them They even picked up the idioms, norms and values which could serve to educate the rural women about the *satyagraha* technique. For instance, addressing the women of Vadthal Village on 6th April 1918, Kasturba Gandhi said : "The true religion of a women is to follow the footstep of her husband like *Sati Sita*.. If she also encourages her husband to stick to the sacred pledge (of non-payment of the revenue dues) her progeny is sure to be brave and India will then win *Swaraj*."[127] Similarly, Ansuyabehn declared at a women's gathering at Navali that they were better halves of their husbands and that it was their duty to boost the moral courage of the Kheda peasants.[128] *Bhajan Mandali's* (the institution of singing devotional songs) also played an important part in organizing the Kheda peasants within the folds of the struggle. Infact, the presence of the rural women was so impressive that it led Vithalbhai Patel to observe that the , "women have become real *Kshtriyanis*... they are not going to budge an inch even though their land, cattle and household material will be confiscated by the government."

He addressed women at Ahmedabad, Anand, Surat, Ras, Borsad in Gujarat, and asked them to donate money to the Tilak Swaraj Fund.[129] He further stated that", If women give us courage, we can endure."[130] It is interesting to note that Gandhiji teaching had an impact and we find that Gangabehn Vaidya collected Rs. 15,000[131] at Ahmedabad. Women instantly responded to his call and contributed a sum of Rs. 1,500 in cash and ornaments.[132]

Also, while composing a new *Satyagraha* pledge against the

Rowlatt Act, the first signatories were women, e.g. Ansuyabehn and Vallabhai Patel.[133]

The important event following the satyagraha pledge was the first non-cooperation movement of 1920-22. Kasturba Gandhi and Ansuyabehn played a crucial role in this movement. Infact, their participation became very significant in Gujarat. They not only asked people in general to boycott Government Schools and Colleges but at the sametime their constructive programme emphasised on the use of Khadi. Gandhi asked women to spin and propagate khadi. He compared British Rule to *Ravana*, and asked the women, particularly of Gujarat not to co-operate with the *Rakshasi Sarkar*. He asked women to participate in their husband's activities like Sita, Savitri and Damayanti. He further added that "Sita had no ornaments or fineries when she went to *vanavas* (Exile). Out country is now in *vanavas*. How can your wear ornaments? Contribute to the Tilak Swaraj Fund".[134]

It was on spinning that Gandhiji laid particular stress. He felt this was an activity which directly linked the educated and the uneducated women with the *Swadeshi* movement. This movement laid emphasis on the use of indigenous goods, particularly *Khadi*. According to him the reason for involving women in the *Swadeshi* movement was....

> "The *Swadeshi* vow cannot be kept fully if women do not help. Men alone will be able to do nothing in the matter. They can have no control over the children, that is the women's sphere. To look after children to dress them is the mother's duty and, therefore, it is necessary that women should be fired with the spirit of *swadeshi*. So long as that does not happen men will not be a position to take the vow."[135]

> "This activity could be undertaken by the educated and uneducated women alike....."

> "All I mean is that it is essential that women make their contribution to the development taking place in the country. This requires no knowledge of letters. It is not true that without such knowledge one cannot take part in national work."[136]

Spinning also had social welfare implications. According to him....

> "I swear by this form of *Swadeshi* because through it I can provide work to the semi-starved, semi-employed women of India."[137]

He further added,"....For the middle class it should supplement the income of the family and for very poor women it is undoubtedly a means of livelihood. The spinning wheel should be, as it was the widows loving companion. But for you who will read this appeal, it is presented as duty, as *dharma*. If all well-to-do women of India were to spin a certain quantity daily, they would make yarn cheap and bring about much more quickly than otherwise the required fineness.....[138] Come with me to the *Khadi* centre of Darbhanga and see the joy and happiness the *Charkha* has brought to those Hindu and Musalman women. If it cannot give work to more, it is not my fault but yours. If you do not care to purchase the products of their hands the work cannot progress. Every yard of *Khaddar* you purchase means a few copper in the hands of those women. A few copper and not more. But it means a few copper where none was carried before. It is for the women of India, a large number of whom do not get even an anna per day that I am going about the country with my spinning wheel and my begging bowl."[139]

Infact, as early as 1908, in Hindu Swaraj Gandhiji had already prescribed spinning wheel as the cure for India's economic ills.

To propagate the spinning project among women, Gandhiji needed women who were committed to the notion and could teach others. Among the first women taught to spin under the auspices of Gandhiji was Avantikabai Gokhale[140] and Ramabai Kamdar.[141]

As a result of his propagation of *Khadi,* in the mill areas of Bombay and Ahmedabad, women made public bonfires of foreign cloth. Infact, Gandhiji asked women to read *Navjivan;* he said that if any women made five other women read it, she was promised a free subscription. He wrote special articles in the non-cooperation movement. He sent a special message to women on 22nd August 1921: "Just as the destruction of articles full of plague germs is the best action from economic point of view, so is the destruction of foreign clothes the best of all. Your blessings can be fruitful by discarding your foreign clothes and by spinning always in your leisure hours for the benefit of the nation.[142] He asked women to hand over their riches apparel when the nation school boys came to their door to purchase *Khadi Sarees* from the *Khadi Bhandars* or Congress House and spin as much as they could.[143]

Thus, spinning linked not only the female intelligentsia but traditional household women directly with the non-cooperation movement.

In Gujarat women presided over meetings and urged their fellow sisters to spin on the *Charkha*, wear *khadi,* send their children to national schools and become *desh sevikas.* In Bombay women were not only encouraged to use *khadi,* but at the sametime large bonfires of foreign cloth took place in July, October and November 1921. The November bonfire, particularly took place at the time of the Prince of Wales visit to Bombay. Meetings that were held at this occasion was presided over by Gandhiji and Sarojini Naidu. It is interesting to note that amongst the 50,000 to 60,000 people who attended it many were women.[144]

Apart from spinnning, Gandhiji laid emphasis on education. He felt that national education would help in combating the process of colonial acculturation and at the sametime become an important instrument for propagating nationalist ideas. There was also a strong realization on his part that education develops and sharpens one's intellect and it stimulates one's power of doing good.[145] Perhaps it was this realization that encouraged him to open a National Girl's School, know as Lokmanya Tilak Girl's School in Bombay on 22nd June 1921. Miss Krishnabai Tuleskar M.A.was appointed principal of the school. When the school was opened there were only 125 pupils and gradually this number increased to 275.[146] This shows that slowly this institution was acquiring a popular base.

Similarly as a result of his efforts in the year 1921, two important organizations came into being , i.e. the *Rashtriya Hind Stri Samaj* and the *All-India Ladies Khilaft Committe.* The early organization was responsible for aiding in introducting *charkha* into all Bombay houses. Also, its main activity was the sale of *khadi.* It held classes for embroidery on *Khadi* from which women could earn a little.[147] The latter organization also propagated the use of *Khaddar.*

Therefore, we find that spinning or the use of *khadi,* which was an important part of his constructive programme brought into the fold of national movement women belonging to urban and rural areas. Infact, it widened the base of the movement. It also encouraged women to outrightly condemn the imperialist government. Women to only condemend the Jallianwallabagh massacre but at the sametime in 1921 openly boycotted the Prince of Wales vist.

Thus, during the Gandhian era, women participated in the struggle for *Swaraj* and in the process acquired self confidence.

The technique of *Satyagraha* and non-violence succeeded in bringing into the fold of nationalism educated and uneducated; modern and traditional women from within the four walls of their homes.

REFERENCES

1. Anil Seal, *The Emergence of Indian Nationalism,* pp. 231-2320 C Dobbin,

op.cit., pp. 32-33.

2. Cornelia Sorabji.... was only nine years old when the Victoria High School was started and she immediately took her place as one of the pupils... For details see E.F. Chapman, *Notable Indian Women of the 19th Century*, p. 128.
3. Helen, S. Dyer, *Pandita Ramabai, The Story of her Life*, p. 10.
   E.F. Chapman *op.cit.*, pp. 9-10.
   Margaret. E. Cousins, *Indian Womanhood Today* p. 19.
4. Trabai Sathe, *Aparjita Rama*, p. 80.
5. Sarojini Vaid, Shrimati Kashibai Kanitkar (Atmacharit-Bui Charit) p. 80-81.
6. Shree J. Joshi, *op.cit.*, p. 223.
   ISR, September 16,1900, p. 23.
7. Kusumavati Deshpande, *op.cit.*, pp. 40,53.
8. Parvatibai Athavale, *op.cit.*, p. 24.
9. Anandibai Karve, *op.cit.*, p. 30.
10. E. F. Chapman, *op.cit.*, pp. 135-136.
    India Calling - The Memoirs of Cornelia Sorabji pp. 128, 130.
11. T.P. Saxena, *Women in Indian History (A Biographical Dictionary)*, pp. 57-88.
12. Pandita Ramabai Saraswati, *op.cit.*, p. 15.
13. Padmaja Phadak, *op.cit.*, p. 442.
14. *The Hindu Magazine Sunday*, November 3, 1991, p. vi.
15. Gail Olivia Pearson, *op.cit.*, p. 120
16. ".......In the Mahratta country, the first writer is Pandita Ramabai. Her "High Caste Hindu Women" printed in America, is beautifully written in English ... Let us mention Mrs. Kashibai Kanitkar who has written the life of Anandibai Joshi....... For details see - *ISR September 2, 1900, Vol. xi, No. 1*, p. 5.
17. *ISR, Sunday*, April 22, 1900, *Vol X*, p. 267, *ISR*, Sunday, May 27, 1900, Vol X, p.306.
18. *Government of India Home Department, Education - Deposit, Proceedings, November 1908, No. 7 "Paper on the Education of Women and Girl's in India which was read at the annual meeting of the National Indian Association*, p. 1.
19. *Ibid.*, p. 3.
20. Devdutt Narayan Tilak, *Maharashtranchi Tejaswani Pandita Ramabai*, p. 220.
21. A Basu *op.cit.*, p. 30.
    Padmini Sengupta, *Pioneer Women of India*, p, 10.
22. Tarabai Sathe, *op.cit.*, pp. 141-42.
23. *Ibid.*, p. 147.
24. *Ibid.*, p. 147
25. *Ibid*, p. 150.
26. Trabai Sathe *op.cit.*, p. 150.
27. *Directory of Womens Institutions in Bombay Presidency Social Section, Bombay and Suburbs*, pp. 2-3.
    Aparan Basu, *op.cit.*, p. 28.

Padmini Sengupta, *op.cit.*, pp. 8-9

Kusumavati Deshpande, *op.cit.*, pp. 75, 82-83.

28. D.D. Karve, The *New Brahmins*, pp. 68-71.
29. Gail Olivia Pearson, *op.cit.*, pp. 58-59.
30. *Ibid.*
31. A. Basu, *op.cit.*, p. 31.
32. *ISR*, March 14, 1909, *Vol XIX, No. 28*, p.314.
33. *ISR*, March 14, 1909, *XIX, No. 28*, p.314 Kusumavati Deshpande, *op.cit.*, pp. 222-23.
34. *ISR*, Nov. 12, 1899, *Vol, X No. 11*, p. 86.
35. Quoted from *Vanita Vishram Golden Jubilee 1915-1965*, in A Basu, *op.cit.*, p. 31.
36. Aparna Basu, *op.cit.*, p. 32.
37. *Bombay Director of Public Instruction on the Progress of Education in the Bombay Presidency in the Quinquiennium* 1912-13 to 1916-17, p. 97.
38. Hiralal Lallubhai Kaji, *op.cit.*, pp. 199-200.
39. Aparna Baus, *op.cit.*, p. 34.
40. Neera Desai, *op.cit.*, p. 158; *Directory of Women's Institutions in Bombay Pesidency*, p. 32.
41. Gail Olivia Pearson, *op.cit.*, p. 148. Ramabai Ranade was the Chairman of Women's Conference between 1907-1920.
42. See Gail Olivia Pearson, *op.cit.*, p. 149.
43. Golden Jubilee Celeberation 1917-1967, Women's Indian Association, p. 1-2
44. *Ibid.*, pp. 1-2.
45. Aparna Basu, *Op. Cit*, p. 36. Gail Olivia Pearson, *op.cit.*, p. 153.
46. Dorothy Jivarajadasa, the founding member of this organization and Herabai Tata who was the secretary belonged to the Parsi Community.
47. Parvatibai Athavale, *op.cit.*, p. 25.
48. ..... Sasipada first broke down the prejudice of his own wife and then proceeded with her assistence ot turn his home into a school.... In 1871 he sailed for England and he was accompanied by his wife, the first Hindu women to cross the seas. For details see S. Natarajan, *op.cit.*, pp. 45-46.
49. Kusumavati Deshpande, *op.cit.*, pp. 77-79.
50. Shree J. Joshi, *op.cit.*, p. 55.
51. Sarojini Vaid, *op.cit.*, p. 75.
52. *Ibid.*, pp. 77-78.
53. Jotiba Phule, *Samagrah Granth*, pp. 294-95.
54. Tarabai Sathe, *op.cit.*, pp. 57-58.
55. Aruna Asaf Ali, "Woman's Suffrage in India" in S.K. Nehru (ed), *Our Cause*, pp. 346-47.
56. *Ibid.*, p. 347.
57. *Ibid.*, p. 349.
58. *Ibid.*, p. 351 Gail Olivia Pearson, *op.cit.*, pp. 210-211. Margaret cousins *op.cit.*,

pp. 58-59. Geraldine H. Forbes, "Vote for Women The demand for Women's Franchise in India 1917-1937", p. 5. in Vina Mazumdar's, (ed) *Symbol of Power - Studied on the Political Status of Women in India.*

59. Gail Olivia Pearson, *op.cit.*, p. 211; Kamaladevi Chattopadhya, *Indian Women's battle for Freedom*, p. 95.
60. S.K. Nehru, *op.cit.*, p. 352.
61. Report from the Joint Select Committee, *op.cit.*, Vol. 11, p. 75, Vol. III, p. 9. In the Ancient Rigvedic period women attended the tribal assembly called *Sabha* (council of elder members).
62. Quoted from "Pamphlet of Women's Indian Association" Madras, June 4, 1919, *A.B. Papers*, Naidu, S. Speeches and Writing p. 198.
63. Prior to 1917, women did have limited franchise in Madras and Bombay, although their participation in public life was limited. In Bombay, particularly women exercised their vote in the municipality. For details, see Vijay Agnew, *Elite Women in Indian Politics*, p. 104.

    Quoted from S. Naidu at the Special Congress 1.9. 1918 in Gail Olivia Pearson *op.cit.*, p. 215
64. B.R. Nanda, *op.cit.*, p. 34. Gail Olivia Pearson *op.cit.*, p. 126. *Golden Jubilee Celebrations 1917-67, Women Indian Association*, p. 2.
65. *Ibid.*, p. 34, Gail Olivia pearson, *op.cit.*, p. 216.
66. *Report of Indian Statutory Commission, Government of India 1930, Vol. 1*, p. 49.
67. Quoted from *Report of the Franchise Committee in B.R. Nanda, op.cit.*, p. 34.
68. S.K. Nehru, *op.cit.*, pp. 352-53. Kamladevei Chattopadhay, *op.cit.*, p. 94-95. Padmini Sengupta, *op.cit.*,p. 21.
69. Gail Olivia Pearson, *op.cit.*, p. 218.
70. *Report from the Joint Select Committee of the House of Lords and House of Commons appointed to consider the Governments of India Bill 1919, Vol. II*, p. 132.
71. *Ibid.*, Vol. II, p. 75, Vol. III, p. 9.
72. *Ibid.*, p. 75.
73. *Ibid.*, p. 32.
74. *Ibid.*, p. 132.
75. *Modern Review, Vol. 26, Nov. 1919*, p. 493.
76. Sankaran Nair was a member of the Southborough Committee. He along with Mr. Hogg, who was also another member agreed that sex disqualification should be removed from the beginning, so far as voting rights were concerned.
77. *Report of the Joint Select Committee, op.cit.*, Vol. III
78. Gail Olivia Pearson, *op.cit.*, p. 222.
79. A.B. Kirth, *A Constitutional History of India 1600-1935*, p. 59.
80. Aparna Basu, "The Role of Women in the Indian Struggle for Freedom," in B.R. Nanda's (ed), *Purdah to Modernity*, p. 16.
81. *Ibid.*, p. 16
82. *Ibid.*

83. *Ibid.*, p. 17
84. Tarabai Modak, *op.cit.*, p. 27.
85. Aparna Basu, *op.cit.*, p. 18.
86. *Ibid.*, p. 18.
87. *Ibid.*
88. The *Bharat Stree Mahamandal* stressed among its objective — the creation of vernacular literature suitable for women. It later proposed the establishment of Home Education for Women. The member of the organization planned to establish a depot for the sale of books for poor women.
89. Aparna Baus, *op.cit.*, p. 18.
90. *Ibid.*, p. 18.
91. Minocher K. Contractor, *Madam Bhikaji Cama - The Patriot whom India had Forgotten,* p. 6.
92. *Ibid.*, p. 7.
93. T.P. Saxena, *Women in Indian History (A Biographical Dictionary)* p. 15. Minocha K. Contractor, *op.cit.*, p. 10.
94. Aparna Basu, *op.cit.*, p. 19.
95. *Ibid.*, p. 19.
96. Gail Olivia Pearson, *op.cit.*, p. 150.
98. *Ibid.*, p. 152.
99. Regarding Women Suffrage Movement and the Franchise Committee an in-depth account is given in the next section.
100. Mrs. Jerabai Mullan Presided at the 8th Annual gathering of the Bombay Women's Indian Association. See *Bombay Chronicler,* October 2nd, 1924, p. 5.
101. *Ibid.*, p. 154.
102. Quoted in *Indian Ladies Magazine Vol. 4, No. 11, 1905*, p. 347, *Indian Ladies Magazine, Vol., 1, No. 4,* 1907 - 1920.
103. Gail Olivia Pearson, *op.cit.*, p. 176.
104. *Ibid.*, p. 176.
105. *Ibid.*
106. Women is the companion of man, gifted with equal mental capacities. She has the right to participate in the very minutest details in the activity of man and she has an equal right of freedom and liberty with him..... *The Collected Works of Mahatma Gandhi,* XIV (October 1917-July 1918), p. 205.
107. *Ibid.*, pp. 202-03.
108. Padmini Sen-Gupta, *op.cit.*, p. 15.
109. *Young India,* 15.12.1921. For detail see M.K. Gandhi, *Women,* pp. 27-28.
110. Padmini Sen-Gupta, *op.cit.*, p. 15.
111. M.K. Gandhi *op.cit.*, p. 38. Frieda Hausuwith, *op.cit.*, p. 232.
112. Aparna Basu, *op.cit.*, p. 20.
113. M.K. Gandhi, *Satyagraha in South Africa,* p. 28.
114. *Ibid.*, p. 285.

115. Aparna Basu, "Gujarati Women's Response to Gandhiji, 1920-1942", in *Samya Shakti,* p. 7.

116. In 1916 and 1917 moves were afoot in the Imperial Legislative Council for the abolition of indentured labour being sent from India to other countries within the British empire. When Pandit Malaviya was refused permission to introduce a bill for the immediate abolition of this labour system Gandhi set out on an all India tour to arouse public opinion on the matter. In the wake of his tour, telegrams were sent from various meetings to the Government protesting against the system. These included atleast seven from various ladies meetings throughout the Country including one from Kasturba Gandhi to Lady Chelmsford, dated Februray 21, 1917. Gail Olivia Pearson, *op.cit.,* p. 156.

117. Mr. J.B. Petit, was an industrialist who provided financial support for Gandhiji's passive resistance in South Africa. See *Gandhi to J. B. Petit March 30, 1916, August 19, 1916 C.W. Vol. XIII,* pp. 265, 92. In February 1917, he organized a meeting in Bombay to oppose Indenture. In indenture. "Mansucripts giving account of works concerning female bonded labour in Fiji. Gail Olivia Pearson, *op.cit.,* p. 157.

118. *Ibid.,* p. 157.

119. Aparna Basu, *op.cit.,* p. 7.

120. *Ibid.,* p. 15.

121. Shirin Mehta, *The Role of Women in the Peasant Movements of Gujarat : A Study in the Gandhian Phase. 1915-28,* p. 166.

122. The strike occurred mainly because the mill-hands in Ahmedabad demanded a commensurate wage increase to make up for the special war-time allowance, arbitrary with drawn by the milliowner. Gandhiji was not anxious to percipitate an agitation. Appealing to the employers to bind the workers with the silken thread of love" he succeeded, On February 14, in getting an arbitrator appointed to look into the problem.... For details see *The Collected Works of Mahatma Gandhi,* XIV (October 1917 - July 1918), p. v.

123. We have said in earlier leaflets that in Satyagraha both the parties invariably succeed.... workers are to resume work tomorrow, i.e. on the 20th, for that day they will get a 35 per cent increase,and for the 21st a 20 per cent increase.

From the 22nd, they will get an increase not exceeding 35 per cent as the arbitrator may decide.

Prof. Anandshankar Bapubhai Dhruwa, M.A. L.L.B., a prominent man of Gujarat and a man of saintly character, a professor in Gujarat College and its Vice-Principal will be the arbitrator.

The arbitrator should give his award within three months. During the period the workers will be paid an increase of 27.5 per cent i.e. the workers give up half of their demand and the employers half of theirs.

Whatever amount is decided by the arbitrator will be adjusted against the 27.5 per cent e.g. if the arbitrator awards more than 27.5 per cent the employers willl give that increase and if he awards less than 27.5 per cent the workers will refund the excess. Two things have been accomplished by this settlement. First, the honour of the workers has been upheld; secondly, it has been accepted as a principle that any serious dispute between the two parties should be settled not by resort to a strike but by arbitration .... *The Collected Work of Mahatma Gandhi,* XIV, (October 1917 - July 1918), p. 269-70.

124. Aparna Basu, *op.cit.,* p. 8.

125. *The Collected Works of Mahatma Gandhi,* XIV, (October 1917 - July 1918), p. iv.

126. Shirin Mehta, *op.cit.,* p. 167.

127. *Ibid.,* p. 167.

128. *Ibid.,* pp. 167-168.

129. The Tilak fund was started to finance the first non-cooperation movement. *Ibid.*

130. Aparna Basu, *op.cit.,* p. 392.

131. *Ibid.,* p. 8.

132. Mahatma Gandhi, *op.cit.,* pp. 392.
The enactment of Rowlatt Act in 1919 led to the abridgment of court procedure in trial of political cases gave the executive extensive powers to arrest and detain person without trial.

133. Aparna Basu, *op.cit.,* p. 8.

134. K. Gopal Swami, *Gandhi and Bombay,* p. 148.

135. *The Collected Works of Mahatma Gandhi, Vol. XV, 1919-1920,* p. 291.

136. *Ibid.*

137. M.K. Gandhi, *An Autobiography,* p. 413.

138. *Young India,* 11.8.1921.

139. *Ibid.,* 10.2.1927

140. Avantikabai Gokhale and her husband Baban Gopal were from a landholding *Chitpavan Brahmin* family from Nagpur. Both of them were members of the Home Rule League and in 1917 she went to Champaran to work with Gandhi in his investigation into the grievances of the labourers against the planters. For details see M.K. Gandhi, *An Autobiography,* p. 35.

141. Ramabai Kamdar was educated at Goculdas Tejpal Girls' School and Chanda Ramji Girls School in Gujarati and Sanskrit, she was married to Mr. N.H. Kamadar, a solicitor, and supporter of the Home Rule League and the Congress, she was involved with the Vanita Vishram and Gujarati *Hindu Stree Mandal* ... See, Gail Olivia Pearson, *op.cit.,* pp.158, 159.

142. Aparna Basu, *op.cit.,* p. 9.

143. Mahatma Gandhi, *op.cit.,* p. 438.

144. *Bombay Chronicle,* November 18, 1921, p. 7.

145. *Collected Works of Mahatma Gandhi, Vol. XIV, 1917-18,* pp. 37-42.

146. Gail Olivia Pearson, *op.cit.,* pp. 173-74.

145. *Ibid.,* p. 177.

5

CONCLUSION

This book has reviewed the growth of women's higher education in western India from 1857 to 1921 and examined its impact on women's lives and status in society. In the early 19th century there was hardly any formal education for women. In the indigenous system of education, prevalent in India in the early 19th century, at the primary level in the village school only reading, writing and arithmetic were taught. Sons of accountants, shopkeepers, moneylenders and petty landlords attended these schools. Education was closely related to the needs of the community and boys got jobs in the offices of Deshmukhs, Sardesais, Patils, and Kulkarnis, etc. The higher schools of learning concentrated on subjects such as logic, astronomy, *Vedas, Upanishads,* etc. and were confined to boys of the upper castes who could become teachers, priests *jotish* (astrologer) or Vaids. Besides certain prevalent beliefs such as that education would lead to early widowhood also retarded women's education.

The initial efforts in promoting women's education were undertaken by Christian missionaries. They were motivated by humanitarian ideals as well as by the zeal for proselytization. They promoted women's education through three important agencies, i.e. Day schools, Orphanages and boarding establishments and *zenana* or domestic system of education. This was informal and was meant for those higher caste women who had missed formal schooling. Their activity was popular among the Parsis, Muslims, Bene-Israel, Catholics, and also from amongst protestant converts. Gujarati and Marathi speaking Hindus also attended mission schools. Though their activity was like a drop in the ocean, they did succeed in laying the basis for the growth of higher education of women.

The thread of missionary activity was picked up by Indian Social

Reformers who had themselves received western education and imbibed some democratic, liberal and rational values of the west. British scholars, administrators and missionaries were all very critical of Indian society, particularly the position and treatment of women. These ideas made educated Indians critically examine their own society and they also came to believe that the progress of Indian society was closely linked with the upliftment of women. They emphasised women's education; for they felt that education would increase awareness among women and prevent them from submitting to unjust social customs and traditions. It would also make them play an effective role as the prime agents of socialization and helpmates of their educated husbands. Reformers like Karve, Ranade, Malabari, Jotiba Phule, Manekjee Cursetjee and others were champions of women's education. Some of them set personal examples, e.g. Karve married a widow, despite, social opposition. He is credited with establishing the *Anath Balikashram* meant for uplifting the condition of child widow; the *Mahaliya Vidyalaya* promoting women's education finally culminating in the establishment of the Women's University in 1916, known as the S.N.D.T. University.

Organized efforts were also made by the male intelligentsia to foster the cause of women's education. One of the earliest of these was the Student's Literary and Scientific Society. It was founded in 1848 and amongst its activities women's issues occupied a prominent place. Debates were held on various issues concerning women and it is credited with establishing some of he earliest schools for girls in Bombay city.

The reformers also helped the state in enacting certain social legislation which greatly effected the position of women in society such as *Sati* Abolition Act of 1829, Widow Remarriage Act of 1856 and the Age of Consent Act passed in 1891.

Many reformers succeeded in educating their wives, sisters and daughters. Pandita Ramabai Saraswati, Anandibai Joshi, Ramabai Ranade, Vidyagauri Nilkant and Sharada Mehta were a few of these women who owe to their husbands or fathers.

It is ironical to note that unlike the Christian missionaries and the male intelligentsia the British government took the responsibility of women's education as late as 1854; while on the other hand, it accepted responsibility for the education of men in 1813. It was Lord Dalhousie, the Governor-General of India, who was responsible in directing the Council of Education, "to consider its function as comprising the superintendence of native female education" and further the Educational Despatch of 1854 approved of these orders. Thus, by this Despatch the cause for promoting women's education was taken up by the government directly. Also, it was made evident that grant-in-aid were to be given to female schools. Similar message was echoed in the Hunter Commissions Report, which was appointed in 1882. Among other things, it clearly mentioned that women's education should be encouraged in all aspects, viz. syllabus, teaching staff, women inspectors and others. In other words it recommendation included an improvement in all aspects regarding women's education. Lord Curzon also supported this view.

The direct involvement of the government not only led to the expansion in primary education but secondary, collegiate and professional education made a gradual advancement. Professions that were available to women were teaching, nursing and midwifery. Also, there was a positive increase in governments expenditure. In the year 1891-92 the expenditure on colleges for general education was Rs. 235.56 and it grew to Rs. 4630.54 in the year 1921-22. This trend was encouraging and positive and led the government and private agency to establish separate colleges for women. Similarly, expenditure on professional education, particularly on training schools for teachers was increasing. This shows that fairly good attention was paid by the government and private agencies for its advancement.

It is interesting to note that in western countries, particularly with regard to Oxford and Cambridge, women had to fight a bitter battle to enter the portals of the University. However, in the University of Bombay there was hardly any conflict over the issue. When the question of admitting women to the University arose, the authorities merely passed a resolution to the effect, "that words in the masculine in the rules of the University shall for the future include also feminine."

Another significant feature pertaining to our period was that the Intermediate Art Courses were becoming popular among women and not Science. However, in 1920-21for the first time three women appeared for the Intermediate examination in Science and passed successfully. There were few women in undergraduate and post-graduate courses. Few women who opted for science course performed well in the examination.

Thus, during our period a beginning in women's higher education had been made though it remained largely confined to the Europeans, Anglo-Indians, Indian Christians and the Parsis who formed only a small percentage of the population. Few women belonging to the reformed Hindu families also took to education.

Education awakened a sense of social responsibility among women and we find that Pandita Ramabai and Ramabai Ranade started organizations to promote social and educational work among women. Pandita Ramabai started the *Sharda Sadan* (Home of learning) and Ramabai Ranade started the *Seva-Sadan* (Home of Service) with the co-operation of Malabari and Dayaram Gidumal. These organizations acted as refuge to child widows and provided them necessary training so that they could make a living. Also they instilled in women the courage to defy customs, e.g. Anandibai married D.K. Karve. Gradually with the establishment of All India Organizations like the Women's Indian Association which cut across caste, communal and linguistic barriers, women belonging to different parts of India could meet and discussion common issues. These promoted communal solidarity and national consciousness among women.

Apart from organizations, some of these women wrote articles; edited journals and wrote their own biographies, e.g. Parvatibai Athavale wrote *Mazi-Kahani* (My Story); her sister Anandibai Karve wrote *Maze Puran* (My autobiography); Sharda Mehta's *Jeevan Sambharna* (Remembrance of my life) and Pandita Ramabai on the other hand wrote *The high caste Hindu Women*. These biographies not only portrayed social conditions existing during the period but acted as a source of inspiration to other women of the Presidency. It also reveals that for the first time few educated women felt that their lives were of some worth which they recorded in their biographies. Some women wrote articles in journals, e.g. Vidyagauri Nilkanth contributed articles to *Buddi Prakash* and along with her husband edited the magazine *Jnan-Sudha*. Miss Rebecca Reuben edited a journal *Hind Mahila* in English. This was first published in Bombay in 1920; from 1923, Avantikabai Gokhal edited another journal of the same name in Marathi. These journals were meant to widen the horizon fo women and also dealt with questions and problems concerning their own lives.

The growth of education among women also promoted political consciousness. We find that from the very inception of the Indian National Congress in 1885, women attended its sessions in different capacities. Some women, e.g. Vidyagauri Nilkanth and her sister Sharda Mehta sang The National Anthem at the Congress session held at Ahmedabad in 1902.

The increasing involvement of women in the suffrage movement enabled them to secure legislative rights. Madras. was the first province to remove sex-disqualification and had also the distinction of having the first women legislator. Dr. S. Muthulakshmi Reddi was chosen Deputy speaker of Madras Legislative Council. Infact, by 1926 women enjoyed franchise on the same term as men in all the provinces so far as elections tothe provincial legislature was concerned.

The coming of Gandhiji brought a new political awakening to western India and saw increasing involvement of women from the urban and rural areas in the freedom struggle. Gandhiji's technique of *Satyagraha* succeeded in bringing into the folds of nationalism educated and uneducated women and also traditional women within the four walls of their homes.

In the first non-cooperation movement in 1921 women from different walks of life in Gujarat participated. Later women also carried out Gandhiji's message of strengthening Hindu Muslim unity and eliminating the curse of untouchability. Similarly, the propogation of spinning on which Gandhiji particularly stressed and the use of Khadi could succeed only because of women's participation. Infact, spinning along with his earlier technique of satyagraha and non-violence once again linked the educated and uneducated urban and rural women to the freedom struggle. This became clearly evident in the Civil Disobedience Movement of 1930 and the Quit India Movement of 1942.

Thus during our period the efforts of the Christian missionaries, male intelligentsia, British government and the female intelligentsia succeeded in laying the base for the growth of higher education of women Though it was limited to few communities and catered to urban areas e.g.. Ahmedabad, Baroda, Bombay, Poona, etc., a trend was set. Infact, this trend continues to exist in contemporary India. We find that all important centres of higher education of women are normally located in urbans areas.

It is significant to note that during our period some educational indicators e.g. literary rate of women increased from 5 per thousand in 1891 to 24 per thousand in 1920-21. This indicates that slowly society was changing and upper caste women so long confined to their homes were beginning to come-out and took to professions like teaching, nursing, midwifery and so on. They defined *purdah* undertook sea voyage, e.g. Pandita Rambai sailed to America and England and Anandibai Joshi went to America to get her doctorate in medicine. This was considered a bad omen in the earlier 19th century and also breach of caste regulations. Women belonging to the reformed familes defined customs, e.g. Tarabai Modak along with her sister rode a bicyle in the streets of Bombay; Anandibai Joshi wore velvet boots and Anandibai Karve grew her hair after joining *Sharda Sadan*. Ansuya Sarabhai drove a carriage in Ahmedabad smoking a cigarette. Among the Parsis this change was more evident, e.g. in 1852 a Parsi couple had created a sensation by driving out together and visiting the European shops. They were also pioneers in spearheading women's education. However, these changes were of a limited nature as the orthodox section continued to oppose it and educated women within their family oftern continued to face stiff opposition, e.g. Ramabai Ranade faced stiff opposition from her sister-in-law and other members of the family while she was being educated by her husband.

The structure of the patriarchal family did not change and men continued to have the decisive say in family matters but in reformed families women were respected and their opinions and views were valued.[1] Similarly, as far as marriage were concerned, it was companionship that was gradually emphasised.[2] Men in reformed families taught their wives and even encouraged them to take to higher education, e.g. Gopalrao Joshi taught Anandibai and even encouraged her to do her doctorate in medicine from America. This kind of relationship that was emerging between husband and wife was gradually breaking the walls of segregation within a partiarchal household. However, this was extremely limited in nature.

The age of marriage also witnessed a change which shows that educated mothers were becoming conscious that early marriage and education would not go together and therefore, they deferred their daughters marriages.[3] The age of marriage rose not within some familes but among various castes and in the country as a whole. A study of the age of marriage through three generations of *Vadnagra Nagars* of Saurashtra shows that the average age in one survey changed from 11.4 to 12.7 to 14.2 and in the other from 11.42 to 13.59 to 14.81.[4]

A few inter-caste marriages began to be performed by 1920's. This reveals that so far as choosing life-partners was conerned certain amount of freedom was given to the girls. This again was limited.

Thus, we find that at a micro-level in a reformed Hindu families, social change gradually started taking palce. In such families women no longer stayed in a segregated way and took an active part in family affairs and in public activities such as debates, speeches and so on. These changes were not revolutionary and therefore, cannot be termed as structural change.

Despite, all these, pioneering efforts women's education has made slow progress. In 1950-51 in Bombay Presidency the female literacy rate was 12.9 which increased to 63. 05 for Maharashtra and 60.91 for Gujarat in 1991. In 1950-51 the total enrolment of girls in educational institutions was 13,56,451 that was about 0.8 per cent of the total population of women in the state. In 1991 total enrolment was 7522240 in Maharashtra and 3749975 for Gujarat which works out to be 19.77 per cent and 18.84 per cent of the total population of women in Maharashtra and Gujarat state respectively.

In 1950-51 the number of women students attending institutions of higher education was 7251 which was 0.54 per cent of total girls enrolment. In 1991 the number of girls enrolled in institutions of higher education was 243778 in case of Maharashtra and 113975 in case of Gujarat. This means that in 1991 only 3.24 per cent in case of Maharshtra and 3.04 per cent in case of Gujarat of total girls enrolled in all institutions attended institutions of higher education. This shows that though in forty years the female literacy rate has increased about five folds and the total enrolment of girls have increased twenty-four folds yet the growth of higher education of women has been only six folds. In forty years the percentage has increased only from 0.5 per cent to 3 percentage approximately.

The participation of women in technical and professional streams which had made a beginning in the late 19th and 20th century has shown marked increase from a little over 6000 in 1950-51 to 1.46 lakhs in 1986-87 which is an increase of 23 times.[5] There has been a noticeable growth in the number of women students in the Engineering and technologies streams in the Indian Institue of Science and Technology and Polytechnics. Thus, the beginning of professional education of women in the 19th and 20th century has now branched off into non-traditional areas as mentioned above especially in those areas which was initially considered as males domain. This trend also extends to other professional courses such as law, medicine and management.

The continuity and change in women's education in western India continues to exist in contemporary India. Various educational indicators points to it e.g. the literacy rate of female has risen from 0.69 in 1901 to 39.29 per cent in 1991. Further according to the latest data available from the Central Education Department, there are 196 university level institutions serving 4.3 million students. The enrolment of women students at the beginning of the year 1993-94 was 16.64 lakhs as against 15.94 lakhs in the previous year. This was an increase of more than four times since independence. At the post-graduate level the enrolment of women was 351 per cent of the total enrolment. Further the participation of women in technical and professional increase since 1947-75, 1992-93 is (i.e. from 1.5 to 8.2 per cent) very perceptible. In other sciences its allied fields the percentage increase was from 22.9 to 33.8 in the above mentioned period.[6]

Thus, the pioneering and initial growth in women's education in 19th and 20th century in western India has now grown and branched off into different fields in contemporary India.

REFERENCES

1. In the household of Bholanath Sarabhai Vidygauri's maternal grand father, his eldest daughter Jithuba had a say Family, women Reformers: A case study of Vidyagauri Nilkanth" in *Samya Shakti: A Journal of Women studies.* Vol. IV and V, 1989-90, Centre for Women's Development Studies.

2. In the case of Vidyagauri, she and her husband jointly edited the magazine Janasudha. They wrote letters to each other which was considered unthinkable earlier. Her children spoke of their marriage as the ideal and perfect marriage, *Ibid.*, p. 69-70.

3. All of Vidyagauri's grand-daughters were married after they were twenty-one and Vidyagauri's grand-daughters married between the age of twenty-one and twenty-eight. Thus there was a distinct rise in the age of marriage between the first and second generations in Vidyagauri's family, *Ibid.*, p. 74.

4. In the previous generation, 20 per cent of marriages took place before the girl was 13 and 50 per cent before she was fourteen. Also Kapadias Survey clearly indicates a gradual rise in the age at marriage *Ibid.*, pp. 75.

APPENDICES

APPENDIX - A

LITERACY RATE AND STATUS OF WOMEN'S EDUCATION IN SOME DISTRICTS OF BOMBAY PRESIDENCY

Literacy of Men and Women in Different District of Bombay Presidency in 1921

District	Population			No. of Literate			Literate per 1000		
	Male	Female	Total	Male	Female	Total	Male	Female	Total
1	2	3	4	5	6	7	8	9	10
Bombay Suburban	88,387	64,453	152,840	19,616	6,428	26,044	222	100	170
Ahmedabad	476,266	414,645	890,911	108,160	21,334	129,494	227	52	170
Broach	158,588	149,157	307,745	44,371	5,202	49,573	280	35	161
Kaira	379,735	331,247	710,982	74,496	10,384	84,880	196	31	119
Panch Mahal's	193,400	181,460	374,866	21,980	2,905	24,891	114	16	66
Surat	337,387	336,964	674,351	95,504	19,041	114,545	283	57	170
Thana	390,021	369,895	759,916	34,336	6,208	40,544	83	17	53
Ahmednagar	369,629	361,923	731,552	41,431	5,409	46,840	112	13	64
Khandesh, East	545,789	530,048	1,075,837	70,564	3,818	74,382	129	7	69

Contd. ....

Appendix A (Contd.)

1	2	3	4	5	6	7	8	9	10
Khandesh, West	324,831	317,016	641,847	28,723	2,267	30,990	91	7	48
Nasik	424,359	408,217	832,576	47,610	5,353	52,963	112	13	64
Poona	516,871	492,162	1,0009,033	74,414	16,170	90,584	121	33	90
Satara	511,480	514,779	1,026,259	42,543	4,470	47,031	83	9	46
Sholapur	382,571	359,439	742,010	35,846	3,515	39,361	94	10	49
Belgaum	487,036	465,960	952,996	50,688	5,527	56,215	104	12	59
Bijapur	405,637	391,239	796,876	48,423	3,103	51,526	119	8	65
Dharwar	528,889	508,035	1,036,924	92,504	8,707	101,211	175	17	98
Kanara	204,165	197,562	401,727	34,125	4,581	38,706	167	23	96
Kolaba	279,596	283,346	562,942	26,009	3,710	29,719	93	11	53
Ratnagiri	525,341	628,903	1,154,244	48,691	4,802	53,493	93	8	46
Hyderabad	322,44	251,006	573,450	25,491	7,517	33,008	791	30	58
Karachi	312,048	230,017	542,065	44,211	8,458	52,669	142	37	97
Larkana	331,217	266,743	597,960	20,603	1,819	22,422	62	7	38
Navabshah	233,830	184,830	418,660	18,261	1,951	20,212	78	11	48
Sabpur	282,306	227,986	510,292	26,919	2,372	29,291	95	10	57
Thar and Parkar	221,095	175,236	396,331	13,134	1,929	15,063	59	11	38
Upper Sind Frontier	134,325	106,294	240,619	5,932	325	6,257	44	3	26
Cambay	37,302	34,460	71,762	8,260	1,791	10,015	221	52	140

Contd. ....

Appendix A (Contd.)

1	2	3	4	5	6	7	8	9	10
Cutch	235,363	249,184	484,547	35,781	5,879	41,660	152	12	86
Kathiawar	1,290,659	1,247,843	2,538,497	238,314	44,111	282,425	185	35	111
Bhavnagar	220,303	206,101	426,404	45,875	10,277	56,152	208	50	132
Gonda	82,995	84,076	167,071	19,955	4,690	24,645	240	56	148
Navanagar	174,275	171,078	345,353	26,651	4,555	31,206	153	27	90
Junagadh	237,264	228,229	465,493	37,105	5,171	42,276	156	23	91
Rest of Kathlawar	575,817	558,359	1,134,176	108,728	19,418	128,146	189	35	113
Palanpur Agency	269,824	248,742	518,566	23,083	1,908	24,991	86	8	48
Palanpur State	122,383	114,311	236,694	110,791	899	11,690	88	8	49
Rest of the Agency	147,441	134,431	281,872	12,292	1,009	13,301	83	8	47
Mahi Kantha	226,974	223,504	450,478	22,780	2,004	24,824	100	9	55
Idar	112,077	114,274	226,351	8,744	680	9,424	78	6	42
Rest of the Agency	114,897	109,230	224,127	14,036	1,364	15,400	122	13	69
Reva Kantha	386,756	366,302	753,058	30,880	4,945	35,835	80	14	48
Rajpipia	86,518	81,907	168,425	11,634	2,524	14,158	135	31	84
Rest of Agency	300,238	284,395	584,633	19,246	2,421	21,667	64	9	37
Surat Agency	92,381	87,373	179,754	7,268	1,363	8,631	79	16	48
Bhar	64,761	65,659	130,420	3,172	377	3,549	49	6	27
Savantvadi	97,006	109,434	206,440	11,440	1,074	12,514	118	10	61

Contd. ....

Appendix A (Contd.)

1	2	3	4	5	6	7	8	9	10
Kolhapur	428,543	405,183	833,726	64,614	6,888	71,502	151	17	86
SMC States	209,952	298,410	608,362	38,107	3,854	41,961	123	13	69
Sangli	113,199	108,122	221,321	16,285	1,885	18,170	144	17	82
Other State Total	196,753	190,288	287,041	21,822	1,969	23,791	111	10	62
Other State in the Presidency Proper	223,230	217,428	440,688	15,606	1,405	17,011	70	7	39
Kaipur	107,216	85,915	193,131	5,344	435	5,779	50	5	30

Source : *Census of India*, 1921, Vol. VIII, Bombay Presidency Part II, pp.104-06.

DECCAN DIVISION AND DISTRICTS

Khandesh

In this district there was hardly any institution promoting higher education for girls. In fact, in 1864 the first girls' school was started at Dhulia. Prior to it there was no separate institution for girls. In the next 10 years the number had arisen to 5, with 282 names on the roll and an average daily attendance of 210 pupils (1857-76). Two of these schools, particularly in Dhulia and Parola were well managed. The latter was under a certificated mistress from Nadurbar Sub-division was particularly meant for muslim girls'. In the Savda division a girls' school was opened in 1878-79 there were in all 7 girls' schools with 390 names on the roll and an average attendance of 269 pupils.[1]

Bombay City

The chief private institution which promoted female education in Bombay city were the Bombay Education Society's boys and girls schools, the *Indo-British Institution,* the Bombay Scottish Orphanage, and *St. Mary's Institution,* the *Convent School at Parel,* the *Sir J.J. Parsi Benovelent Institution,* several school of *American Mission,* the *Robert Money School* and *12 Vernacular* schools belonging to the *Scottish Missionary Society.* Sectarian School education was represented by the Prabhu seminary and a Bhattia School, was also attended by Khojas, Memons and Lohanas. Female education apart from missionary efforts, was stimulated by Students Literary and Scientific Society, which supported a vernacular free school for girls and was attended by 654 pupils, of whom 136 were Marathi speaking Hindus, 120 Gujarati Hindu nd 398 Parsis. Muhammodan education was represented by only one Hindustani school, opened by Governmen in Kazi street in 1844. However, the bulk of Muhammad population evinced no ardent desire for education on western lines and were quite content with the ability to read *Quran.*[2]

Regarding the spread of female education the Education Department did little; it was left almost entirely to private enterprise and benevolence to found schools for the weaker sex. Among the most notable institutions privately endowed prior to 1865 were the Parsis girls schools opened in 1858 , Convent school in the Fort, Byculla, and Lower Mahim, the St. Joseph's School at Mazagon and Cavel, St. Anne's school at Byculla, the Cowasji Jehangir Readmoney school at Ketwadi, the Alexandra Native Girl's English Institution founded in 1860, and a Marathi school for the propagation of the Gospel in 1864.[3]

However, female education received a philip by an annual assignment of Rs. 10,000 made by the Government of India in 1868 and by the visit of Miss Carpenter to India and the consequent establishment of female training schools at Ahmedabad, Poona and Bombay. The Bombay School was endowed with 12 scholarships, ranging in value from Rs. 15 to 25, and it existed till 1872, when irregular attendance obliged the authorities to close it. However, the ony legacy of Miss Carpenter's Philanthropic mission which continues to this day is the Mary Carpenter scholarship for girls', which are annually awarded by the National Indian Association of London to pupils of recognized girls' schools in Bombay. More successful than the Bombay normal schools was a Gujarati girls' school opened in the Fort in 1859 by the Trustees of the Gokuldas Tejpal Charities to which all Gujarati-speaking Hindu girls were admitted free of charge. It is significant to note that the school that was opened with 60 pupils now contained more than 200.

The history of education from 1872, when Mr. K.M. Chatfied became Director of Public Instruction, to 1882 when the Education Commission was appointed, was chiefly concerned with the extension of primary education and the improvement of higher and collegiate tuition. The former object occupied the chief attention of the Bombay Government who decided that any large increase in secondary and higher schools should result rather than direct action of their own education agency.[4]

Nevertheless, the policy of government bore fruit and the census officer of 1881 was able to point out that since the census of 1872 very considerable progress and been made in the education of the population. The percentage of the male population under instruction had arisen from 5.0 to 7.6 and of the female population from 1.8 to 2.8, while the proportion of educated males and females, had arise, respectively from 17.5 to 24.9 and from 4.0 to 6.3. This increase was mainly because more new schools were opened. Further impetus to education came when in 1873 the first Government Gujarati Girls' School at Charni-road was opened. This was followed by the opening of the first Marathi Girls' School at Kamathipura in 1876. The Parsis also did not lag behind and in 1871 the Merwanji Sethna school was established to provide education for women.

The missionaries who were pioneers n female education also did not lag behind. In 1874, the missionary belonging to the Methodist Episcopal mission founded a school in 1873-74 at Grant road in Bombay. The Zenana Bible and Medical mission also did not lag behind and a high school for girls was soon established in 1874.[5]

Thus by 1874 private institutions along with the missionaries helped in the foundation of girls school in Bombay city. These schools encouraged primary as well as higher education.

The proliferation of education institutions clearly reveal that the age old prejudice against female education was gradually being overcome. This is further supported by the fact that the municipal girls school rose from 11 to 23 and aided girls schools from 25 to 33 in 1909.

Bombay also became a sea of higher education. College as well as doors of the University gradually began to be open for women, e.g. Wilson college which was opened in 1832 admitted male as well as female students. It is interesting to note that the number of pupils in the college gradually arose from 18 in 1870-71 to 64 in 1880-81, this figure reached to 22.3 in 1890-91. Next five years also saw an increase of 500 students. Similarly the beginning of the 20th century also saw a continuous increase of scholar in this institution. The roll of college also included 31 lady students of whom 19 were Parsis, 8 Hindus and 3 were Christians only one student was Muhammadan.[6]

These figures clearly reveal that higher education of women in Wilson College was popular among the Parsis.

Also, University education was open to women without much difficulty as compared to Cambridge and Oxford where women had to wage a bitter fight. Infact, in 1888 Cornelia Sorabji was the Ist women in the Presidency to receive a University degree. This had a positive impact and we find that in 1901-02, as many as 75 girls were attending and reading in college.[7]

Nasik District

In the district of the Deccan division it was only in 1861 that first superior Anglo Vernacular School was established. In 1871 it was transformed into Nasik High school. In fact, it was the first secondary school in this district. Female education was almost negligent. The literacy rate among the female also portrays that women's education was very limited.

The percentage of literacy in the district for total male and female since 1901 is as follows :

Year	*Total*	*Male*	*Female*
1901	4.31	8.13	0.39
1911	4.37	8.08	0.60
1921	6.36	11.22	1.31

These figures clearly reveal that as compared to male's female literacy was extremely minimal. Perhaps, this was because of social factors, i.e. child marriage and enforced widowhood as discussed in chapter two that prevented women from taking to higher education.

Satara

In this district female education had gradually begun. Most of the girls' schools in this district was inspected by the Inspectress of Girls' School, Poona. The important function performed by the Inspectress was to inspect girls' secondary and special schools in the district. Primary schools were also inspected. The main reason for inspection was to suggest improvement regarding girls' school at primary and secondary levels.[9]

A significant development in this district was the establishment of a voluntary education institution namely *Rayat Shikshan Sanstha* by Bhaurao Patil in 1919. The main aim of the institution was to educate the low caste people in rural areas also the Sanstha had a number of schools' and training colleges for women.[10]

Poona

During the period under review it was Poona which became and important nucleus of higher education. In 1896 Hindu Widow's Home Association was established by D.K. Karve. As stated in Appendix 'A' this institution was purely an educational institution. Its main activity was to educate widows. The other important institution begun by him was the *Mahila Vidyalaya.* The final culmination of Karve efforts was the foundation of S.N.D.T. College for Women in 1916. Infact, it was the nucleus of the Indian Women's University.[11] Among the declared objects of this institution was to make provision for the higher education of women through modern Indian language as a medium of examination and instruction by starting, aiding and affiliating institutions for such education, and secondly to formulate and lay down courses of studies specially suited to the needs and requirement of women. Upto 1923, this institution was housed in a small building in Hingne.

Also, Poona was a seat of various organizations begun by women, Pandita Ramabai's *Arya Mahila Samaj* which was started in 1882 had its branches not only in Poona but it had its branches spread all over Maharashtra. Similarly, *Sharda-Sadan* which was founded in 1889 was shifted to Poona in 1890.

Both these organizations promoted womens education and discouraged child marriage. The latter institution trained women, especially widows as teachers, nurses and mid-wives.[12]

A similar kind of institution was established by Ramabai Ranade, i.e. the *Seva Sadan*. Initially the institution started functioning in Bombay in 1908 and within a year a branch was opened in Poona. This institution like the earlier one not only provided education to widows and unmarried girls but also encouraged women to be self-reliant. In 1909 under the guidance of Ramabai Ranade Poona Seva-Sadan started classes for adult women, industrial classes, hostel for women, a training college, a high school and a nursing and medical department[13] was also begun.

Dharwar

It was only 1867 that the first girls' school was opened at Dharwar. During the six year's ending 1873-74, the number of girls schools rose to 11 with 429 names on the rolls and an average attendance of 295.2, of these two were maintained by the Basel German Mission Society and the rest werc government schools. In 1890 the number was 20 with 979 names on the roll and an average attendance of 625. Of these schoolsthere were Basel German Mission Schools, 2 Estate or jagir schools, one each at Lakshemeshwar and Savanur and the rest were government schools. In 1880, four few girls schools were opened and in 1881-82 the number of schools reached 24 of which 17 were government three mission and 4 Estate school,[14] with an attendance of 1484. In 1882-83, 2 new estate schools were opened and the attendance rose from 1484 in 1881-82 to 1859- in 1882-83. Besides these separate girls school 2450 girls attended boys school, so that the total number fo girls' attending school is 4309.

In 1881 the state of Education in Dharwar was as follows[15] –

Age	*Hindus*		*Muslims*		*Christians*	
Under instruction						
Below 15	15,031	460	1323	47	118	161
Above 15	2,791	24	276	10	27	11
Instructed						
Below 15	1,124	72	97	12	17	9
Above 15	28,536	215	1879	45	195	79
Illiterate						
Below 15	133,100	142,499	18,596	18,941	342	321
Above 15	209,526	246,407	28,478	30,960	502	574
	390,198	389,677	50,599	50,023	1201	1155

Kolaba

Before the British took up the education of this district under their care every big village had a school, kept generally by a Brahmin and attended both by boys and girls, under 12 years of age. Since the introduction of state education these private schools gradually vanished.

In this district the first girls' school was opened at Alibag in 1861. This number gradually increased to 23. Co-education was also prevalent in this district. Thus, in this particualr district girls' generally attended primary school.[16]

Thana

Before 1867 there were no schools for girls' in the district. In 1871-72 there were six schools for girls' with 248 names on th rolls. In 1879-80 the number of schools continued to be six but the number of pupils had risen to 363. In the town of Bhiwandi, particularly there were 3 Government schools, two for boys and one for girls......[17] This increase in number of schools clearly indicate that female education, particularly schools education was becoming gradually popular in this district.

The percentag of literarcy regarding male and female population in this district since 1901 is as follows -

Year	*Total*	*Males*	*Females*
1901	5.31	9.09	1.21
1911	5.88	9.99	.61
1921	5.34	8.80	1.68

These figures clearly indicate that female literacy had gradually advanced since 1901, however as compared to the male population literacy rate continued to be very low in this district.

KONKAN

Ratnagiri District

In this particular district the most significant development regarding female education took place in 1918. In this particular year --- The Women Education Society, Malvan, came into existence. The initial significant step taken up by the society was totake over the management of the girls' high school at Malvan. The main object before the society was to start, conduct, and manage education institution principally for women and to make best possible efforts to spread education among women.[18]

Ahemadnagar

In this district the first school was opened in 1840. Prior to this period there was hardly any girl's school. In 1868 there were 59 names on the roll with an average attendance of 25.2. In 1872-73, an additional school was opened in this district. The number of pupils in both the schools amounted to 148 of whom seven were Parsis. Similarly in 1882-83, there were 19 schools with 1, 123 names and an average attendance of 598.5. Thus, we find that in this district, Girl's school was gradually coming up. Higher education was nearly negligent. The literacy figure of the district also indicates this fact.

Year	*Total*	*Males*	*Females*
1901	4.67	8.93	0.43
1911	4.65	8.59	0.65
1921	6.40	11.21	1.49

Baroda State

The Baroda state was in fact the vaneguard in the sphere of female education. It was in 1885, His Highness Maharaja Sayaji Roa III stressed the importance of female education in memorandum which ran as under :

> "I would particulary emphasise the importance of the education of girls'. It is the unremitting watchfulness and conciliatory supervision of intelligent and educated mothers which form powerful factors in giving right tone to infant minds, and which are the best agents for the eradication of crooked ways. Women regulate the social life of a people, and men and women rise or fall together. To fit the girls for their function in our social life, I could give my special attention to the opening of girl's school".

It was the declared policy of the State or Department of education (Baroda State) to open separate schools for girls in all places where sufficient number of students were forthcoming. Similarly, where a sufficient number of girls students were not forthcoming, girls under twelve years of age were admitted to the boys school. In all cases inducement in shape of special prizes and scholarships were given to encourage regular attendance of girl's.

In order to further promote education in 1892 compulsory education was experimentally introduced in the town of Amreli and in nine villages of the Amreli taluka. Compulsion was introduced in the first three standard. All boys between the ages of 7 and all the girls between 7 and 10 year living within a mile of the school were compelled to attend the school. In 1893, Compulsory Education Act was passed in 1906 and modified successfully in 1910, 1916 and 1926.

The Education Act of 1906 fixed the age limit at 7 and 12 for boys and 7 and 10 for girls. Later on the compulsory age for boys as well as for girls was fixed at 7 and 12 respectively. Also, there were a number of exemptions on prescribed ground for non-attendance such as those who were physically handicapped, girls who were under purdah and children who happened to be the only son of cultivator, etc.

Thus, by introduction of compulsory education, the state of Baroda was advanced educationally as compared to other states in India.

As a result of this Act, the total number of girls' schools' at the end of 1911-12 was 351 while it was 347 in the preceding year. The number of girls' learning in these 351 institutions was 28, 045 against 26,396. Moreover 32, 496 girls learnt along with boys in mixed schools in those villages where separate girls' schools could not be maintained.The corresponding figure of last year was 28,083. Thus, the total number of girls' attending schools was 60, 541 against 54, 479. It is interesting to note that inspite of famine it is indeed satisfactory to find that the number of girls' has not only been steadily maintained but it has greatly increased. This increase in number may be ascribed to greater vigilance in enlisting the girls' of compulsory age, as well as to the relief work to add to the wage-earning capacity of the family. At the same time, the numberof girls in higher classes was gradually advancing. The total number of Girls High School by 1911-12 was one and the number s of pupils was around 28. Most of the girls' in highest classes were provided with better teachers. Probably, this reason explains the steady increase of pupils.[20]

A significant development that took place in 1911-12 was the affiliation of Baroda High School with University of Bombay mainly for the purpose of matriculation examination. At the end of the year under Report there were 187 girls ' learning English against 171 in the preceding year. Of these 187, 28 belonged to the High School proper against 23 of the preceding year. They were distributed as under[21] –

Matriculation	8
Standard VI	5
Standard V	6
Standard IV	9
Standard III	23
Standard II	33
Stardard I	40
Primer Classes	63
	187

By 1913-14, the Baroda High School for Girls' showed slow but steady sign of growth. At the end of the year total number of girl's enrolled was 101 girls. Library and laboratory facililties were all equipped to carry out practical work in Physics and Chemistry.

As a result of the facilities provided by the school during the year 6 students of Baroda High School appeared for the University Matriculation examination. Out of these six, two passed. One of the students even secured the Chatfield prize awarded by the University for passing with the highest number of marks from among the female candidates.

The subjects generally taught in these school generally emphasised on domestic sciences. The logic or rational behind it was that it would be of immediate relevance to girls in their later life. Thus, needlework, knitting, embroidery and cookery were especially taught not only in Baroda but also in schools located near Baroda, i.e. at Patan, Navsari, Gandevi, Petlad and Visnagar.

It is of significance to note that such subjects taught in school found favourable supports from the parents. Infact, the emphasis of these subjects encouraged girls' to continue their education in schools.

In primary schools, there were no special teachers for these subjects, they were generally taught by the mistresses, who received training in Training College for Women. In fact, the demand of separate teachers for these subjects continue to be pressing in Baroda.

This increasing demand for teachers led to the opening up of a professional institution for women known as Training College for Women. This college was started in Baroda in 1882. The number of trained women teachers gradually went on increasing and we find that by the end of 1914 there were around 104 stipendiary scholars. The total amount of scholarship given to women under training was Rs. 700/ per month.

Women who joined the college came from varied background. Caste-wise the 104 scholars were distributed as follows ---

42	-.	Brahmins
20	-	Kshatrias
5	-	Banias
3	-	Patidars
22	-	Other Hindus
7	-	Non Aryans
1	-	Parsi
3	-	Jains
1	-	Luhana

These figures clearly reveal that professional education, particulary teachers training was popular amongst the Brahmins and Kshatrias in Baroda.

As a result of gradual expansion of female students in high school and establishment of female training college a fillip was given to higher education of women. It is interesting to note that at the end of 1914 there were six lady students out of 550 students enrolled in Baroda college. Despite the number being less a ground was laid in Baroda for the growth and development of higher education of women.

Similarly, women who could not avail the facilities of formal institution of learning could seek education through the *zenana* classes. These zenana classes imparted instruction to women who were desirous of learning. Age was not a consideration. The subjects taught consisted of Reading, Writing, Accounts and Needle work. Classes were generally held in the afternoon from 2 to 5 p.m. By 1914, there were 3 zenana classes, one in Baroda city, another at Petlad and third at Mehsana sub-division. There were 184 women on the role. Out of this number 99 appeared for the examination of whom 71 passed.

In order to further encourage women's education, on 8th February 1915, the Rulers of Baroda opened the "Chimnabai Industrial Home". This home owed its being to the efforts of H.H. the Maharani of the State. The chief objective of this institution was to relieve as far as possible the misery of womenfolk. In his institution household industries like knitting, sewing and lace-making were intended to be imparted. In his speech made at the opening of the institute, Dewan Madhava Rao said —

> "Institution of this kind are alien to the genius of the Hindu people; put Her Highness has noticed, with this insight that comes of the sympathy for her subjects, the change are slowly taking place in the condition of the family life and caste organization and has realized that many Hindu widows will have to be provided with means of earning a livelihood if they are not to be left utterly destitute."

Thus, we find that in Baroda state, the rulers actively encouraged female education. It is because of this encouragement that women not only enrolled themselves in colleges but also in Professional Institutions like the Teachers Training College.

REFERENCES

1. *Gazetteer of the Bombay Presidency Vol. XII,* Khandesh, p. 330.
2. *The Gazetteer of Bombay city and Island, Vol. III,* p. 108.
3. *Ibid.,* p. 111.
4. *Ibid.,* pp. 115-16.
5. *Ibid.,* p. 117.
6. *Ibid.,* p. 133.
7. *A Review of Education in Bombay State 1855-1955,* p. 390.
8. *Maharashra State Gazetteer* Nasik District, pp. 786-87.
9. *Maharashtra State Gazetteer,* Satara District, p. 718.
10. *Ibid.,* p. 728.
11. *Gazetteer of Bombay State,* Poona District, p. 557.
12. Helen S. Dyer, *op.cit.,* p. 29.
13. Kasumavati Deshpande, *op.cit.,* p. 222-23.
14. *Gazetteer of the Bombay Presidency,* Vol. XXII, Dharwar, p. 613.
15. *Ibid.,* p. 613-14.
16. *Maharashtra State Gazetteer's* Kolaba District, p. 643.
17. *Maharashtra state Gazetteer's,* Thana District, p. 868.
18. *Maharashtra State Gazetteer's,* Rantnagiri District, p. 729.
19. *Maharashtra State Gazetteer's,* Ahmednagar District, p. 739.
20. *Report on Public Instructin in the Baroda State for the Year 1911-12,* p. 35.
21. *Ibid.,* p. 35.
22. *The Indian Review,* January 1915, Vol XVI, p. 186.

APPENDIX - B

IMPORTANT MALE AND FEMALE INTELLIGENTSIA AND THEIR CONTRIBUTIONS TO WOMEN'S EDUCATION

Baddruddin Tyabji (1844-1906) – He did his best for the amelioration of the condition women of his community and for the advancement of their education. His daughters were the first in the Bombay Presidency to receive their education in England. At the Annual Mahommedan Educational Conference of 1903 at Bombay he delivered an impressive speech advocating the weakening of the power of the *zenana* system of the Mahommedans and strongly urged the necessity for liberal education of Muslim women.

Bal Gangadhar Sastri Jambhekar (1812-1846) – provided a powerful intellectual incentive for the younger generation of mid 19th century in Bombay. He urged widow remarriage, liberalization of caste formalities and the readmission to Hindu society of persons who had been baptized christians. His weekly journal the *Bombay Durpan,* was the first in western India to espouse social reform causes in the late 1830's. Another journal that was published by him was *Digdarshan* (Show the Way). He was not, however, a revolutionary; he observed orthodox patterns of behaviour and pressed for social reform that did no entail giving up religious beliefs.

Bal Gangadhar Tilak (1856-1920) – He belonged to the highest caste in Maharashtra, i.e. the *Chitpavan Brahmin* community. He graduated from high school in 1872 and enrolled himself at the Deccan College. Later he completed his B.A from the Elphinstone College which had earned the credit of producing many social reformers. He founded the two Newspapers, *Mahratta* and *Kesari* which carried social message to the people. He was a man of strong views and a lover of traditions and ancient history; he decided to launch a vigorous campaign against those who ere concentrating their energies on social reform. He challenged the right of a foreign bureaucracy to sit and legislate on Indian society. In his views social condition could not be improved until political conditions were bettered. He strongly held that slow and spontaneous action by society would bring about the desired result; education and consciousness of social evil would eradicated the defects. He opposed the Age of Consent Bill vehemently and condemned Malabari's suggestion for Indian Marriage law as absurd and as involving an interference with Hindu religion.

Behramji Malabari (1853-1912) — Gujarati born in 1853, Malabari was educated in a missionary school and never attended college, he was profoundly influenced by Dr. Wilson, the Scottish missionary and the first Vice-Chancellor of the University of Bombay, who patronized Malabari's early writings, which included pieces of social reform. Malabari was deeply moved by certain customs like infant marriage and enforced widowhood. The sight of mistreated widows, he said "burn themselves into my brains. It is not merely that I know the miseries of widowhood, not merely that I feel them feel for and with the widows; I am the widow for the time being." With fervous matching that of the great social reform publicists of the West, Malabari spread widely his description of personal tragedies due to infant marriage and enforced widowhood. His appeal was to the sentiment of all Indians not merely to the minds of the educated classes. Malabari began issuing tracts and delivering lectures on reform, and when his "Notes" on "Infant Marriage in India", and "Encoroed Widowhood" were publishe don August 15, 1884, they were the product of years of training in the effectiveness of the printed word. These "Notes", which were circulated among officials and private persons, British and Indian, marked the beginning of the All India Social Reform Movement. His chief proposals to check infant marriages were : that, after five years, universities should prohibit married students from taking examinations; that heads of government departments should give preference in hiring unmarried men; and that education departments insert material in school books describing the evils of early marriage. To improve the conditions of life for widows, he asked the government to assure that all widow learn of their rights to remarry under Widow Remarriage Act of 1856; to use its authority to protect widows from involuntary seculusion and "social ill-usage", and to prohibit priests from excommunicating any one who assisted in a widow remarriage.

Dadabhai Naoroji (1825-1917) — Played a great part in educational and social reform in the Western Presidency. It was in 1849 that the Students Literary and Scientific Society was formed and this society encouraged discussions on women's education. In the organization of the society and in giving effects to the confusion arrived at by its discussions, Dadabhai Naoroji occupied a key position. From 1849 to 1865, he helped in bringing together scattered workers and giving ungrudingly his spare time. He took an active part in the establishment of the Bombay Association, the Framji Institute, the Irani Fund, the Parsi Gymnasium, the Widow Marriage Association and the Victoria and Albert Museum. He launched two journals devoted purely on social reform, e.g. The *Stri-Bodh* which was for women in 1857 and the *Rast Goftar* in 1851.

Dadoba Pandurang (1814-1882) — Was born in a *Vaisya* family. It was he who wrote the first Marathi Grammar. He was man of wide learning on world religions. He founded the *Paramahans Mandali* (Divine society) in 1840 with the object of abolishing caste and idolátry, and fostering widow remarriage. Typical of the Bombay reformer, who were not seeking dramatic personal break with society. The society's meetings were held in secrecy.

Dalpatram (1820-1898) — Belonged to the Gujarat Vernacular Society. he was a strong advocator of women's education. He felt that society could only advance in women were educated. He edited *Buddhi Prakash,* a periodical published by the society (Gujarat Vernacular Society) since 15th May, 1850.

Dalpatram has, for the most part written poetry. He also wrote dramas and instructive essays. His poetic compositions include among other, *Vijaya Kshama, Hamsa-Kavya-Shataka, Hunnar Khanni Chadai, Gamar Barvani, Ritu Varnana* and so on. Soem of the plays written by him are *Lakshmi Natak* and *Mithyabhimana Natak.*

Framji Cawasjee Banarjee (1786-1851) — Belived in giving English education to girls of his community. Though he was not highly educated, nor imbued with ideas of religious or social reform, he had a shrewd common sense and he appreciated the value of education. Later he was to overcome the prejudice of the community against medical education by providing rooms for the students near the college, where they could undergo the necessary purificatory ceremonies. His pioneering efforts in girls education bore fruits in 1849 when the Students Literary and Scientific Society started its morning classes for women. This work was entirely voluntary and attracted other Parsis who helped in the foundation of three Parsi Schools.

Gopal Hari Deshmukh (1823-1892) — Wrote under the penname of 'Lokahitwadi'. He wrote against out-dated customs and usages in Hindi Society and the inhuman treatment meted to women and the lower caste in his Shatapatre (Hundred letters), 1848-50. In 1840 he had written in Marathi that "The priests are very unholy because they repeat things without understanding their meaning and profanely reduce knowledge to such repetition. The Pundits are worse than priests, because they are more ignorant and also haughty... Who are the *Brahmins* and in what respects do they differ from us? Have they twenty hand and do we lack something in us ? When such questions are now asked the *Brahmins* should give up their foolish concepts; they must accept that all men are equal and everybody has a right to acquire knowledge."

Ishwar Chandra Vidyasagar (1820-1891) — Often referred as thé "father of Bengali prose style", and noted for his vast scholarly books and educational materials. Be became the principal of the Sanskrit College in 1851 and held the position of Hony. Secretary of Bethune' School. In his individual capacity he founded girls' schools in the districts of Hooghly, Burdwan and Midnapore in Bengal. However, his greatest contribution was his crusade for remarriage of widows and the abolition of polygamy. Infact, his agitation in favour of widow remarriage started in the early 1850's and culminated in the publication of his major work on the subject, *Marriage of Hindu Widows,* in 1856. In that book he sought to prove *Shastric* sanctions for the remarriage of widows and stated his unwillingness to rest the case on reason alone. His efforts bore fruits and in 1856 the Government passed the Hindu Widwo Remarriage Act.

Jagannath Shankarset (1803-1856) — He was born in a rich upper class family of Bombay in 1803 and entered public life at the early age of 19. He was keenly interested in the spread of education and was covinced that the missionary enterprise would never succeed in solving this national problem. He gave his full support to the official and non-official secular attempts to spread modern education. He was a prominent member of the Bombay Native Education Society from its inception in 1822 to its closure in 1840. He was a member of Bombay University Senate from its establishment in 1857 to his death in 1865. He was a great champion of women's education and when the Students Literary and Scieitific Society began to open girls' schools, he gave liberal support by housing one of its school in his own compound and by sending his daughters to it.

Sir Jamsetjee Jejeebhoy (1870-1904) — Was a pioneer of social reform. He particularly sympathised with the movement for the education of girls and the emanicipation of womehood from the tyranny of the social customs of the time. He is credited of having established many schools for girls and started an institution named — "Parsee Benevolent Institution"

J.E.D. Bethune (1801-1851) — Was the law member of the Executive Council of the Governor-General and the President of the Council of Education from 1848 to 1851. Prior to his coming to India in 1848 he held several important offices under his Majesty's Government in England. He was keenly interested in the education of women and soon after his arrival in Indian began to consider the ways and means to foster it. Since the company at this time was now prepared to countenance any efforts at the education of women the channel of official enterprise was closed to him. He, therefore, decided to establish a secular school for girl's in his own individual capacity and to bear all the expenses thereof. The school began in 1849. Within a short span of time it began to attract a fairly large number of girls'. He died in 1851 and, in his will endowed the school with all the lands and propery he had in the city. It was then taken over by Lord Dalhousie who paid for it from his own private purse until the company took it over.

Jotiba Govind Phule (1827-1890) — Belonged to the lower caste, i.e. shudra gardner. He viewed British rule as godsend, and though never entered th civil service, was publicly honoured by the government on several occasions for his tireless efforts and impressive achievements in every field of social reform. Champion of the "Untouchables" and leader of the *Non-Brahmins, Mahatma* (great-soul). Phune as he came to be called, concluded that the British had conquered India, "to liberate the disabled *Shudras* from the slavery of the crafty *Aryas*". He started a society for the welfare of the depressed known as the *Satyashodhak, Samaj* in 1873 and is credited of having established the first private school for girls in 1851. He taught in the school personally and when the number of pupils increased and he could not get an assistant teacher, he taught his wife and made her assist him in the cause. Both he and his wife had to face tremendous opposition in this task from the conservative section of society, but they continued their work undaunted and made it successful. He carried on propaganda in favour of widow remarriage and brought about the remarriage of a Brahmin Widow in 1864. He also founded an Orphan Home where widows in difficulty might deliver and leave their illegitimate children.

Karmaveer V.R. Shinde (1873-1944) – He tried to harmonize our traditional culture with modern western culture or tried to synthesise the both. Being acquainted with condition of women in England, he found that women's status in India was very low because of the existing customs, and traditions and prejudices. He felt that unless the condition of women in society was improved there could be no social progress.

Shinde believed that if education was given to girls of lower classes they would release themselves from the shakles of superstition and slavery. They would improve their families and bring about a general elevation of their class to higher culture. He educated his sister Janakka and thereby enabled her to live a life of independence. When he opened the Depressed Class Society, he took special efforts to uplift the condition of women of the Depressed classes by looking after their material and moral progress. He also renderd a very important service in initiating and spreading the demand for compulsory primary education for girls.

Kashinath Trimbak Telang (1850-1893) – At the age of 14 Telang passed matriculation examination in 1864, and joined the Elphinstone College. He did M.A. and LL. B. simultaneously. His earliest efforts were primarliy academic and literary. He joined the Student's Literary and Scientific Society in 1868. But in the prime of his intellectual vigour he was greatly devoted to the social and cultural movement. Telang was instrumental in introducing compulsory primary education in Bombay. He was the first Indian Vice-Chancellor. He also served as the judge of the Bombay High Court in 1889.

Mahadev Govind Ranade (1842-1901) – Was a product of Elphinstone College which had the credit of producing social reformers who were determined to eradicate social evils plaguiging the society. As a student of History and Economics he had an in-depth knowledge of the society, particularly the status and position of women. He pleaded for emancipation of women and denounced certain customs like early marriage, enforced widowhood, caste system and so on. He laid the foundation of an All India Organization, to carry the struggle for social reform. He founded the National Social Conference, an organ of the social reform movement on organized basis. This was in pursuance of his view that the social reform movement to be effective should not be based on the efforts of individuals or groups but should be conducted by a central national, organization and there collective efforts. He strongly expoused the cause of female education. He not only educated his wife but started a Girl's High School in 1884.

Manekjee Cursetjee (1808-1887) – He was one of the pioneers of Female Education in Bombay. He was a son of a well-known Parsi contractor, who was a friend of the great Duke of Wellington; was the foremost pioneer of English education for native girl's, the father and founder of the Alexandra Native Girls English Institution, the dauntless *vakil* of the *Sudder Adawlut,* the friend and correspondent of the aristocracy of England and Europe, the "Byron of the East" as he was sometimes facetiously called, the sheriff of Bombay, one of the first natives of India who was lionized in Europe about the middle of the last century, the genial warm-hearted, humorous and old Manekjee Cursetjee was indeed an ornament to his community.

Mehtaji Durgaram Mancharam (1809-1876) – He was one of the pioneering social reformer in western India. He was a product of the new elementary educational system set up under Elphinstone administration. A government teacher in Surat from 1828, Mehtaji never knew Enlgish, but despite that handicap he held views on the ideal position of women which evidenced western inspiration and composed attacks on idolatry and witch-craft which were similiar in essence to Rommohan Roy's. In 1838 he began public protest against treatment meted to widows and in 1844 he organized the Many Dharma Sabha, Universal Religious Society to discuss social problem including those arising from caste.

Maharshi Karve (1858-1962) – Was a great crusader regarding women's right and position in society. Throughout his life he constantly strove to do away with customs like child marriage and enforced widowhood. To put his ideas into practice he not only married a widow in 1893 but also started the Widow Marriage Association. This was open to those who had married widows or those who did not hesitate to dine with persons who had married widows. Like many other reformers of his age there was a realization on his part that no amount of social legislation would have a meaningful effect on the position and status of women unless they were educated. Education would make women aware of their position in society and perhaps prevent them from succumbing to irrational customs and traditions. It would also make them self reliant. In order to promote women's education Karve opened institutions which carried his ideas to logical consequence. He began with the Hindu Widows Home Association which was purely educational institution and went on to establish the Mahila Vidyalaya which finally, culminated in the foundation of the S.N.D.T. University solely meant for women.

Naoroji Ferdoonji (1817-1885) – Belonged to the first batch of English educated youth in Western India who took to social and educational reforms in the early years of the last century. Born at Broach in March 1817, he was but eight years senior to his more celebrated namesake, Dadabhai Naoroji, with whom he worked in intimate companionship for the uplift of his countrymen. He was a great social reformer to him is chiefly due the establishment of the first girls school, the first Native Library the first literary society, the first debating club, the first political association, the first body for improving the condition of women, the first institution for social and religious reform, the first law association, and the first educational periodicals.

Narmada Shankar (1833-1886) – Was a Gujarati social reformer who took up the cause of women's education, urged widow remarriage, attacked caste barrier's and advocated travel to England in order to acquire western scientific knowledge.

Raja Rammohan Roy (1772-1833) – Aptly described as the father of Modern India. He came from an ancient and respectable *Brahmin* family. Throughout his life he stood for more equitable and humane treatment of women; advocated the grant of property rights to them; was a champion of their education; roundly condemned polygamy and, in his will, disinherited any son or descendant who would have more than one wife at a time; had his grand-daughter married at the age of 16 and was obviously opposed to child marriage. Infact, he was the earliest champion of women's right in Modern India. On the basis of his study of all religions, he evolved a purificatory movement within Hinduism itself --- the *Brahmo Samaj* which later carried on social and religious reform activity.

Sir Vithalda Thackersey (1873-1922) – Was a strong supporter of women's education. He realized that the progress of country was intimately connected with the emancipation and uplift of women and regarded the status and progress of women as an index to the general advance of the country in the scale of nation. His greatest service to women's education lay in the fact that he contributed financially to the tune of 15 lakhs to the Women's University established by D.K. Karve. He contributed handsomely and the Women's University came to be named after Sir Vithaldas mother, "the S.N.D.T. Indian Women's University." The second institution which owed his generous and financial support was the *Vanita Vishram* started by Shivagauri Gajjar and Bai Bajigauri Munshi. Sir Vithaldas gifted Rs. 1,00,000 for the purpose of providing for the boarding, lodging and education of atleast 24 Gujarati Hindu Ladies and at least 16 Bhatia Ladies and of maintaining a school to be named the S.N.D.T. Mooljee Vanita Boarding School. One of the Branches of the institution at Rajkot also received his financial support. His various contributions to institutions promoting women's education showed his deep dedication to the cause he withstood for.

Sorabji Shapurjji Bengalli (1831-1893) – Was a great reformer, educationist and philanthropist, and one of the leaders in the public life of his time. Among the many men of light and lustre that have illumined the historic period of the 19th century, Bengalli stands forth as the pioneer of female education. He was associated with the Parsi Girls School Association and played a pioneering role in establishing the first female hospital in Western India known as the Cama Hospital.

Vishnu Parashuram Shastri Pundit (1827-1876) – He is known as Ishwarchandra Vidyasagar' of Maharashtra. The work which Pandit Vidyasagar started in Bengal — the work of educating public opinion in favour of the remarriage of widows was taken up in Maharashtra with great zeal by a band of workers among whom Vishnu Shastri Pandit was prominent. He wrote articles on social reform in the *Indu Prakash*. Some of his articles focussed on the evil effects of enforced widowhood. In 1856 he founded the *Vidhava-Vivahottejak Mandal* (Society for the encouragement of widow remarriage).

Anandibai Joshi (1856-1887) – Was born in Poona. She was married at the age of five to Gopal Rao Joshi who taught her personally. She was the first high caste women to leave her country and study medical science in America. In 1886 she took her degree in Medicine from Women's Medical College at Philadelphia. She was offered the post of Resident Physician to the women's ward of the New Albert Edward Hospital at Kolhapur with a salary of Rs. 300. However, she was one destined to carry out this assignment.

Anandibai Karve (1865-1950) – She was the first student of *Sharada Sadan* opened by Pandita Ramabai. She broke the prevailing custom of widowhood and married D.K. Karve on March 11th, 1893. She got a certificate in midwifery form Nagpur. She joined her husband in his effort of uplifting the condition of widows.

Annie Besant (1847-1933) – Annie Wood was born in 1847 at London. She became the President of the Theosophical Society in 1907, being regularly re-elected thereafter and made India her permanent home. She passionately took up the cause of Indian independence and Indian education. Her activities were crowned with success in 1917 when she was interned by the Government and elected President of the National Congress, and in 1921, when her Central Hindu College was merged with the Hindu University of Benaras. She preached *Swadeshi* and raised voice against casteism. At the 1913 Congress session, she espoused the cause of Indian National Movement which was to embody religious, education, social and political reforms. She started a weekly Commonwealth and a daily New Premier. She mooted the idea fo Home Rule and asked the British government or promise India Self Government as a right and not as a reward for the loyalty of Indians during the war. She was arrested in 1917. She was deeply interested in the progress of women and joined a deputation led by Mrs. Sarojini Naidu that called on Mr. Montague, Secretary cf State to ask for political right for women. In 1917 she founded the Indian Boys Scouts Association. Mrs Besant was opposed to Gandhi's non-co-operation movement and characterized it as a revolt. This made her unpopular. She vented her feeling against the setting up oi Simon Commission with only Englishmen as its members.

Avantika Bai Gokhale (1882-1949) – A dedicated social worker who was a close associate and disciple of Mahatma Gandhi, took a leading part in the Champaran Satyagraha' 1917. She wrote the first biography of Mahatma Gandhi, and together with Kasturba, opened his eyes to the poverty in India, which came to influence his spinning wheel philosophy. In 1918 she founded 'The Hindu Mahila Sabha' in Bombay, which still strives for the uplifment of needy women with its educational, medical and other welfare programmes. She was an active political worker form 1920-46 and was imprisoned many time.

Kadambini Ganguly (1861-1923) – Daughter of Brajakisore Bau, zamindar of Bengal. She appeared in the list of successful candidates at the B.A. examination of the University of Calcutta in 1882. She was one of the first lady graduates in India (the other was Chandramukhi Bose), she was also one of the first graduates in Medical Science, taking her M.B. degree from the Medical College, Calcutta in 1887. After serving for about 5 years in the Eden Hospital, Medical College, she proceeded to Glasgow and Edinburgh for higher studies in Medicine. She attended the Bombay session of the Indian National Congress in 1889 as one of the lady delegates; she was the first women to speak from the Congress platform, when she was called upon to move the vote of thanks to the Chairman. Kadambini was one of the organizers of the Women's Conference held in Calcutta along with the session of the Indian National Congress in 1906. In 1908 she organized a meeting in Calcutta, where she presided as well, sympathising with the *Satyagraha* workers at Transvaal., S. Africa, under the leadership of Gandhiji. She collected money tohelp the workers at Transvaal.

Kashibai, Kanitkar (1861-1947) – Was encouraged to take to education by her husband. She read George Elliot, Marie Correlli Lord Lytton and the Arabian Night. She wrote extensively and her article, "An advise to an upcoming writer" was published in the 1890 issue of *Manoranjan.* She became the Vice President of *Seve-Sadan* (Home of Service).

Kasturba Mohandas Gandhi (1869-1944) – She was born at Porbandar in 1869. She married Gandhiji when she was 13. Her public life began after she joined her husband in South Africa in 1897. From 1904 to 1914, she was the soul of the Phoenix settlement and became Kasturba 'mother' to the inmates, a role she continued at Kochrab, Sabarmati and *Sevagram, Ashrams* in India. She led the women's Satyagraha in the final fight in South Africa. She was imprisoned and came out of jail in an emaciated condition. She joined Gandhiji in the Champaran *satyagraha* and taught cleanliness, discipline, reading and writing to the village workers women and children. In 1918 she took an active part in the Kaira *Satyagraha.* Infact, she taught the women the art of non-violent resistance. Later during India's non-violent fight for freedom she took up the leadership of the movement whenever Gandhiji was arrested; she plunged into the struggle, addressed meetings, collected funds and kept up the morale of the people.

She presided over the backward *Rani Paraj* Community's second conference, which resulted in their giving up drinking and taking to spinning and khadi. In 1930 and again in 1930, she courted arrest by picketing liquor and foregin cloth shops. In 1939, she participated in the Rajkot satyagrha for political reforms and was kept in detention at Tramba. Later in 1942 when Gandhiji was arrested inthe morning of August 9, she decided to address the meeting which Gandhiji was to have addressed, however she was arrested and later taken to the Aga Khan Palace detention camp at Poona.

Madam Bhikaiji Cama (1861-1936) – Was born to Sorabji Faramji Patel, a prominent businessmen of Bombay. She took her education at the Alexandra Parsi Girls School in Bombay and from the very beginning was interested in social and political work. At the age of 40 she went ot England and Paris and there she came in contact with Indian revolutionaries like Vir Savarkar, Virendra Chattopadhya, Mukund Desai and others. Along with them she carried propaganda for India's liberation from British rule. She started the *Vande Mataram* English Weekly from Geneva in 1905 and ran it for 10 years, advocating the cause of India's independence. In 1907 on 18th August she attended the World Socialist Congress at Stutgart (Germany) where over a 1,000 delegates from various countries of the world had come and Mada Cama moved a resolution demanding complete independence for India, and it was here for the first time India's National Flag was unfurled by her. During the world war she appealed to the Indians not to help the allies.

Margaret E. Cousins (1878-1954) – She was an active member of women suffrage movment in England and Ireland. She came to India in 1915 to join Annie Besant at Adyar and became keenly interested in female education. She was an active member of the Women Indian Association founded in 1917, and strove hard to win voting rights for women. In 1926 she founded the All India Women's Conference which became the most important platform for women's movement.

Muthulakshmi Reddi (1886-1968) – An Andhra *Brahmin,* was one of first women medical graduates in India. She was the first women legislator in the British India. She was subsequently elected as Deputy President of the Madras Legislative Council. She was one of the member of the deputation which met the Secretary of State in connection with the women's franchise. Mrs. Reddi was also in the Council, Welfare of Women, of which she was the staunch advocator. She was in favour of an enactment for the abolition of the Devdasi system; and law's to close brothels.

Pandita Ramabai (1858-1922) – A pioneer social reformer and an advocate for the education and emancipation of Indian women. At the age of 12 she mastered 20,000 sacred verses in sanskrit. From her parents she acuired good knowledge of Marathi, and later acquired theknowledge of Canarese, Hindustani, Bengali and English Languages. She is credited of having founded the *Arya Mahila Samaj, the Sharda Sadan,* and *the Mukti Sadan.*

Ramabai Ranade (1865-1922) – Was born in a hill town of Satara District. She was married to Mahadev Govind Ranade at the age of 13. She was personally taught by her husband and by 1875 with the help of a tutoress she studied upto the 5th standard. She mastered both Marathi and English languages. In 1882 she read an address in English at a public meeting, advancing the project of starting a Girls' High School in Poona. She formulated plans for a Home of Service and finally started the Poona *Seva-Sadan* with branches all over the Bombay Presidency. She established the *Seva-Sadan* Nursing and Medical Association at which High Caste Hindu widows and girls volunteered to work and she did a wonderful piece of pioneering work, when she took the first batch of probationeers to the Sassoon hospital Nursing Department. At the Indian Women's Conference held in Bombay in 1904, she defined her life work the motto: "Life is a sacred trust", and these words she scrupulously followed all her days She was very much in favour of women franchise and threw her heart and soul in the campaign.

Sarojini Naidu (1879-1949) – Was born in Hyderabad on February 13, 1879. She passed the Matriculation examination in her twelfth year in the first class standing first in the Madras Presidency. In her early life she became a poet. At thirteen she wrote a long poem - 'Lady of the Lake'. She wrote many books the most important being *The Golden Threshold*, took the English world by storm. It became the best seller. Her other collection of poems 'The feather of the Dawn', 'Bride to Time' and The Broken Wing were applauded by the readers. She strongly campaigned for women rights and in July 1919, she went to England as a member of the deputation of the All India Home Rule Leauge, where she pleaded for the right of women. She appeared before the Joint Committee on Indian Reforms. She supported franchise for women. She was elected President of the Congress Session at Kanpur in December 1925. In her inspiring address, she made a fervent plea for unity. Her Presidentship was an occasion for women to come forward and entre public life. She took part in the salt *satyagraha* in 1930 and was sent to jail. In 1931, she accompanied Mahatma Gandhi to London to attend the Second Round Table Conference. She represented Indian women there. In 1932 she was arrested for taking part in the Civil Disobedience movement. However, she was released on March 21, 1943. She presided over the Asian Relations Conference in New Delhi in March 1947. She was the chosen leader for Asia and India. When the nation became independent Sarojini Naidu became the first Governor of U.P.

Sharada Behn Mehta (1882-1970) – Born in a well known family of Gujarat. Her father Gopilal Manilal Dhruv, and her mother, Balaben, were eminent reformers. She got good education and along with her sister Vidyaben were the first two lady graduates of Gujarat in 1901. In 1889 she was married to Sumant Misra and both husband and wife played a remarkable role in social and political life of Gujarat since 1921. She worked particularly in the field of women's welfare, abolition of caste and untouchability and against exploitation of women and child labour. In 1919 she helped in editing Mahatma Gandhi's paper *Navjivan.*

Swarnakumari Devi (1885-1932) – The 10th child of Maharshi Debendranath Tagore was born in Calcutta in 1885. She wrote a number of books - novels, essays and poetries. Her work include *Dipnirvan* (1876) *Chinnamukul* (1879) *Hughlir Imambari* (1294). *Bidroha* (1890), *Vichitra*

(1920), she was on the editorial board of the monthly *Bharati* from its inception. Later on she became its editor (1884). In 1886 --- she started a women's organization, the Sakhi Samiti and became its secretary. This Samiti was set up to facilitate free exchange of thoughts among Bengali women. She attended the 6th session of the Indian National Congress as a women delegate. In the 1929 session of the Bengali Literacy Conference in Calcutta she was elected the general President as well as the sectional President of the Literature section. In 1927 she was awarded the Jagattarini Gold Medal by the University of Calcutta. She was the first women author of Bengal who won this prize.

Tarabai Modak (1892 1973) – Belonged tothe reforming Parthana Samajist family. She received her education in famous institutions such as the Hozoorpaga Girls School, Pune, Alexandra Girls School and the Elphinstone College. She like most of the women intelligentsia of our period attended the Congress Session at Surat in 1907. She delivered her initial lecture on Women's Education at Vidyamandir in Amravati and supported female education, as she felt for political participation and social change education was essential. Later she became the principal of Barton Female Training College at Rajkot in 1921. Infact, she became the first lady principal of the College. Later she joined Dakshinamurti-Bal-Mandir a school for children aged 8 to 18. This schools ideology was influenced by Gandhiji. Here she translated various books, e.g.

1. Mountessori in the Home.
2. Mangesh Parrot.

This became very popular. Infact, Tarabai tried to spread Montessori system of education. She also became a champion of Adult education in Maharashtra and extensively toured and lectured on the subject at Pune and Satara. She also started *Balwadi* in Amravati for Harijan children. She established *Shisu Vihar* at Bombay in 1936 worked for the expansion of children's education. She became M.L.A. Maharashtra *Vidhan Sabha* in 1946 and was awarded *Padma Bhushan* in 1962.

Vidyagauri Nilkanth (1896-1958) – She was married at the age of 13 to Ramanbhai Nilkanth whose father was a well known social reformer. She continued her education even after marriage, and graduated in 1901. She devoted her life for the uplift and education of women and was associated with almost every social educational and cultural institution of Ahmedabad. She started the *Mahila Mandal* in 1914.

APPENDIX - C

LIST OF REMARRIAGES IN BOMBAY PRESIDENCY

Year	*Name*	*Caste*
1165	Bai Bayabai Pense	N. Chitapawan Brahmin
	Mr. Narayan Jagannath Bhide	
1876	Bai Dhankorebai	Kapole Bania
	Mr. Madhaodas Rugunathdas	
1882	Bai Bhulibai	Pathare Prabhu
	Rao Bahadur Moroba Kanoba	
1872	Bai Shyamkore	Kapole Bania
	Sha Pragji Lalji	
1872	Bai Jivkorebai	Visa Khadayita Bania
	Sha Lalloobhai Mathuradas	
1872	Bai Krishnabai	Koknasth Devrukh
	Mr. Wasoopew Babaji Navrange	Brahmin
		Devrukh Brahmin
1872	Bai Durgabai	Koknasth
	Mr. Gangadhar Balkrishna Gadre	Brahmin
1873	Bai Kandoobai	Deshastha Brahmin
	Mr. Gajanad Pandoorang Mohrir	
1874	Bhai Diwalibai	Deshaval Bania
	Sha Kevaldas Amarji	Dosakhadaita Bania
1874	Bai Kushabai	Kokanastha Brahmin
	Pandit Vishnu Parshuram Shastri	Brahmin
1874	Bai Gangutai	Gaud Brahmin
	Mr. Laxmanrao Vithal Bhandre	
1874	Bai Gitabai	Deshastha Brahmin
	Mr. Krishnaji Dhonod Panje	
1875	Bai Jadavbai	Visha Shrimali Bania
	Sha Lalloobhoi Khushalchand	
1876	Bai Gangabai	Dasa Lad Bania
1877	Bai Sakhoobai	Deshastha Brahmin
	Mr. Dinkar Bhikaji Joshi	Konkastha Brahmin
1878	Bai Dimatbai	Dasa Oswal Danias
	Sha Lalji Hardore	
1878	Bai Durgabhai (alias) Umabai	Deshastha Brahmin
	Mr. Sadashiv Pandurang Kelkar	Koknastha Brahmin
1879	Bai Tejanbai	Dasa Oswal Dania
	Sha Devji Ramji	

1879	Bai Fulbai Sha Kanji Devji	Dasa Shrimati Brahmin
1879	Manekbai Sha Damodar Devehand Vakil	Modh Bania
1879	Baid Revabai Sha Gorhandas Lalloobhai Shroof	Nagar Bania
1879	Bai Aitai Mr. Balvantrao Govind Godbole	Deshastha Brahmin Koknastha Brahmin
1880	Bai Diwalibai Dave Jetharam Shivram	Khedaval Brahmin
1883	Bai Bainji Bhaiji Mr. Shaishankar Harishankar	Khedaval Brahmin
1880	Bal Baniji Tarvadi Bhaiji Dayaram	Brahmin
1880	Bai Goduabai Mr. Krishnaji Govind Pendse	Deshastla Brahmin Koknastha Brahmin
	Bai Venubai Mr. Pandurang Vinayak Kanmarkar	Koknastha Brahmin
1881	Bai Suraj Mr. Abheyram Kuberji	Brahmin
1881	Bai Tanubai Mr. Dwarkaath Raghoba Turkhadkar	Brahmin
1882	Bai Dhibai Thakar Chaturbhuj Kallianji	Bhatia
1882	Bai Mankorbai Mr. Vamanji Goverdhan	Dasa Shrimaji Bani Modh Bania
1882	Bai Jamnabai Gor Primji Vallabh	Shrimali Brahmin
1882	Bai Mabai Sha Damji Rattanji	Dasa Oswal Bania
1882	Bai Laxmibai Mr. Mhasukh Surchand	Dasa Shrimali Bania
1882	Bai Rambai Sha Nathji Gopalji	Dasa Shrimali Bania
1882	Bai Ramha Sha Nagji	Brahmin
1882	Bai Gitabai Rao Bhadur Wamanrao Mahadeo Kolatkar	Deshastha Brahmin Koknasth Brahmin

1883	Bai Jamnabai Mr. Himatlal Dalsukhram	Audich Brahmin
1884	Bai Diwali Thakar Oghad Dayalji	Audich Tolakia Brahmin Paenwal Brahmin
1884	Bai Veubai Mr. Vishnu Vithal Shrikhande	Karade Brahmin
1884	Bai Yamunabai Mr. Raghunath Sitaram Alarkar	Deshastha Brahmin
1884	Bai Narabadabi Mr. Raghunath Sitaram Alarkar	Deshastha Brahmin

APPENDIX - D

INSTITUTIONS ESTABLISHED BY D.K. KARVE

Hindu Widow Home

> "...... the best way to advance the cause was, I thought, to educate widows. Education would make them self-supporting and would enable them to think for themselves.... widows when educated would understand their own interest and if able to muster sufficient courage, would be ready for a practical step...."[1]

The Hindu Widows Home which was purely educational institution was formally established on 14th June 1886 with Dr. R.G. Bhandarkar as President and D.K. Karve as its secretary.

In the initial stages the growth of the institution was rather slow. It began with one widow in 1899 at the end of year, the number rose to four only. In the second year the number rose to eight and the home also included two unmarried girls. Results of the third year were very encouraging, there were eleven widows and three unmarried girls. Number of inmates increased in the fourth year, i.e. there were fourteen widows and five unmarried girls.[2]

The increasing number of un-married students in the *ashrams* clearly reveals that the institution which began purely for the needy widows was now increasingly becoming popular among the women at large in our Presidency. The 21st Annual Report 1916 of the Widows Home Association states that there were 216 students on the roll, of these 86 were widows and 109 were unmarried girls, 21 were married.[3]

The Report also mentions in detail the community from which the students came. Generally the students belonged to ---[4]

Konkanastha	-	68	Vidurs	-	5
Deshasthas	-	51	Telis	-	3
Karhadas	-	26	Vanis	-	3
Saraswats	-	21	Telugus	-	2
Kayasthas	-	12	Gujarathis	-	2
Daivadnyas	-	8	Naidu	-	1
Marathas	-	7	Jina	-	1
Devarukhe	-	1	Dravida	-	1
Kunbi	-	1	Vaishna Madras	-	1
Shimpi	-	1	Brahmakshatri	-	1

These figures clearly indicate that the institution not only catered to the Brahmin community but also to the lower castes. This clearly reveals that Karve did not believe that education was the preserve of the Brahmin community alone. Though the participation of women from the lower caste was less the fact that they joined the institution shows the desire on their part to get the benefits of education. An interesting feature of the Widow's Home Association was that it was gradually acquiring a wide base among women as mentioned earlier.

Another significant feature of the Home was that its inmates came from different parts of India chiefly from central and southern India. The 21st Reports mentions that the student came from[5] –

Poona District	-	28	Bijapur	-	4
Kolapur and S.M. State	-	27	Gujarat	-	4
			Belgaum	-	3
Central Province	-	20	Baroda	-	3
Bombay	-	19	Nizam Dominion	-	3
Thana District	-	17	Berar	-	12
Rathnagiri District	-	4	Kolaba Distt.	-	10
Nasik District	-	4	Mysore	-	3
Sholapur	-	9	Mangalore	-	1
Central India	-	7	Khandesh	-	1
Ahmednagar	-	7	Rajamundey	-	1
Gwalior state	-	6	Goa	-	1
Satara District	-	5			
Indore	-	5			
					216

The inmates of the association were instructed in Marathi, Sanskrit, and English as languages. Also, Arithmetic was taught. In the initial period the highest classes had advanced in some subjects to the level of high school standard V.[6]

The widows were trained in printing, weaving, craft, knitting, music, and so on. These courses were particulary meant for those widows who were elderly and weak intellectually. By undertaking these courses they could become self-reliant.[7]

According to the 14th Annual Report for the year 1909 the Ashram completed the Marathin Seventh Standard, i.e. it reached the highest stage in primary instruction. The course was so arranged that those who learned English along with these standards were able to compete the first three Anglo-Vernacular standards with the completion of Marathi courses.

The significance of the *Ashram* came to the forefront in the same year when five girls were sent up for the vernacular final examination of the Education Department. Three students were successful. In the list of one hundred and fifty successful candidates at this examination arranged according to merit, the number of those passed were 5, 12 and fifty.[8]

The 16th Annual Report of the Ashram gives an in-depth information about the status of 250 students who left the Ashram :[9]

S.No.	*Qualifications*	*Number*
1.	Matriculation	8
2.	College Certificate	13
3.	Passed Midwives and Nurses	12
4.	With certificate of Vernacular Final or the Marathi 7th Standard Examination	11
5.	Unqualified Teachers	5
6.	Fit to work as Teachers though without certificate	37
7.	Engaged in Industry	6
8.	Learning in other School and Colleges	57
9.	Those who have simply passed from the illiterate into literate class	101
		250

These figures highlight the point that the education imparted in the *Ashram* (Home) enabled most of the students to go in for higher education and also professional courses. Infact, the kind of education acquired by the students in a way helped in achieving the objective of the institution.

Scholarship and prizes were awarded to successful candidates in order to encourage them. These had a lot of meaning for poor students for whom they proved to be an added incentive. Infact, it acted as a motivating force for retaining students in the *Ashram* (Home).

The growing popularity of the Widows Home can be gauged from the fact that visitors came to the home from different parts of India. According to the 16th Annual Report for the year 1911, 105 persons visited students. The following table gives the different localities from which the visitors came---[10]

Bengal	-	2	United Province	-	5
Berar	-	25	Central Province	-	44
Bombay	-	142	Deccan	-	109
Carnatic	-	33	Foreign countries	-	2
C. India	-	22	Gujarat	-	64
Madras Presidency	-	9	Konkan	-	52
Nizams Dominion	-	25	Mysore	-	4
Punjab	-	7	Poona	-	473
Sindh	-	7	Southern most state	-	31
					105

These figures indicate the popularity of the institutions not only in Bombay Presidency but in other Presidencies as well.

A discussion of the Home would be incomplete without taking into account the contributions of Parvatibai Athavale. She was the sister of Anandibai Karve. Her greatest contribution to the Home was the donation she collected for it. Her efforts bore fruits and she not only acquired financial assistance but also popularized the name of the institution and got many students enrolled in it.

Apart from the efforts of Parvatibai Athavale, the Home succeeded in acquiring the services of Mrs. Kashibai Devdhar, Mrs. Venubai Namjoshi and Banubai Deshpande who later on became the life workers of the Home.

Mahila Vidyalaya — 1907

Karve drew his inspiration of setting up Mahila Vidyalaya while he was teaching girls of Alexandra and Cathedral Girls High School. An idea dawned on him that if he too established a similar kind of institution the cause of women could be effectively dealt with.

The growing popularity of the *Anath Balikashram* (or Hindu Widow Home) particularly among the unmarried and married women compelled Karve to establish an institution which would cater to women's education in general. Since the members of the Widow's Home Committee were not prepared to expand their work a need was felt to open a new institution. Therefore, it was on 4th March 1907, the *Mahila Vidhyulaya* was founded.

The principal aim of the institution was to raise the age of marriage of girls so that they get enough time to complete their studies. A Brahmacharya fund was constituted to help the poor girls.

In the initial stage the school was intended to be a boarding school but Karve discovered certain practical difficulties in the scheme. It was found that the girls admitted to the Vidyalaya had reached different stages in the curriculum and it became impracticable to have a large number of classes for a comparatively small number of students. Therefore, Karve tried to experiment co-education in secondary schools. It was at the New English School, which served as the feeder for the Fergusson College and that girls form *Mahila Vidyalaya* were admitted.

This however, was temporay arrangement and in 1912 the *Mahila Vidyaluya* was shifted near the Widows Home. In the initial stage the number of girls who attended the New English school was 20. Gradually the number of girls began to increase. The Committee of Widows Home realized that the best practical course would be to have a common school for the students of the *Vidyalalya* and the Home, especially once it was shifted near the Widows Home. It was therefore, agreed to admit girls from the *Vidyalaya* to the Widow's Home and this amalgamation took palce in November 1913. The two institutions were conducted as two separate entities till the beginning of 1915 when the differences were made up and they were amalgamated.

The S.N.D.T. Indian Women's University

It was while preparing for his role as the president of the National Social Conference Session of 1915 that Dr. Karve came across the brochure on the Women's University of Japan in Tokyo. He was inspired by it and discussed the whole question of women's education in his address and proposed a plan for a women's university for our country.[11]

The establishment of the University i.e. S.N.D.T. (Shreemati Nathibai Domodar Thackersey) saw the final culmination of the sincere efforts of Karve regarding promotion of female education. Infact, it portrayed the last stage of his development of ideas and achievements. It came into being in 1916 with Shri Ramkrishna G. Bhandarkar as Chancellor and Shri Raghunath Paranjape as Vice-Chancellor. It received its present name in 1920 when the late Shri Vithaldas Thackersey gave a donation of Rs. 15

lakhs to the University, subject to certain conditions among which one was that it should be named after his mother, Shreemati Nathibai Damodar Thackersey. The object of the University as originally constituted, were as follows -[12]

1. to make provision for the higher education of women through modern Indian language (mother-tongue) as the media of instruction;
2. to regulate pre-university education, to start, aid, maintain and affiliate institutions for such education and to formulate courses of studies specially suited to the need and requirements of women;
3. to make provision for the training of teachers for primary and secondary schools;
4. to institute and confer; such degress and grant diplomas, titles, certificates and mark of honour in respect of degrees and examinations as may be prescribed by the regulations; and
5. such other objects, not inconsistent with these as may be added from time to time by the Senate. The University made slow; but steady progress between 1916 and 1937 partly because the idea was not then accepted by a lage section of the intelligentsia, partly because it did not obtain recognition from the government and other Universities and also due to financial stringency. It is interesting to note that one lady graduated from the University in 1919 and three in 1920.

REFERENCES

1. Dhondu Keshave Karve, *op.cit.*, p. 59.
2. *The Hindu Widow's Home Association Poona 21st Annual Report - 1916,* p. 2.
3. *Ibid.*, p.2
4. *Ibid.*
5. *Ibid.*, p.2.
6. See *9th Annual Report for the Year 1904,* p. 2.
7. *Thirteenth Annual Report for the year 1908,* p. 4-5.
8. *Fourteenth Annual Report for the year 1909,* p. 3.
9. *Sixteenth Annual Report for the year 1911*, p. 3, 105.
10. *Ibid.*, p. 2.

11. Panandikar S, Neera Desai, Kamalini Bhansali, ed., *Future Trends in women's higher education and the role of the S.N.D.T. Women's Unviersity, Report of the Round Table Discussion,* p. 6.
12. *A Review of Education in Bombay State 1855-1955,* pp. 261-62.

BIBLIOGRAPHY

PRIMARY SOURCES

A. Reports

Adam, William, *Report on the State of Education in Bengal 1835-38,* ed. A. Basu, Calcutta, 1941. *Report of the Indian Education Commission Appointed by the Resolution of the Government of India dated 3rd February 1882,* Calcutta, 1883.

______, *A Review of Education in Bombay State 1855-1955. Bombay Educational Series No. I.,* Poona 1958.

______, *The Countess of Dufferins Fund Ninth Annual Report of the National Association for Supplying Female Medical Aid to the Women of India for the year 1893,* Calcutta, 1894.

______, *Report of the Director of Public Instruction, Bombay, for the year 1859-60,* Byculla, 1861.

______, *Report of the Director of Public Instruction, Bombay for the year 1869-70,* Bombay, 1870.

______, *Report of the Director of Public Instruction, Bombay for the year 1889-1890,* Bombay, 1890

______, *Report of the Director of Public Instruction, Bombay for the Year 1899-1900,* Bombay, 1900.

______, *Report of the Director of Public Instruction, Bombay for the year 1909, 1910,* Bombay, 1910.

______, *Report of the Director of Public Instruction, Bombay for the year 1920-21,* Bombay 1922.

______, *Report of Public Instruction in Baroda for the year 1911-12* Baroda, 1913.

______, *Report of Public Instruction in Baroda for the year 1913-14, Baroda, 1913-14,* Baroda, 1915.

Cotton, J.S., *Progress of Education in India 1892-96-97, Third Quinquennial Review.* London 1898.

Croft, A., *Review of Education in India in 1886 with Special Reference to the Report of the Education Commission,* Calcutta, 1888.

Nash, A.M., *Progress of Education in India 1887-1891-92, Second Quinquennial Review,* Calcutta, 1893.

B. Educational Record's

Richey, J.A. ed., *Selections from Educational Records Part II,1840-59,* Calcutta, 1922.

Sharp, H., Selection from Educational Record Part I, 1781-1839, Calcutta, 1920.

C. Contemporary Biographies in Marathi and English

Athavale, Parvatibai, *Mazi Kahani,* Poona, 1936.

Karve, Anandibai, *Maze Puran,* Bombay, 1944.

Karve, D.K., *Atmava-va-charit,* Poona, 1958.

Carpenter, Mary, *Six Months in India,* London, 1868.

Karve, K.D., *Looking Back,* Poona 1936.

D. Contemporary Speeches, Writings and Memoirs

Besant, Annie, *Wake up India,* Madras 1913.

Gandhi, M.K., *Speeches and Writings Relating to Women,* Edited by Anand T. Hingoram, Karachi, 1941.

Nehru, Shyam Kumari, Our Cause — A Symposium by India Women, Allahabad, 1938.

Raleigh, Thomas, *Lord Curzon in India,* Being a Selection from his speeches as Viceroy and Governor-General of India 1889-1905, London, 1906.

Sorabji, Cornelia, *India Callings, the Memoirs of Cornelia Sorabji,* London, 1935.

Tennant, A. Carrie, *On Marriage Reform and Female Education Lecture Delivered at Baroda under the distinguished auspices of His Highness the Maharaja Saheb, Who graciously presided: March 30th-1911,* Published under the auspices of the Hindu Marriage Reform League" of Calcutta.

———, *"Women's Possibilities Evils of Early Widowhood and Poverty from Marriage Expenses" Delivered at Trichinopoly on Decem-*

ber 18th 1911, Published under the "Hindu Marriage Reform League" Calcutta.

E. Gazetteer

Imperial Gazetteer of India, Provincial Series, Bombay Presidency, Vol. 1, Calcutta 1909.

The Gazetteer of the Bomay Presidency, Vol. XII, Khandesh, Bombay 1880.

The Gazetteer of the Bombay Presidency, Vol. XIII, Part II, Thana, Bombay 1882.

The Gazetteer of the Bombay State, Poona District, Bombay, 1954.

The Gazetteer of the Bombay City and Island, Facsimile Reproduction, Vol. III, Bombay 1978.

Maharashtra State Gazetteer, Satara district, Bombay, 1963.

Maharashtra State Gazetteer, Nagpur district, Bombay, 1966.

Maharashtra State Gazetteer, Nasik district, Bombay 1975.

Maharashtra State Gazetteer, Kolaba district, Bombay 1964.

Gujarat State Gazetteer, Surat district, Gujarat, 1962.

Gujarat State Gazetteer, Kheda district, Ahmedabad, 1977.

Gujarat State Gazetteer, Mehsana district, Ahmedabad, 1975.

Imperial Gazetteer of India, Baroda Calcutt, 1908.

F. Census Report

Sedgwick,L.J., *Census of India, 1921. Vol. VIII, Bombay Presidency, Part II,* Bombay 1922.

G. Contemporary Newspapers

Metha, M., Pherozeshah, *The Bombay Chronicles* 1913.

Natarajan, K., *The Indian Social Reformer,* 1890 (Weekly).

Tilak, B., *Kesari,* 1881.

H. Contemporary Letter's in Marathi and English

Agarkar Letters. *Poona, Dated 25th Nov., 1890, Nehru Memorial Museum and Library,* New Delhi

H.V. Mote, ed., *Vishab Sharda, Khand Pahila - 1897-1947*, Bombay, 1972.

Government Records

Dalhousie Muniments - Sec : 6 No.' 258, Home Department, National Archives, New Delhi.

Government of India, Home Department Education-Deposit Proceedings, November 1908, No. 7, National Archives, New Delhi.

Government of India, Department of Education, Education-A Proceedings, April, 1911-Nos. 84-88, National Archieves, New Delhi.

Government of India, Finance Department - Leave and Leave Allowance, No. 94 of 1911, National Archives, New Delhi.

I. Secondary Sources

Aiyar, Ramaswami, *The Cultural Heritage of India. Vo. II*, Calcutta, 1969.

Agnew, Vijay, *Elite Women in India Politics*, New Delhi, 1979

Albuquerque, Teresa, *Urbs Primain India: An Epoch in The History of Bombay, 1840-1865*, Bombay, 1985.

Altekar, A.S., *The Position of Women in Hindu Civilization from Prehistoric Times to the Present day*, Delhi 1962.

Asthana, Pratima, *Women's Movement in India*, Delhi, 1974.

Bagal, Jogesh, C., *History of the Bethune School and College*, 1849-1949, Calcutta, 1949.

Bagwat, A.K., *Maharashtra - A Profile.*

Balfour, I. Margaret, Young, Ruth, *The Work of the Medical Women in India*, Bombay 1929.

Bana, I.H., *History of Institution Supported by Parsi Philanthropy and Enterprise in Education*, Bombay 1946.

Basak, N. L., *History of Vernacular Education in Bengal 1800-1854*, Calcutta 1974.

Bhandari, R. K., *Educational Development of Women in India*, New Delhi, 1982.

Bhansali, Kamalini, Desai, Neera and Panandikar, S., *Future Trends in Womens Higher Education and the Role of the S.N.D.T. Women's University. Report of the Round Table Discussion*, Bombay,

1975.

Butler Clementina, *Pandita Ramabai Saraswati,* London, 1922.

Chandavarkar, G.L., *Maharshi Karve,* Bombay, 1958.

Chapman, E.F., *Sketches of Some Distinguished Indian Women,* London, 1981.

Chattopadhyaya, K., *Indian Women's Battle for Freedom,* New Delhi, 1983

Chattopadhyaya, Kamaladevi, *The Awakening of Indian Women,* Madras, 1939.

Chiplunkar, G.M., *The Scientific Basis of Women's Education,* Poona, 1930.

Contractor, M.K., *Madam Bhikaji Cama - The Patriot whom India had Forgotten,* Surat, 1961.

Cousins, E. Margaret, *Indian Womanhood Today,* Allahabad, 1941.

Cowan, G.M., *The Education of the Women of India,* New York, 1912.

Darukhanawala, H.D., *Parsi Luster on Indian Soil,* Bombay, 1939.

Das, R.M., *Women in Manu and his Seven Commentators,* Varanasi, 1962.

Das Gupta, Jyotis Chandra, *A National Biography for India,* Dacca, 1911.

Das Gupta J.C., *A National Biography for India,* Dacca, 1911.

Datta, V.N., *Sati : A Historical, Social and Philosophical Enquiry into Hindu Rite of Widow Burning*, New Delhi, 1988

David, M.O., *John Wilson and His Institution,* Bombay, 1975.

Desai, Neera, *Women in Modern India,* Bombay, 1975.

______, *Social Change in Gujarat,* Bombay 1978.

Deshmukh, C.O., *Report of the National Committee on Women's Education,* May 1958 to January 1959, Government of India, 1959.

Deshpande, K.Tr., *Ranade, His Wife's Reminiscences,* Delhi, 1969.

Dobbin, Christine, *Urban Leadership in Western India, Political and Communities in Bombay City.* (1840-1885), London, 1972.

Dongerkery, S.R., *The History of the University of Bombay 1857-1957,* Bombay, 1957.

Durgabai Deshmukh, *Report of the National Committee on Women's Education,* May 1958 to an 1959, Ministry of Education, Government of India, 1959.

Dyer, S. Helen, *Pandita Ramabai, The Story of Her Life,* London, 1900.

Fatak, Padmaja, *Tarabai Modak,* Bombay, 1981.

Framjee, Dosabhoy, *The Parsees, Their History, Manners, Customs and Religion,* London, 1858.

Fuller, B. Marcur, *The Wrongs of Indian Womanhood,* London, 1900.

______, Fourth World Conference on Women: Beijing 1995: Country Report Government of India, Deptt. of Women and Child Development : Ministry of Human Resources Development, New Delhi, 1995.

Gandhi, M.K., *Young India 1927-1928,* Madras, 1935.

______, *An Autobiography : The Story of my Experiment with Truth,* Ahmedabad, 1959.

______, *Woman and Social Injustice*, Ahmedabad, 1942.

Ghugare, Shivaprabha, *Renaissance in Western India,* Karmaveer, V.R. Shinde,1873-1944, Bombay, 1983.

Gidumal, Dayaram, *The Life and Life Work of Behramji M. Malabari,* Bombay, 1888.

Hanswirth, Frieda, *The Status of Indian Women,* London, 1932.

Heimasath, H. Charles, *Indian Nationalism and Hindu Social Reform,* New Jersey, 1964.

______, *Indian Worthies, Vol. I, Bombay Manoranajak Grantha Prasarak Mandali 1906,* Bombay, 1906

Jha, D.N., *Ancient India : An Introductory Outline,* New Delhi, 1981.

Jyotiba Phule, *Samagrah Granth,* Poona, 1963.

Kaji, L.H., *Life and Speeches of Sir Vithaladas Thackersey,* Bombay, 1934.

Karkaria, R.P., *India, Forty Years of Progress and Reform, Being a Sketch of the Life and Times of Behramiji, M. Malabari,* London, 1869.

Karlekar, Malavika, *Voices from Within-Early Personal Narratives of Bengali Women,* Delhi, 1991.

Karve, D.D., *The New Brahmans, Five Maharashtrian Families,* Los Angeles, 1963.

Keer, D., *Mahatma Jotirao Phooley - Father of our Social Revolution,* Bombay, 1964.

Kirth, A.B., *A Constitutional History of India 1600-1935,* London, 1959.

Kolasker, M.B., *Religious and Social Reform A Collection of Essays and Speeches By Mahadev Govind Ranade,* Bombay, 1902.

Kumar, Radha, *The History of Doing : An Illustrated Account of Movements for Women's Rights and Feminism in India 1800-1990,* New Delhi, 1993.

Kumar, Ravinder., *Western India in The Nineteenth Century : A Study in The Social History of Maharashtra,* London, 1968.

Mardi, M.G., *Krantijyoti Savitribai Jyotirao Phule,* Poona, 1980.

Malabari, M., *Infant Marriage and Enforced Widowhood in India,* Bombay, 1887.

Mathur, Y.B., *Women's Education in India - 1966,* Bombay, 1973.

Mazumdar, Vina (ed)., *Symbols of Power : Studies on the Political Status of Women in India,* New Delhi 1979.

Misra, Lakshmi, *Education of Women in India 1921-1966,* Bombay, 1966.

Mitra, S.M. and Maharani of Baroda, *The Position of Women in Indian Life,* Bombay, 1912.

Ministry of Information and Broadcasting, *Great Men and Women of India,* Delhi, 1973.

Mookerjee, S., Ed., *The Wilsonian, 1832-1957,* Bombay, 1956-57.

Nag, Kalidas (ed)., *Bethune School and College Centenary Volume 1848-1949,* Calcutta, 1949

Nanda, B.R. (Ed.), *Indian Women, from Purdah to Modernity,* Delhi, 1976.

Natarajan, S., *A Century of Social Reform in India,* Bombay, 1962.

Nurulla, S., and Naik, J.P., *A Students History of Education in India 1800-1916,* Calcutta 1962.

______, *A History of Education in India (During The British Period).* Bombay, 1951.

Parasnis, N.R., *The History and Survey of Education in Thana District,* Bombay, 1967.

Parulkar, R.V., *Survey of Indigenous Education in the Province of Bombay, 1820-30,* Bombay, 1951.

______, *A Source-Book of History of Education in Bombay Province, Part-I Survey of India, General Education 1820-30,* Bombay, 1945.

Parvate, T.V., *Mahadev Govind Ranade : A Biography,* Bombay, 1963.

Patwardhan, M., *Autobiography and Character of D.D. Karve,* Poona 1958.

Sarasvati, Pandita Ramabai, *The High Caste Hindu Women,* New Delhi, 1901.

Sardar, G.B., Metha, Shakuntala, Desai, *Neera Golden Jubilee Commemoration Volume 1916-1966,* Bombay, 1968.

Sathe, Tarabai,*Aparajita Rama,* Poona, 1985.

Saxena, T. P., *Women in Indian History, A. Biographical Dictionary,* New Delhi, 1979.

Seal, Anil, *The Emergence of Indian Nationalism,* London. 1968.

Sengupta, Padmini, *Pandita Ramabai Saraswati Her Life and Works,* Bombay, 1970

______, *Pioneer Women of India,* Bombay, 1944.

Sergeant, W. Philip, *The Rulers of Baroda : An Account of the Life and Works of the Maharaja Gaekwas,* London, 1928.

Sheering, *The History of Protestant Mission in India,* London, 1975.

Shinde, V.R., *Karamveer, Renaissance in Western India (1873-1944),* Bombay, 1982.

Shrigaonkar, S.R., *The Education of Girl's in Maharashtra in Maratha History Seminar,* May 28-32, 1970, Kolhapur, 1971.

Singh, J. Sirdar, *B.M. Malabari : Rambles with the Pilgrim Reformer,* London, 1914.

Swami Madhavananada and and Majumdar, R.C., *Great Women of India,* Calcutta, 1953.

Thackersey, Premlila, *Education of Women,* Government of India, 1970.

Tilak Devdutt Narayan, *The Brilliant Lady of Maharashtra, Pandita Ramabai,* Nasik 1960.

Tyabji, B. Husain, *Badruddin Tyabji a Biography,* Bombay, 1952.

______, *University Grant Commission Report for the Years 1974-75 to 1992-93,* New Delhi, 1993.

Vadgama, Kusoom, *India in Britian : The Indian Contribution to the British ways of Life,* London, 1984.

Viad Sarojini, *Shrimati Kashibai Kanitkar Atmacharit–Anicharit,* Bombay, 1980.

Vohra, Ropa and Sen, Arun, K., *Status Education and Problems of Indian*

Women, Delhi 1986.

Weitbrecht, M., *The Women of India and Christian Work in the Zenana,* London, 1875.

Wilson, John, *A Memoir of Mrs. Wilson of the Scottish Mission, Bombay,* London, 1837.

Wolpert, A. Stanley, *Tilak and Gokhale : Revolution and Reform in the Making of Modern India,* Berkely, 1962

Journals and Articles

Apte, L. Mahadeva, Lokahitavadi and V.K. Chiplunkar, Spokesmen of Change in 19th Century Maharashtra", *Modern Asian Studies, Vol., VII,* 1973, Cambridge, 1973.

Basu, Aparna, Gujarati Women's Response to Gandhi 1920-42 *"Samaya Shakti, A Journal of Women's Studies Vol. 1, No. 2, 1984,* Centre for Women's Development Studies.

______, "The Reformed family, Women Reformer: A Case study of Vidyagauri Nilkanth", *Samya Shakti, A Journal of Women Studies Vol. IV &V, 1989. Centre for Women's Development Studies.*

______, "A Century's Journey: Women's Education in Western India 1820-1928"' in *Socialization Education and Women Explorations in Gender Identity.* Ed. Karuna Chanana N.M.M.L. New Delhi, 1988.

Chanana, Karuna, *"Social Change or Social Reform The Education of Women in Pre-Independence India"* Chanana, Karuna, *in Socialization Education and Women Explorations in Gender Indentity,* N.M.M.L., New Delhi, 1988.

Forbes, Geraldine, "Missionary Women in 19th Century India" Forbes, Geraldine, in *Economic and Political Weekly.* April 26, 1986.

______, Vote for Women --- The Demand for Womens franchise in India, 1917-1937" *Symbols of Power: Studies on the Political Status of Women in India. (Ed.),* Vina Mazumder, New Delhi, 1979.

Gumpers, Mc. Donald, "City Hinterland Relation and The Urban Development of A Regional Elite in 19th Century Bombay" *Journal of Asian Studies 1973-74.*

Joshi, J. Raghunath, "Anandibai Joshi - Triumph and Tragedy" *Span,* December 1988.

Kadam, V.S. "The Institution of Marriage and Position of Women in Eighteenth Century Maharashtra". *The Indian Economic and Social History Review,* 25, 3, 1988.

Karlekar, Malavika "Construction of Feminity in Nineteenth Century Bengal : Reading from Janaika Grihabadhur Diary" *Samya Shakti, A Journal of Women's Studies Vol. IV and V 1989-90* Centre for Womens Development Studies

Mehta, Shirin, The Role of Women in the Pesant Movemnent of Gujarat : A Study in the Gandhian Phase. 1915-28" *The Indian Historical Review,* July 1985-January 1986, Vol. XII" No. 1-2.

K. Reviews

Chattarjee, Ramananda, "The Modern Review" July to December 1909, Calcutta 1909. *The Modern Review* July to December 1917, Calcutta, 1977.

Gandhi, M.K. *Women and Social Injustice,* Ahmedabad, 1942.

Natesan, G.A., Ed., *The Indian Review,* A Monthly Periodical Devoted to the Discussion of All Topics of Interest.

______, *The Indian Review,* January 1915, Vol. XVI.

Hingorani, T. Anand, ed, *To the Women by Mahatma Gandhi*, Gandhi Series Vol. II Karachi, 1941.

L. Unpublished Thesis

Pearson, Olivia Gail, *Women in Public Life in Bombay City with Special Reference to the Civil Disobedience Movement,* Jawaharlal Nehru University, 1979.

Kapadia, K. Rupa, *A Compilation of the Life of Maharshi Karve with Special Referene to the Growth and Development of S.N.D.T.* University, University of Bombay, 1972.

INDEX